The New History in an Old Museum

THE NEW HISTORY

Creating the Past at Colonial Williamsburg

DUKE UNIVERSITY PRESS

IN AN OLD MUSEUM

Richard Handler and Eric Gable

DURHAM AND LONDON ■ 1997

© 1997 Duke University Press
All rights reserved
Printed in the United States of America on acid-free paper ∞
Typeset in Monotype Garamond by Keystone Typesetting, Inc.
Second printing, 1998

Library of Congress Cataloging-in-Publication Data
Handler, Richard
The new history in an old museum : creating the past at Colonial
Williamsburg / by Richard Handler and Eric Gable.
Includes bibliographical references and index.
ISBN 0-8223-1978-0 (cloth : alk. paper). —
ISBN 0-8223-1974-8 (paper : alk. paper)
1. Colonial Williamsburg Foundation—History.   2. Colonial
Williamsburg Foundation—Management.   3. Williamsburg (Va.)—
History.   I. Gable, Eric.   II. Title.
F234.W7H27   1997
975.5'425202'0747554252-dc21   96-6519 CIP

For Adria LaViolette and Jennifer Nourse

Contents

Acknowledgments   ix

1   The New History in an Old Museum   3

2   Imag[in]ing Colonial Williamsburg   28

3   Why History Changes, or, Two Theories of History Making   50

4   Just the Facts   78

5   Social History on the Ground   102

6   The Company Line: Aspects of Corporate Culture
     at Colonial Williamsburg   125

7   The Front Line: Smile Free or Die   170

8   Picket Lines   208

9   The Bottom Line   220

Notes   237

Works Cited   249

Index   258

Acknowledgments

In a book that is critical of Colonial Williamsburg, it may seem disingenuous to begin by thanking its loyal employees for help received. Nevertheless, we wish above all to thank several members of the Colonial Williamsburg staff (at the time of our fieldwork) who went out of their way to make our research possible: Cary Carson, Edward Chappell, Rex Ellis, Connie Graft, Brenda Leclair, Christy Matthews, Dennis O'Toole, and Mary Wiseman. To thank them is not to claim that they would agree with our critique; it is to praise them for practicing the kind of openness that intellectual inquiry requires. We also thank the many dozens of other Colonial Williamsburg folks who took the time to talk to us about the complex world of their museum.

Our field research in 1990 and 1991 would not have been possible without a generous grant from the Spencer Foundation. The National Endowment for the Humanities has been equally generous, providing us, through its Collaborative Research program, with support for data analysis and for completing this book (grant no. RO-22633-93). We thank the program officers of those organizations who took an interest in our project and helped us to construct the grant proposals that funded it. Finally, the University of Virginia, through its Center for Literary and Cultural Change and through the dean of the Faculty of Arts and Sciences, has supported this work for the past six years.

Over the many years we have worked on this project, we have talked with dozens of friends, relatives, and colleagues who have encouraged us, criticized us, given us new ideas and references, and above all tolerated our fascination with Colonial Williamsburg. Without trying to name each and every person who has taken an interest in our project, we would like to single out a few individuals who have been consistently supportive interlocutors: Gary Downey, Jeff Hantman, Adria LaViolette, Jennifer Nourse, Chuck and Nan Perdue, Dan Segal, Bonnie Urciuoli, and June Webb. We are also grateful to our editor at Duke University Press, Ken Wissoker, who (as always) has been a joy to work with. Finally, we especially thank Anna Lawson, who collaborated with us during the fieldwork stage of the research and went on to write her doctoral dissertation on African American history at Colonial Williamsburg. We have drawn on her work throughout the present book.

As with any collaborative undertaking, we have learned as much from each other as from anyone else. Collaboration is a wonderfully enriching endeavor. To recognize each other's efforts, we decided when we began this project to give Gable's name first on the articles we wrote together and Handler's on the book you have in front of you. To put either name second, however, belies the true and ongoing collaboration this book represents.

To think deeply in our culture is to grow angry and to anger others; and if you cannot tolerate this anger, you are wasting the time you spend thinking deeply. One of the rewards of deep thought is the hot glow of anger at discovering a wrong, but if anger is taboo, thought will starve to death.—Jules Henry, *Culture against Man*

Suppose we continue to neglect discipline for the mob and stop teaching thick and thin patriotism? I admit it isn't exactly honest business; America isn't so wonderful as nations go, but must we not make Americans believe it wonderful? Can we emphasize the fact that Lincoln told smutty stories and Washington held slaves and Jefferson begat bastards, and Webster drank more than was good for him? —W. E. B. Du Bois, *Dusk of Dawn*

The New History in an Old Museum

Visitors at the Courthouse on the Duke of Gloucester Street.
(photo by Eric Gable)

1 ∎ *The New History in an Old Museum*

Road Apples

There is no more evocative symbol for the current state of American history museums than the horse droppings that decorate the neat streets of Colonial Williamsburg—America's premier outdoor history museum. Manure is authentic dirt, an instance and symbol of natural disorder. Museums are carefully managed realms of classification where every thing is kept in its place. If Colonial Williamsburg lets the horse chips fall where they may, and indeed wants those chips to be something every visitor notices, what does that signify?

Colonial Williamsburg is a place not ordinarily associated with a dirty past. For many years, the museum has attracted a million visitors annually, people who come to see a tidy and elegant Revolutionary-era community. They come to watch the fife-and-drum corps and the militia parade down the Duke of Gloucester Street, or to observe the many craftspeople—blacksmiths, gunsmiths, silversmiths, weavers, coopers, cooks, and many others—hard at work. On sweltering summer days, these visitors are willing to stand in long lines to enter the well-appointed homes of the colonial burghers, where they will admire the furnishings of a satisfying domesticity—the wallpaper, the draperies, the furniture, the prints, the dried flowers, the china on which are set the simulacra of meats, pastries, and fruits. They wish to gaze at the good life, and they eagerly buy expensive reproductions or facsimilies of what they see displayed in the town's restored houses. Ultimately these visitors come, so nearly every one of them will tell you, to learn about "the past," "their past"—the collective truth about the way life "really was" back at the founding of the great American nation.

At Colonial Williamsburg, manure on otherwise clean streets signifies something about the way Americans generally think of life in "their past." Life was at once less pleasant and more organic—closer to nature. But the recent purposeful leaving of horse droppings on the streets also signifies something about a change in the way Colonial Williamsburg wishes to portray the past. The manure represents the coming of the new social history.[1]

Social history came to Colonial Williamsburg in the 1970s. It had developed, so say its acolytes, out of the turmoil of the previous decade as a new way of telling the American story. And it was brought to Colonial Williamsburg at a time of declining visitation. According to social history's proponents in the museum, the entrenched version of the American story focused too narrowly on "great men" and elites, and ignored the works and lives of the vast majority of the American population. Moreover, it was too exclusively celebratory. It privileged national consensus and ignored social conflict, thereby cleansing American history of oppression, exploitation, injustice, and struggle. That fewer Americans were coming to Colonial Williamsburg indicated that after Vietnam, Watergate, and the turmoil of the Civil Rights movement, the public was no longer willing to buy the old history of consensus and celebration. The new social history was meant to redress the balance and reclaim Colonial Williamsburg's market share. The museum would continue to celebrate American identity and American community, but it would no longer be silent about past injustices and their ramifications in the present. In short, the past that social history introduced into the museum was to be a dirtier past, both literally and metaphorically.[2]

The new social history challenged established history making in another, perhaps more profound way. It was more explicitly "constructionist" or "relativistic" than the histories it sought to supplant. Its proponents argued that historical truths are socially produced by particular people with particular interests and biases. The truths embodied in historical stories are thus not absolute or universal, but relative to the cultural context in which they are made. Other people, elsewhere, might use the same events and facts to tell different histories or, prompted by the desire to tell different stories, might work to discover previously overlooked facts. The new social historians wanted to acquaint the public with these constructionist arguments. They wanted to encourage their audiences to think critically about the relationship of present-day politics and culture to the histories they were hearing, reading, or seeing. If history, anybody's history, had an agenda, how was one to recognize it? From this critical perspective the authoritarian objectivism of history museums had to be challenged, and the museum had to be made to teach a different theory of history.[3]

When they were brought onboard in the mid-1970s, the new generation of social historians and administrators knew that changing Colonial Williamsburg would not be an easy task. Blocking the way, first, were the interests and attitudes of those who sponsored the patriotic ideology the institution had always purveyed. Critics of museums in general, and of Colonial Williamsburg in particular, have long pointed out that these venerable institutions represent hegemonic values, values congenial to the elites who establish, fund, and administer them. At Colonial Williamsburg, the American story had been a story celebrating the success of the colonial upper crust, and, by extension, of wealthy individuals like the Rockefellers who used philanthropy to link their genealogies to the American founding fathers. Not only did this version of the Williamsburg story celebrate these great men, it also celebrated America's greatness, asserting that every American citizen has a fair chance of achieving similar success because the American social order, based on universal democratic values, is fundamentally just. The entrenched Williamsburg story, then, affirmed the status quo. Thus it was (and is) reasonable to suppose that those who profited from the status quo—those who controlled the museum—would resist changing that story.[4]

A second obstacle to change was built into the very structure of the institution. Colonial Williamsburg was set up, in the late 1920s, as a hybrid organization, a nonprofit foundation with one "side" devoted to the general business of running the place and the other devoted to the museum's cultural and educational work. When the museum became a mass tourist destination after World War II, it developed increasingly complex organizational structures and routines for dealing with a large, paying public. Like many other large museums, it increasingly found itself operating on the border between mass entertainment and mass education.[5] The Colonial Williamsburg Foundation's mission statement spoke of high educational principles, but the museum catered to an audience that was not captive, and one, moreover, that was often "on vacation." If the social historians were to change the history that Colonial Williamsburg told, they would have to prove that a new history was what their audiences wanted, or at least that revisionism could be compatible with commercial viability.

Despite these obstacles, Colonial Williamsburg's new historians and administrators launched bold initiatives, both historiographical and organizational, to remake the foundation. And certainly by the time we began extended field research there, in early 1990, the stories that were being told on the "front line"—that is, on the museum-city's streets, where museum staff members meet visitors—were rather different from those reported for earlier times. For example, it is difficult to imagine a newspaper journalist in the 1950s beginning a feature article on Colonial Williamsburg with a discussion of "road apples," but that is what we found in the Sunday paper as we were writing this chapter in the summer of 1994. The lead article in the travel section, entitled "Authenticity: Colonial Williamsburg Strives for That 18th-Century Atmosphere, Right Down to the Road Apples," began:

> Road apples.
> That was my mother's euphemism for horse droppings. Road apples.
> When I first, uh, stumbled upon them as I was strolling down the middle of Nicholson Street in Colonial Williamsburg, I was—elated!
> Would you find road apples littering Main Street, U.S.A., in Florida's Walt Disney World? Never!
> You'll find them here, though; and that fact says a lot about what Colonial Williamsburg is—and what it isn't.
> For years, Colonial Williamsburg was burdened with a reputation—among a somewhat cynical group of travelers who, no doubt, thought of themselves as the cognoscenti—as a too-cute, too-contrived, Disneyesque re-creation of what was once the capital of the British colony of Virginia. A historical theme park.
> But that is precisely what it isn't. . . .
> It is authenticity that the Colonial Williamsburg Foundation . . . has sought since John D. Rockefeller Jr. began funding the restoration . . . in 1926.

Having asserted that authenticity is Colonial Williamsburg's mission, the author continued by describing a sampling of the museum's offerings. Highest on his list was the Other Half Tour, which offered "an education about one of the sorrier chapters in the nation's history," teaching that "it was the large slave population that allowed this town's residents to maintain their atypically high-level colonial lifestyle." Here, in a nutshell, we found two of the key topics the social historians had worked into the revised Williamsburg story: the history of previously excluded people such as African American slaves, and the social history of consumerism, of the material culture of everyday life.

The rest of the article, however, dwelt on themes and scenes that have played at Colonial Williamsburg for half a century: the Raleigh Tavern and the Capitol, where "the first stirrings of the movement for American independence found root"; the Peyton Randolph House and the Governor's Palace, "where visitors can get the best view of how Williamsburg's 18th-century gentry lived, dressed, ate and amused themselves"; and the ubiquitous costumed colonial craftworkers. Finally, the two color photographs that dominated the article on the printed page countered the social historians' road apples with thoroughly conventional images of Colonial Williamsburg: tulips, white clapboard buildings and white picket fences, and (as the caption puts it) the "fife and drum corps deliver[ing] a splash of color as well as Revolutionary War period music."[6]

In this newspaper article, road apples and tulips, slavery and patriotism coexist in textual space as if they belong together. Assembled, they add up to a single thing—"authenticity." Yet, as we were to discover as we conducted anthropological field research in the museum-city over a period of two years, these images can also represent mutually contradictory paradigms of a collective past. To people who work at or visit Colonial Williamsburg, shit and tulips, slavery and Revolutionary-era soldiers can be seen as opposing icons representing the struggle between critical history and celebratory history, a dirty past and a Disney past, a new history and an old one.

As juxtaposed paradigms, new history and old also have come to represent opposed sides in what conservative intellectuals have managed to characterize as a "culture war." According to them, the so-called tenured radicals have infiltrated American institutions of higher learning and subverted them, waging an insurgent campaign against every foundational value—the true, the good—that makes this civilization great. Although they assert that the insurgency is widespread in the liberal arts, they emphasize that a particular point of subversion has been in the teaching of history.

Recently, conservative critics have found museum exhibits mounted by social historians to be particularly apt targets for what they envision as a counterattack against an entrenched academic radicalism. The controversies surrounding "The West as America" exhibit at the National Museum of American Art and the attempt by curators at the National Air and Space Museum to portray a revisionist history of the nuclear bombing of Hiroshima and Nagasaki have made public and plausible the conservative critique. In the more extreme forms of the conservative position, American history is a narrative of progress, which, however, is constantly in danger of losing its pedagogic power if it is stripped of its essential optimism. From such a perspective, there is a fine line between putting manure on the streets of an American shrine for the sake of verisimilitude and besmirching American identity by dwelling on what is dirty about the nation's collective past. The new social history is often portrayed as crossing that line and erasing virtue by rubbing Americans' noses in their collective villainy or victimhood.

Unlike the curators who mounted "The West as America" exhibit or those who tried to mount the *Enola Gay* exhibit, Colonial Williamsburg's social historians have never been a prominent target of conservative critique. Yet because the new social history has been assimilated into Colonial Williamsburg's narrative of nationhood, this site is a perfect place to study how Americans who work at and visit it recognize and reconcile conflicting versions of the past in the vernacular. This book is our attempt to put into an ethnographic context what for the most part has become uncontested polemic. A guiding question for us is: To what extent have the radical messages of the new social history become common belief and practice at Colonial Williamsburg? By looking at what happens to history on the ground in a particular place, at a particular time, we will show that social history has hardly had the kind of insurgent effect its critics claim for it.

The Museum as a Social Arena

This book is an anthropological study of Colonial Williamsburg, an American history museum and a modern nonprofit corporation. Our work is part of a burgeoning new scholarship focusing on museums as arenas for the significant convergence of political and cultural forces. Intellectual developments both within and beyond the academy have made it impossible to continue to view museums as simple repositories of cultural and historical treasures. Questions about what counts as a cultural treasure—or even what counts as culture—about what history means, and about who has the power to assign value to cultural and historical productions have been too pointedly raised to allow established cultural institutions to continue business as usual.[7]

The new scholarship on museums originates in a variety of disciplines— anthropology, archaeology, art history, cultural studies, history, literature, and philosophy. Despite differing disciplinary traditions, most of this work addresses a common set of interconnected concerns. First are questions about cultural representation: How do museums collect, classify, and display material artifacts to convey images of various human groups understood to be culturally different? And in what terms, more generally, is cultural difference evaluated in museums? Next are questions about the ideologies and interests that underpin or are reinforced by those representations of culture: Who establishes museums and who chooses their contents? What ideological propositions subtend those choices? Whose interests are served by the particular visions of cultural difference that museum displays authorize? Finally, there are questions about audiences: How do museums construct their audiences by welcoming some visitors but discouraging others? How do audiences receive—accept, resist, or reinterpret—the messages museums convey?[8]

These common questions can be pursued in a variety of ways, but most museum scholarship to date has confined itself to a rather narrow range of what anthropologists sometimes call data. Museums produce messages, or meaningful statements and actions. Scholars and critics of museums try to answer the sorts of questions mentioned above by reading, or interpreting, those messages. Due largely to disciplinary conventions, most scholars who study museums work from already produced messages—that is, they examine museum exhibits, texts about such exhibits (whether the catalogs that accompany them or the critical responses they provoke), other texts produced by museums (gift catalogs, public relations and fund-raising brochures, glossy periodicals such as *Smithsonian* and *Colonial Williamsburg*), and, for those whose topic is historical, the usual array of documents that can cast light on the values and intentions of earlier generations of museum founders, patrons, directors, and curators. A partial exception to this generalization is research on audience response, for this sort of work in a sense creates texts by interviewing or surveying museum visitors and recording their responses. Still, most audience research is conducted after the fact—after the visit has occurred—and in this sense remains a study of a completed text, a past response (although, clearly, visitors tailor their account of their responses according to the interview or survey situation in which they find themselves).[9]

As valuable as much of this research is, very little of it focuses on the museum as a social arena in which many people of differing backgrounds continuously and routinely interact to produce, exchange, and consume messages. Some scholars have attended to aspects of institutional histories and dynamics, but there has been almost no ethnographic inquiry into museums as arenas of ongoing, organized activities. As a result, *most research on museums has proceeded by ignoring much of what happens in them.* Museum scholars have exhaustively studied what we have called already completed museum messages, but only rarely have they examined the institutional life through which museum workers and audiences create those messages.[10]

Anthropological fieldwork is a research method well suited to avoid this oversight. The basic intention of our research project was to study the production and consumption of museum messages in relation to the institutional context in which those processes occurred. How, we asked, might museum exhibits take shape and change as they pass through the various phases of their development within a large organization like Colonial Williamsburg? What do different people—curators, historians, education specialists, frontline interpreters, visitors—contribute to the making of those messages? What are the different kinds of social interactions in which museum meanings are generated?

Put more simply, our object was to study what goes on in museums, not only onstage, as it were—where visitors take in exhibits—but behind the scenes, where scores of museum employees work weeks, months, even years to produce the completed museum displays that visitors so casually consume. We were interested, we told ourselves in our most ambitious moments, in the total social life of a contemporary museum.

Such a project is hopelessly grandiose and, we gradually learned, impossible to accomplish. Yet our ambitions were informed by the research conventions of our own discipline, anthropology, and the totalizing implications of its central theoretical concept, culture. Anthropologically trained fieldworkers try to immerse themselves in a social situation without predetermining what is and isn't important in it. Of course, researchers are always swayed by unconscious prejudices, and even the most indiscriminately inquisitive ethnographers will miss much of what is going on around them. Nevertheless, we believe that we approached Colonial Williamsburg with a more open-minded attitude concerning what might be relevant to the study of a museum than is characteristic of many museum researchers. By this we mean that we treated Colonial Williamsburg as a complete social world—a reconstructed village and a nonprofit corporation—and tried to be curious about everything that went on in it, from history making to merchandising to labor relations to after-hours socializing. We tried persistently to ask how the activities that took place there—some of them apparently far removed from the foundation's publicly asserted educational mission—might nonetheless come to influence the accomplishment of that mission.

Although we fell short of our goal to study all of Colonial Williamsburg (for reasons we will discuss), the beneficial results of our attempt to do so are threefold. First, in our research we have been able to consider a wider range of museum messages than that considered in most museum scholarship; second, we have been able to study some of the social processes of message making that such scholarship largely ignores; and, third, our approach makes it possible to complicate the triadic model of cultural producer–cultural product–cultural consumer that has become the norm for the critical interpretation of cultural representations (like museum displays) in mass societies.

With regard to our first point, examining a wide range of museum messages, we noted above that most students of museums focus on already completed messages—exhibits, catalogs, reviews, and visitor surveys. We noted also that those messages result from only a small fraction of all the communicative events that occur within museums. It is obvious that the museum's publicly foregrounded messages are influenced by other messages and communicative processes not normally open to public inspection— messages and processes that contribute to the final, public product. Studying backstage messages, then, should lead to new interpretive insights about the kinds of museum exhibits and discourses to which most critical analysis has heretofore confined itself.*

To illustrate: during our fieldwork we gradually came to understand that internal audiences are at least as important as the visitors who are conventionally thought to be the museum's audience. This became clear when we attended a three-week training session for a group of new interpreters and saw historians, curators, and educators teaching frontline personnel how they were to teach the public. In other words, in this scenario, museum professionals rehearsed for other museum professionals selected episodes of the Colonial Williamsburg story. The teachers did not in any simple sense tell their trainees what to say. Rather, they outlined the themes (politics, family life, religion) the museum had decided to emphasize, the stories appropriate to each, the artifacts available to convey those stories, the historical documents underpinning both the stories and the artifacts, the particular interpretive difficulties that various artifacts and buildings posed, and the questions visitors were likely to ask.

---

*At Colonial Williamsburg, and at many other museums, onstage versus backstage is more than a simple dichotomy due to the pervasive front-staging of backstage scenes during which visitors, assigned temporary VIP status for one reason or another, are taken behind the scenes to see how the museum "really" works. Needless to say, these backstage scenes are themselves carefully staged, and the preparation and planning that go into them are not available to public scrutiny. As ethnographers, we gained some access to back stages from which most visitors are excluded; but even those back stages were prepared, we presume, in ways beyond our ken.

During our research we were able to compare the stories told during such training sessions with the stories interpreters delivered to visitors on the front line. We could also look at planning documents and research reports produced before the time of our research by the foundation's researchers and administrators; those guiding documents could then be compared with the messages disseminated in training sessions. And we were able to interview people involved in every stage of a museum message's passage from the drawing board to the public. This meant that we could ask Colonial Williamsburg insiders why such-and-such a story was told in this setting, why or how it had changed from setting to setting, and whether they thought the storytellers' intentions were served or thwarted by the final versions that reached the public. None of the answers we received to such questions were definitive; nor, indeed, could they be, since the messages we were studying were multiply authored and beyond the control of any one person, no matter how highly or strategically placed within the institution. Still, the differing commentaries of the foundation's many storytellers challenged our evolving interpretations of history making in the museum.

As museum messages are translated through the institution, they change. This brings us to the second point mentioned above, the social production of museum messages. To study how historical research is transformed into educational programs to be impressed on frontline interpreters who in turn tell stories (based on those programs) to the public is to study not only changes in meaning but the social factors that influence such changes. To take an example that we will develop later in the book, the museum historians' notions of what a critical social history should include developed in dialogue with the research and ideas of their colleagues in the academy. In its initial stages, the revised Colonial Williamsburg story was significantly informed by this audience of professional historians. Not only did (and do) the foundation's historians interact at professional meetings and through professional publications with their academic colleagues, their relationships to those colleagues were (and are) influenced by the institutional relationships of museums to universities (relationships marked by vexing assessments of relative scholarly prestige).

Now, to develop this example one step further: as this academically informed version of the Colonial Williamsburg story is translated into stories for a broader public, a second group of interlocutors, the visitors, plays a role in its production. This is a complicated business that we will examine later in some detail; for now, suffice it to say that museum professionals have definite ideas about what audiences will tolerate, and that "what" entails not only the content of museum stories but the manner of their presentation. In brief, teaching history to the public is a social encounter with rules of its own, some of which are imposed on the situation by the museum (its values and expectations), and some by what the visitors bring to it. The result is that the history told on the front line at Colonial Williamsburg is in some respects different from the history that appears on the printed pages of foundation planning documents. This is hardly surprising, but neither should it be overlooked in the study of museum messages.

Focusing on the social production of museum messages caused us to rethink the dominant model of cultural production that guides research in museum studies and cultural studies. Scholars working in these fields typically pursue three interrelated sorts of questions. As we suggested above, they ask about the ideological meanings contained in cultural representations, about the relationship of those ideological meanings to the interests and intentions of the producers of cultural products, and about the ways consumers interpret the products they receive, either reproducing or resisting the meanings intended by cultural producers.

This model too neatly delineates producers and consumers of messages, in effect reifying them as isolable agents and neglecting the complex ways in which the parties to communicative exchanges are mutually constituted in the very process of exchange. At Colonial Williamsburg, for example, are the internal audiences—the frontline employees—producers or consumers of museum messages? They are, of course, both. At the very least, then, an analysis of their role in the production of Colonial Williamsburg's messages will have to consider the separate moments in which they receive, or consume, a version of those messages and then reauthor them vis-à-vis the visiting public.

But even making this adjustment leaves intact the model of discrete producers and consumers of messages; frontline employees may play both roles, but this sort of analysis does not question the distinctiveness of the roles themselves. We found, however, that producers of messages at Colonial Williamsburg held certain distinctive ideas about their audience that profoundly affected their communicative work. Museum professionals have become increasingly concerned with "visitor response." At Colonial Williamsburg, they were constantly trying to monitor their audience—to discover how visitors were consuming historical products—and to use that information to modify those products according to the needs and desires of their consumers, as the institution defined them. Every new program they instituted, every shift in interpretive focus they argued for, arose at least in part, they claimed, out of visitor needs and desires. In short, the producers of history at Colonial Williamsburg portrayed themselves as responding to an audience—one, to be sure, whose interests were often hard to fathom, but one whose interests were nonetheless salient.[11]

More generally, Colonial Williamsburg's producers operated with the same three-part model of producer-product-consumer that museum analysts presuppose. This means that the theoretical schema that guides much museum research is itself part of the field of study. The cultural representations generated at Colonial Williamsburg were full of self-conscious talk about the producers' intentions; and moreover, intent itself was always entangled in a "native" version of a dialogical relationship between producer and consumer. Because of this, we have eschewed the producer-product-consumer schema as an organizational framework within which to present the results of our research. As explained above, we, too, are interested in the production and consumption of cultural representations, but in our fieldwork we found that we could not neatly dissociate the moment of production from the moment of consumption, or producers from consumers.

To recapitulate: the questions that informed our work at Colonial Williamsburg did not differ fundamentally from those asked by other scholars of museums. We wanted to learn about the meanings conveyed in the history told at Colonial Williamsburg and about the cultural and ideological motivations of its producers and consumers. As anthropological fieldworkers, however, we considered more aspects of museum life than most museum scholars consider. And this, we feel, adds significantly to what we have to say about Colonial Williamsburg and, more generally, about the cultural politics of history museums.

Serendipity and Structure in Field Research

We began field research in January 1990. Almost every week, accompanied by Anna Lawson, a doctoral candidate in the Department of Anthropology, we traveled 120 miles from the University of Virginia in Charlottesville to Williamsburg, returning home after a stay of one or two (or, during the summers, three or four) days. We continued this sustained field research through the summer of 1991, after which our visits to Williamsburg tapered off.

In Williamsburg, we interviewed people employed by the foundation, from vice presidents to department managers to frontline interpreters to backstage "support" personnel (secretaries, researchers, seamstresses, gardeners, etc.). We repeatedly toured all the museum's buildings and attended as many special programs and events as we could. We tape-recorded (and then transcribed) almost all interviews, tours, and programs, and tried to return copies of transcripts to interviewees to provide them with a record of their remarks as well as to pursue further interviews. We presented occasional workshops to staff interested in our developing research. And we worked regularly in the foundation's byzantine archives, sorting through administrative documents to track changing policies and attitudes as well as to glean statistics on visitors, ticket sales, and budgets.

We gradually learned that our plan to study the entire foundation was infeasible, even for three researchers. Colonial Williamsburg is, as Kenneth Hudson puts it in *Museums of Influence*, "the site museum to end all site museums."[12] Its core is the restored portion of the city of Williamsburg, which runs for about a mile along the broad Duke of Gloucester Street. The 173-acre Historic Area, as this district is called, included at the time of our research "over one hundred gardens and greens" and eighty-eight "original" buildings, plus "an additional fifty major buildings and a large number of smaller structures" that had been reconstructed from the ground up "on their original sites."[13] In all, the reconstructed and restored capital had more than five hundred buildings, of which three dozen or so were open to the public. They included impressive public edifices like the Governor's Palace and the Capitol (both reconstructed); several places of business (taverns, stores, and craftshops); elegant private homes; and the outbuildings, or "dependencies," including a few used to depict the living and work quarters of black slaves, who made up half the population of the eighteenth-century city.

Just beyond the Historic Area is Bassett Hall, an eighteenth-century house that served as the Williamsburg residence of John D. Rockefeller Jr. and his wife, Abby Aldrich Rockefeller. This, too, was open to the public during the period of our research, as was Carter's Grove, a James River plantation which, though eight miles from the center of Williamsburg, is "owned and operated" by the foundation. In addition to a mansion house, Carter's Grove includes a reconstructed slave quarter, the "partially rebuilt structures of Wolstenholme Towne, one of the earliest English settlements in the New World," and (opened to the public at the end of our fieldwork) the Winthrop Rockefeller Archaeology Museum. The Abby Aldridge Rockefeller Folk Art Center and the DeWitt Wallace Decorative Arts Gallery are museums immediately adjacent to the Historic Area. So large, then, is this site museum, Colonial Williamsburg, that it contains other large museums.[14]

The educational work of the foundation is carried out by a large and varied staff. Frontline interpreters, most of whom are costumed in eighteenth-

The Governor's Palace. (photo by Molly Handler)

Street scene. (photo by Eric Gable)

Wetherburn's Tavern. (photo by Molly Handler)

The Wythe House. (photo by Molly Handler)

century clothing, talk to the public about American history and colonial life. The categories of interpreters are constantly changing at Colonial Williamsburg, but during the time of our field research the most important were the following. "Historic interpreters" led groups of visitors through particular buildings or on outdoor walking tours focused thematically on such topics as Colonial Williamsburg's gardens or women's history. "Character interpreters" were "living history" performers who spoke to the public in the "first person" (as opposed to the "third person" employed by the historic interpreters), that is, as eighteenth-century people. (Since these characters were "living" in 1770, they feigned ignorance when anachronistic questions were posed to them—about, for example, the American Revolution.) The dozen or so members of the all-black Department of African-American Interpretation and Presentation (AAIP) employed both first- and third-person techniques to teach black history. They also created an array of programs—musical and dramatic presentations, storytelling sessions, and videos—to get their messages across. Craftspersons simultaneously practiced their "historic trades" (about three dozen different ones at the time of our research) and "interpreted" them to the public, as did the workers who tended to the museum's livestock—oxen, horses, cattle, sheep, and poultry. "Visitor aides" took tickets, monitored crowds, and answered the questions, both practical and historical, of passers-by. Costumed "sales interpreters" staffed the cash registers in the shops selling period merchandise to the public and were expected to be able to provide historical information about the wares on display.

The frontline personnel are "supported" by a large complement of specialists and "trained" by still others. Curators, historians, archaeologists, archivists, and librarians work backstage to provide the information, stories, and programs the museum conveys to its public. Many of these specialists deliver lectures and presentations to specialized audiences (like groups of donors) or to the general public concerning both eighteenth-century topics and the work they do to learn about them. Education specialists train the museum's frontline employees and also work with elementary and high school teachers to devise special programs for the many student groups that visit Colonial Williamsburg every year.

So much for the education, or museum, side of the foundation. There is also the business side. From its inception, the project known to the public as Colonial Williamsburg was established as two corporations, as explained in *Colonial Williamsburg: The First Twenty-five Years* (1952): "Colonial Williamsburg, Incorporated, was formed to serve the historical and educational purposes of the organization, and holds title to properties within the designated historic areas. Williamsburg Restoration, Incorporated, is a business organization and holds title to properties which have been purchased for business uses. The term 'Colonial Williamsburg' has been adopted as the institutional name to define the entire project and includes both corporations."[15] Over the years the legal relationship between the two corporate entities has been changed several times with an eye to efficiency, the maximization of income, and in response to changing federal tax codes. In 1970, the two corporations mentioned above were merged to become the Colonial Williamsburg Foundation. In 1983, the foundation's board approved "the formation of a new hotel subsidiary . . . Colonial Williamsburg Hotel Properties, Incorporated," which was to operate "on a budget separate from the parent corporation."[16] This was the legal relationship of the foundation's two sides at the time of our research.

More important, for our purposes, than the formal corporate structure of the foundation is the fact that so much of what goes on there occurs in organizational units devoted to business and administration. There are divisions or departments for advertising and marketing, for the foundation's four hotels and seven restaurants, for facilities and property management, for products (from expensive reproduction furniture to trifling souvenirs), for corporate planning and finance, and for personnel, or "human resources." As is the case with most large, bureaucratic institutions, the specifics of corporate organization change continually, and it is beyond the purpose of this book to attempt to chart them. What is crucial is to recognize that in addition to the highly visible historically costumed employees, the vast majority of the backstage staff who work at Colonial Williamsburg are not historians and curators but waiters and waitresses, maids and bellhops, janitors and laundresses, secretaries and computer specialists, gardeners and construction workers, bus drivers and security officers, and the scores of supervisors and managers who oversee those workers' routines.

And then, of course, there are the visitors—since the early 1970s, a million paying visitors each year, give or take a hundred thousand. Colonial Williamsburg published marketing research data profiling the museum's visitors during the period of our fieldwork. "Most of our visitors come from within a 500-mile radius, primarily from the Northeast states," the marketers announced. The "top markets" (in order of importance) were New York City, Washington, D.C., Philadelphia, Boston, Baltimore, Norfolk, Harrisburg,

Street scene. (photo by Eric Gable)

Cleveland, Chicago, and Pittsburgh. Important markets not from the eastern half of the United States included Los Angeles (eleventh), Canada (thirteenth), San Francisco (fourteenth), and Dallas (nineteenth). Typical visitors, according to these data, "are between the ages of 35 and 64," "are married," "have gone to college," "earn $30,000 or more per year," "travel primarily in pairs or with children," and "have visited before."[17] From our own observations, we would add that visitors to Colonial Williamsburg are predominantly white, except for urban school groups. Families with children are prominent among the museum's visitors, but although the foundation nurtures an image of itself as family oriented, its survey data indicate that families are in the minority; the commonest social unit visiting Colonial Williamsburg is the couple. We should also note that the composition of the visiting public varies with the seasons: families with children are most common in the summer, school groups tour in the late spring and early summer, and retired people tend to come in the autumn and winter.[18]

We have said that the size and complexity of Colonial Williamsburg thwarted our ambition to study the place in its totality. Our academic expertise had prepared us to study the business of history making but not the business of business. Yet the business aspects of Colonial Williamsburg were both central to its daily life and a frequent topic of conversation among

The Williamsburg Inn. (photo by Molly Handler)

employees, even (perhaps especially, as we will discuss below) those on the museum side. Thus, in our ambition to study *everything* that was going on around us, we inquired about business operations as well as history making.

We gradually learned, however, that we would never have enough time to make a detailed ethnographic study of each administrative unit or functional specialty within the foundation. In part this was due to the ethnographer's predilection to focus closely on what we might call the microsociology of human interaction and, in the process, to try to learn something of the life histories and motivations of the participants. In doing so we came to know more than casually perhaps two dozen people at Colonial Williamsburg. We also conducted more than two hundred interviews with individual employees at various levels of the foundation and more than fifty interviews with visitors (these lasted anywhere from less than an hour to seven hours and ultimately yielded many hundreds of typed pages of transcripts). But what one gains in depth one loses in breadth; inevitably, we learned more about some people and some aspects of the foundation than about others.

The choices that ethnographers make as research unfolds (at times it seemed to unravel!) are prompted both by serendipity and by a developing understanding of what is important. Serendipity comes in the form of personal relationships that engage or satisfy both researcher and "native consultant"—as opposed to those that fail; the kinds of access the researcher is granted to files, to closed meetings, and to backstage programs and facilities; the kinds of events that one happens on, from after-hours parties to once-only presentations of special programs—including such "historic" events as the picketing of Colonial Williamsburg by the foundation's unionized hotel and restaurant workers early in 1991; and the particular collection of mostly public, but sometimes strictly internal, documents the researcher happens to amass.

An anecdote is in order here. While working in the archives, we learned of a class of documents that we thought might be useful but were not available to us without special permission. We raised the matter with the appropriate corporate vice president, who, after some consideration, denied us access on the grounds that the documents in question might refer to delicate personnel matters. When we mentioned this casually to another vice president, he immediately gave us a stack (several years' worth) of the documents in question—which, though they circulated only among administrative officers, were apparently little read by them. He would eventually, he told us, discard his copies anyway, and he let us keep them. We found that they contained few delicate personnel matters, and in any case we have not drawn on them for such material.

In the end, we focused most of our attention on five aspects of museum life. First was the museum's public educational programs. We toured every building that was open during the time of our research at least once, usually several times; for each, we taped and transcribed at least one example of a complete tour and often several examples using different interpreters and audiences. We also attended (and usually taped) at least one version of most of the special programs (plays, lectures, and backstage demonstrations) that occurred regularly during our research. And we conducted extensive interviews with frontline personnel and visitors.

Second, we conducted a series of interviews with the staff members who worked with objects and artifacts. This included both museum-side personnel in the Department of Collections and business-side personnel responsible for developing and marketing products, as well as archaeologists and architectural historians.

Third, we paid close attention to the hotel and restaurant workers' union during early 1991, when its members picketed Colonial Williamsburg during a contract dispute.

Fourth, we tried to be systematic in studying the foundation's corporate culture by interviewing most of the seventeen or so vice presidents as well as many department heads, managers, and supervisors. We also collected and studied the endless public relations literature that Colonial Williamsburg addresses to a range of audiences, both internal and external.*

Fifth, we realized quickly that African-American history was the linchpin of historical revisionism at the foundation, and so our associate, Anna Lawson, agreed to focus her research on the Department of African-American Interpretation and Presentation.[19]

These five areas of concentration were decided in part by serendipitous factors that led us in some directions rather than others, but the trajectory of our research probably owed more to our developing sense of what was significant and to the questions we brought with us. We explained above the kinds of questions that recent museum scholarship has raised. Those questions—about the meaning of history, how that meaning changes, and whose interests particular historical meanings serve—were profoundly engaging to Colonial Williamsburg insiders, who, after all, work in a world that is shaped in important ways by the critical literature on museums. As we explained at the outset, the arrival of social history and, more generally, the changing Colonial Williamsburg story were major concerns for most of the museum-side staff, as they were for us.

A second "native" concern that came to preoccupy us was the tension or contradiction between the foundation's two sides. This was epitomized, during the first year of our research, by the many conversations we heard about a nine-million-dollar golf course the foundation was planning to build. Some employees, especially frontline personnel, thought that the addition of a third (!) golf course indicated excessive commercialization at the expense of educational integrity. Others accepted management's contention that the facility was necessary to help Colonial Williamsburg compete in the lucrative conference business, which accounts for a significant portion of the hotels' and restaurants' revenues. Internal criticisms moved in the opposite direction, too. Some business-side personnel worried that the museum was moving too far in the direction of social history, at the expense of the great men—

---

*Colonial Williamsburg generates an amazing variety of printed material, both for internal consumption and for various audiences beyond the foundation. We cite these sources fully in the notes, but as an aid to the reader we mention here the publications we used most frequently: the foundation's annual reports, the *Colonial Williamsburg News* (an in-house newspaper that has been published biweekly or monthly since 1948), *Colonial Williamsburg* (a glossy quarterly publication sent to donors), the *Visitor's Companion* (an eight-page newspaper-style list of events given to visitors during the period of our research), and various editions of the official Colonial Williamsburg guidebook.

Thomas Jefferson, George Washington, Patrick Henry, Peyton Randolph, George Wythe—about whom visitors were (it was presumed) most curious. They wondered whether audiences are willing to be exposed to the harsh conditions of slavery, or whether a pleasant past is the only history that is marketable. In short, the Colonial Williamsburg we came to know was pervaded by an institutional identity crisis. Was it a "Republican Disneyland" or a "living history museum," a "megaresort" or a "serious educational institution"?—to ask the question with phrases that insiders used repeatedly. Or, to ask it another way, but still sticking to terms used by the natives, what is the ideal balance between "education" and "entertainment" at Colonial Williamsburg?

Questions such as these are certainly not absent from the literature on museums,[20] perhaps because they are closely related to questions about historical revisionism. In any event, our research took shape in response to both sorts of questions. We wanted to understand the relationship between critical social history and celebratory patriotic history at Colonial Williamsburg. We also wanted to understand the relationship of business and education within the foundation, and the relationship between that duality, on the one hand, and the duality of critical and celebratory history, on the other.

The pursuit of such questions led us to engage current debates in cultural studies and museum scholarship. We believe that the analysis presented in this book both follows and complicates the notions of hegemony and resistance that dominate those discussions. As we explained at the outset, the work of the social historians seeking to revise the Colonial Williamsburg story had to overcome (or at least work around) an entrenched social elite and a hegemonic ideology. They knew this as well as any of the institution's critics. Elite self-interest, middlebrow values, commercial zeal, and the exigencies of the mass-leisure market are all social facts with which revisionist history makers had to contend as they tried to change Colonial Williamsburg. Yet because these social facts figured in the stories that Colonial Williamsburg insiders told about themselves, they must be treated not simply as forces impinging on museum professionals from the outside, but as elements these people have to a large extent internalized. Or, to put it another way, the insiders' habitual talk about those social facts is a social fact in its own right, and a crucial one, for their decisions and actions are influenced by the way they anticipate the impingements of class conservatism and commercialization. This sociological self-consciousness on the part of the natives must be reflected in the anthropologist's account of the fate of social history at Colonial Williamsburg. Indeed, as we will argue, the significance of those social facts derives as much from the natives' belief in them as from their independent efficacy. Those disembodied abstractions "commercialization," "middlebrow taste," even "the public" itself are like the ghosts and ancestor spirits of classical ethnographies. The anthropologist need not pronounce on the ultimate reality of such concepts, for the natives, by believing in them and by talking for them even when they are otherwise silent, make them socially real.

The upshot is that the workings of hegemony prove to be more complicated than any simple model of cause and effect suggests. Like many critics of museums, when we first considered the question of hegemony in the museum, our initial position was that Colonial Williamsburg's social historians had been co-opted by the combination of conservative political and business values that seemed to dominate the museum. Such a position was informed as much by our place, as intellectuals, in American society as it was by the results of our research: it was easy for us to reproduce, rather uncritically, the ideas (heard frequently at Colonial Williamsburg) that business corrupts education and that patriotism sells better than a dirty past. But as anthropologists, our method was to listen to the natives, as David Schneider suggests in an important book about American culture.[21] And as we listened to the foundation's educators and business people, we began to think that their relationship entailed more than the mere domination of one set of values by another. We began to discern something like a mutual blurring of responsibilities, wherein each of the foundation's "sides" talked about its goals in the language of the other. There was, in other words, no simple way to know whose values were dominant at Colonial Williamsburg, or whose interests were served by them.

Our attempts to find a neat answer to questions such as these have frustrated us—we have not been able to reduce our account of social history at Colonial Williamsburg to a single-stranded narrative. The chapters that follow, then, are ethnographic explorations of aspects of the institution which, we believe, impinge crucially on the making of social history in this American museum and nonprofit corporation. Chapter 2 examines some prevailing images of Colonial Williamsburg and the ways the foundation's messages are constantly inflected by attempts to enhance images that are considered positive and to parry those deemed negative.

There follow three chapters concerning history making proper. Chapter 3 looks at theories of history making at Colonial Williamsburg; that is, at historiography. Chapter 4 concerns what we might call epistemological politics; that is, the relationship between historiography and internal struggles over interpretive choices. Chapter 5 presents an ethnographic account of the social history programming that was being presented in 1990 and 1991.

The next three chapters examine other factors that affect the production of social history at Colonial Williamsburg. Chapter 6 sketches some of the central values of the foundation's corporate culture. Chapter 7 is an ethnographic account of the front line, where the museum's history is delivered to the public who consume it. Chapter 8 looks at labor relations at the foundation, focusing on a struggle between management and the hotel and restaurant workers' union. Whether the conclusion, chapter 9, succeeds in tying these strands together in a useful way we must leave for the reader to decide.

On the Use of Quoted Material

Our analysis relies heavily on what people at Colonial Williamsburg told us, often in formal interviews, and on what employees told the public during guided tours, staged demonstrations, and the like. We tape-recorded most interviews and most of the public events we attended; in all such cases, we asked the permission of those whom we wished to tape before doing so. Furthermore, when taping, we promised that we would not quote people by name in any publications resulting from our work. Thus, most of the quoted material from people at Colonial Williamsburg is not attributed to named individuals, except when we draw on the published (and therefore publicly available) writings of the foundation's scholars and administrators.

By disciplinary convention, anthropologists quote informants or consultants anonymously or pseudonomously. This is not without problems. For example, as James Clifford points out, placing quotations in the mouths of generic tribesmen implies that all members of a group think alike.[22] It will be clear from the following that all Colonial Williamsburg insiders do not think alike—there is no generic "Colonial Williamsburger." But we have stuck to the convention of anonymity because much of what people at Colonial Williamsburg told us concerned the politics of the place, and many people would have been reluctant to talk if they thought their "backstage" ideas would become publicly available in a form that identified them personally. Furthermore, we have by and large not been concerned to relate people's arguments to their personal lives and backgrounds. It was their place within the corporate structure, not their individual personalities, which, we thought, was most salient in shaping the conversations we had with them. Therefore, although we do not quote people by name, we consistently identify speakers by their position at the foundation (e.g., "as one vice president told us").

Such solutions or the use of pseudonyms are not without problems. In *Plainville Fifteen Years Later,* anthropologist Art Gallaher tells of conducting a restudy of an American small town and finding in the local library a well-worn copy of his predecessor's book, *Plainville, U.S.A.* In the margins people had written in the real names of the people to whom the first anthropologist had given pseudonyms.[23] Not surprisingly, ethnographies arouse the curiosity (and often the ire) of their subjects. Colonial Williamsburg is a large enough local community that the speakers we identify in this book by structural position (vice president, frontline interpreter, etc.) cannot be personally identified with certainty. In any case, it was not our intention to name individuals. Our ethnography is an analysis of the culture of a corporate world, not a story about individuals within that world.

Quotations from people at Colonial Williamsburg are taken verbatim either from our notes or, in most cases, from transcripts of taped interviews or tours. We use quotation marks to introduce terms and phrases routinely used at Colonial Williamsburg or more generally in the museum world (e.g., "interpreter"), but after the first use, such terms are no longer placed within quotation marks.

2 ∎ *Imag[in]ing Colonial Williamsburg*

Mechanical Squirrels

Costumed employees in the Historic Area at Colonial Williamsburg some-times like to ridicule the "clueless" visitor, "the rube from Toledo," the one who gets off the bus at the Duke of Gloucester Street and expects to find a theme park, complete with thrilling rides. This visitor is part of the mythol-ogy of the place. Interpreters tell and retell the story about the visitor who, stooping to get a closer look at one of the nearly tame squirrels that are everywhere scurrying or begging for tidbits, asked: "Is it mechanical?"

The clueless visitor who thinks live squirrels are clever simulacra is a kind of stereotype. Such people do, however, exist—as we discovered while inter-viewing, at random, visitors on the streets of the reconstructed city. Once, for example, when we tried to initiate an interview with a couple from South Dakota by explaining that we were "writing a book about how a museum reconstructs the past," both seemed nonplussed. Why did we want to talk to them? When we explained that we wanted to know what visitors to Colonial Williamsburg thought of the way the museum reconstructed the past, the woman (a teacher of "gifted children K through 12") exclaimed: "Oh, this is a museum? I thought it was an attraction—a theme park!" When we asked her why she thought Colonial Williamsburg was a theme park and not a museum, her husband, a Lutheran minister, chimed in, "They charge like a theme park." Because the museum charged so much, he was suspicious that the place might not be exhibiting anything like a close approximation of "the past": "Being a tourist, you're always getting the feeling that they're doing things for the attraction and not the history." "Of course," he added, "we just came from Disney World so we're a little wary."*

The impression that Colonial Williamsburg had made on these educated middle-class visitors from America's heartland is one of the foundation's nightmares. If visitors can mistake Colonial Williamsburg for a theme park, they have not been convinced of its reality, its historical authenticity. Further, instead of seeing Colonial Williamsburg as an altruistic cultural institution whose lofty mission is public education and historic preservation, they have mistaken it for a commercial enterprise, a business that sells phony experiences to make a profit. To see Colonial Williamsburg as a theme park, then, is doubly injurious, for such an interpretation violates both the foundation's historical integrity and its civic purpose.

Colonial Williamsburg has, in short, an image problem. But that image problem is not easy to shed, for it stems, at least in part, from the foundation's hybridity, its dual character as educational institution and business concern. In American culture, the relationship between business values and educational values is complex. On the one hand, business and educational values can be understood to support one another. Business is work, the work that sustains life; more particularly, business in America is a rationalized method of pursuing and quantifying work and its products in order to sustain "the ever higher standard of living," as the anthropologist Jules Henry puts it in his study of American culture.[1] Education is training for work. A good education, as Americans often define it, provides students with the skills they will need to be successful in landing and keeping good—that is, "high-

---

*Stephen Fjellman's ethnography of Walt Disney World is entitled *Vinyl Leaves,* and the main body of the text begins with a description of a Disney Corporation fake tree made of pre-stressed concrete, steel mesh, paint, and 800,000 vinyl leaves. Interestingly, Fjellman's preface is sited at Colonial Williamsburg, which is portrayed as a kind of prelude to Disney World: "It was about as nice as late April gets in Colonial Williamsburg. . . . As I stood there . . . I threw my figurative arms out shoulder-high and bellowed in my mind, 'I love it here!' How could I spend more time in places like this, places where I am endlessly entertained? Where would I hang out if I could? And two thoughts came to my mind simultaneously, jostling and connected: I have tenure, and I'm going to Disney World!" (Fjellman 1992:1, xv).

paying" and "interesting"—work. Candidates for public office in the 1990s often justify their stated commitment to education by saying that America needs the "best-trained workforce" to compete in the global economy.

Business and education are understood by many Americans to fit together in a second way. Education is itself an important component of a high standard of living. One of the rewards of success in business is that individuals and society in general can devote economic resources to "spiritual" or "cultural" activities. Citizens benefit from such activities—from higher education, the arts and religion—in ways beyond those that can be calculated in economic terms.[2]

On the other hand, Americans also experience tension between the values of business and those of education. First, Americans often judge what they conceive as purely cultural activities—art for art's sake, for example, or abstract historical speculation—to be impractical and wasteful, or, at best, a luxury that can be sacrificed in hard times. Second, even when they grant the value of impractical endeavors, Americans want to know how to measure success in them. In other words, granted that purely cultural activities have value in and of themselves, how is that value to be calculated? How, for example, can university professors and museum professionals demonstrate their "productivity"? Finally—this time from the side of education and culture—business can be seen to compromise, corrupt, or pollute "higher" activities that should not have to be justified in economic terms. In sum, business demands that education and culture prove their value in business terms, while education and culture can reject those terms as unworthy of or irrelevant to their endeavors.

The intersection of business and education in one institution, Colonial Williamsburg, requires careful impression management. The public, and employees as well, must be taught that a correct relationship obtains between the two sides of the foundation. This gives rise to a standard and pervasive script that the foundation produces about itself. In this script, Colonial Williamsburg is a business—indeed, it is a "well-run" business. But—and the *but* looms large—it is unique because its product is not the food it sells in its restaurants, the colonial-era reproductions it makes available through an upscale home-furnishings catalog, the pleasant ambiance of a stroll down its tree-shaded streets, the thrill of chatting with a person who acts and looks like someone straight out of the eighteenth century. No, Colonial Williamsburg produces education. The rest—the historical entertainment, the smooth arrival of the meal at your table, the invisible endowment that quietly grows—is all in the service of education.

In the correct image of Colonial Williamsburg, then, business is important but secondary; it "supports" education, the ultimate purpose of the institution. As we shall see, Colonial Williamsburg works hard to produce what it considers to be proper images of itself for its various publics. But as we shall also see, such a project can never be successful. Thus we find that the concern—indeed, the obsession—with image has become a guiding and characteristic problematic that shapes the way the institution works and ultimately the kinds of messages it can produce. Proper image becomes an end in itself. A great deal of pedagogic work goes into creating and maintaining a proper image—a great deal of work goes into impression management.

The Image of Profit in the Second Yankee Reconstruction

Colonial Williamsburg was born in impression management. As the frequently told story has it, the Reverend Mr. W. A. R. Goodwin, rector of Bruton Parish Episcopal Church in Williamsburg, convinced John D. Rockefeller Jr. to put up the money to restore the "one remaining Colonial village" in America.[3] Goodwin was a visionary. Sensitive to the presence of the ghosts of the American Revolution in Williamsburg, he wanted to turn the town into a national shrine. To do so he needed a patron, and to convince a patron he needed to make that person see through the shabby modernity of the town—its "garages and gas tanks . . . and . . . Ford cars"—to the hidden but still extant colonial reality. Henry Ford refused Goodwin's advances, but Rockefeller, whom Goodwin pursued tenaciously for several years, eventually accepted them. Goodwin's approach to Rockefeller between 1924 and 1927 involved a negotiation of the proper image of Williamsburg. The story is full of surveying, measuring, mapping, and platting. When Goodwin wrote to architect William G. Perry to engage him to prepare some of the first maps of what was to be the restored Historic Area, he asked: "I find myself wondering whether you would be interested to join with me in trying to visualize, and then work out a plan which might be used to interest others in the work of preserving and restoring" the colonial city. With the help of Perry's maps, Goodwin was able to create an image of Williamsburg that persuaded Rockefeller to undertake the project.[4]

The Rockefeller family, too, was deeply concerned about images—in particular, maintaining a proper image of itself vis-à-vis the American public. In an egalitarian culture, great wealth is almost by definition under public suspicion.[5] In a society in which everyone is equal in their fundamental humanity—one in which it is high praise to be called "ordinary" and "just like everyone else"—the extremely wealthy are set apart as extraordinary and, even worse, as above the masses of ordinary people. Philip Kopper, in his sumptuous and informative history of Colonial Williamsburg, noted that John D. Rockefeller Jr.'s "life's work [was] to manage his father's empire and achieve the public rehabilitation of the man who had come to personify (somewhat unfairly) the evils of great wealth. The scion devoted most of his . . . highly disciplined energies to the systematic support of worthy causes." The younger Rockefeller, according to historian Peter Dobkin Hall, "appears to have felt compelled to invent a tradition that would explain and justify the fact of the family's wealth."[6]

It is probably a mistake to reduce Rockefeller philanthropy to simple impression management. John Ensor Harr and Peter J. Johnson, biographers of the Rockefeller dynasty, have argued that it is a "myth" to understand the philanthropy of the dynastic founder, John D. Rockefeller, as an attempt to "expiate his guilt for his years of greed and riding roughshod over everyone in building his monopoly." Rather, Rockefeller's philanthropy, and that of his son and heir, "was born out of religious principles, not public relations or a sense of guilt." The Rockefellers apparently conceived of themselves as stewards of societal wealth, wealth to be used for the good of society.[7]

Yet public relations, if not guilt, was a crucial issue for the Rockefellers, both because they felt they had to counter public images of the dynastic founder as a robber baron and because they were constantly stalked by people seeking money.[8] Thus, for example, when Rockefeller authorized Goodwin to begin buying up properties in Williamsburg at the end of 1926, he enjoined the strictest secrecy concerning the patron's identity, apparently fearful that public knowledge of the identity of Goodwin's backer would drive up real estate prices in Williamsburg.[9] Not only would that make the project more expensive, it would also open the Rockefellers to charges of exploiting an unsuspecting public, swindling them of their property for private gain. (Later, when the restoration was a public and going enterprise, an architectural adviser cautioned that "promiscuous looting" [of buildings, to salvage old materials] *or its appearance* should be avoided.")[10] The enjoined secrecy caused Goodwin no small trouble, as his parishioners speculated about *his* motives in buying property after property. Some felt that he abused his "pastoral responsibilities" by "unfairly influenc[ing] many naive parishioners." In any case, by the time Goodwin announced the identity of his patron at a town meeting in June 1928, he had spent more than two million of Rockefeller's dollars.[11]

Rockefeller philanthropy differed from that of earlier generations of

American elites not only in scale but in organization: it was, in Hall's words, "scientifically targeted" and "rationally administered." Once Rockefeller committed himself to the restoration of Williamsburg, he turned the project over to administrators and experts. The restoration was quickly incorporated in 1928 as Colonial Williamsburg, Inc., and the Williamsburg Holding Company (renamed Williamsburg Restoration, Inc., in 1934). Teams of experts with the best academic credentials, mainly architects and architectural historians, were hired, both as permanent staff and as outside consultants.[12]

Once the restoration was under way, the citizens of Williamsburg had to be persuaded that it was a good thing. At the June 1928 public meeting, Goodwin argued that the restoration would provide not only spiritual rewards but material ones as well. There was some opposition—one local citizen, Major S. D. Freeman, presciently argued that Williamsburg citizens would lose control of their town as they became museumified, like "a butterfly pinned in a glass cabinet"—but Goodwin carried the day.[13]

More interesting for our purposes than the politics of real estate development is the politics of culture that accompanied the restoration. Not only was it necessary to persuade the citizens of Williamsburg to reimagine their relationship to their local polity, it was necessary to teach them to reimagine their local culture and history. The identity of Williamsburg's white citizens had to be remade with the American Revolution rather than the Confederacy as its focal point, and the scientific authority of the restoration's experts was crucial in this matter.[14]

The relationship of Rockefeller philanthropy to academic and scientific expertise is important to note because it has remained central in the corporate culture of Colonial Williamsburg. "All my life I have employed experts," Rockefeller Jr. once remarked. "I listen to what they say and then I exercise my own good judgement."[15] The statement neatly shows that apparently neutral expertise is not unconnected to value judgments. But to establish one's judgments as authoritative, their basis in expertise must be stressed and their connection to what are ultimately personal values downplayed.

The problem of authorizing a value-laden point of view on the basis of scientific or academic expertise is neatly illustrated by another Rockefeller history project, the writing of a biography of the senior Rockefeller. This preoccupied Rockefeller Jr. throughout the 1920s and 1930s (perhaps not coincidentally, the early years of the Williamsburg project). The family's problem, according to Hall, was to find a biographer with the academic credentials to inspire critical respect in the final product and still exercise some control over that product: "Yearning for the legitimacy that a credible biography by an independent scholar would provide the family and its mission, yet deeply—and not unreasonably—afraid of giving any author, however eminent, the independence necessary to produce such a work, Junior was paralyzed. On the one hand, he did not want to offend his father, and on the other, he feared the impact on public opinion of too candid a treatment of him." Eventually Columbia University historian Allan Nevins was chosen for the task, and his 1940 biography "served to crystallize and legitimate the myth of the Rockefeller family's goodness and greatness."[16]

At Williamsburg, Rockefeller's hired scholars provided the knowledge, the historiographical perspective, and, no less important, the cultural taste that served as the basis for the restored, reimagined city. The reminiscences of Williamsburg residents who lived through the first years of the restoration—referred to by some as a second "Yankee reconstruction"—contain evidence of the battle that was fought as newly introduced standards of truth and authenticity gradually displaced indigenous ones. During the early years of the restoration, many Williamsburg residents continued to live in their houses as these were being restored. Both residents and tourists debated the virtues of the architectural and decorative choices that were made. Such debates could occur only if they could be couched in terms of personal choice. As one resident wrote in her diary in 1931, "Mr. Rockefeller is considered personally responsible for everything and his taste much criticized." But the restoration proceeded resolutely to act on the advice of its architectural experts, and on the belief that their accumulating knowledge was authoritative. Quite early on, buildings began to be "re-restored" to take account of new research, thereby legitimating research as a self-correcting, hence objective, process. When, for example, it was decided that a building had been reconstructed six feet away from its original foundations, Rockefeller provided funds to move it. "No scholar," he said, "must ever be able to come to us and say we have made a mistake." (Rockefeller, however, was never as interested in historical scholarship as he was in architectural restoration; according to Kopper, in the early years the foundation pursued historical research only because President "Chorley insisted on it to save Rockefeller possible embarrassment lest the Restoration err in its building . . . programs.")[17]

Gradually, Williamsburg residents accepted the new standards, although not without some resistance. Consider the following 1932 excerpt from the diary quoted above: "Of course the work has met with storms of criticism and disapproval. Intimate as we are with our surroundings, and each one of us brought up with firm convictions of the authenticity of the legends connected with different houses, it has been very irritating to have them exploded or ignored by strangers primed with information gained by 'research.'" Yet, as the diary makes clear, research eventually won the day: "We have all become house-conscious of course. . . . Those of us who have lately removed an old picket fence, or obliterated the traces of an old smoke house which was falling down in the backyard, are overcome by shame and remorse, while others who have not been able to afford new front steps or to have a little attic room remade, with a higher ceiling, are filled with pride as if their actions had been restrained by good taste and correct knowledge instead of by a lean purse. We became very wise also in antique furniture, china, etc. . . . We used to speak of 'Aunt Jane's Teapot' and 'Uncle James' sideboard,' but now it is 'the Spode Teapot' or 'the Sheraton sideboard.'"[18]

In this diary entry, "good taste" and "correct knowledge" are conflated. Indeed, such conflation recurs constantly in the foundation's attempts to market the proper image of itself to the public. Colonial Williamsburg's reputation for authenticity is also a reputation for good taste, and the foundation can, quite literally, trade on both. The oldest standing committee at the foundation today is the Products Review Committee (originally known as the Craft Advisory Committee). This committee has met regularly since 1937 to pass judgment on the authenticity and suitability of products to be marketed to the public as reproductions of Colonial Williamsburg antiques. From the first days of the restoration, visitors wanted to buy items similar to those exhibited in the restored buildings. When Colonial Williamsburg began marketing products to satisfy that demand, it decided that to protect its integrity, it could not yield to the temptation to reproduce objects unconnected to Williamsburg: "In order to preserve the dignity of the hall-mark, Mr. [Vernon] Geddy stated that he felt we should not put the hall-mark on any reproduction, the original of which was not on exhibition in Williamsburg, and the Committee ruled that hereafter, as a matter of principle, only furniture and furnishings which are used in Williamsburg or approved for use in Williamsburg by the Furnishings Committee, will be hall-marked as authentic reproductions by Williamsburg Craftsman, Incorporated."[19]

This principle states literally that authenticity is a function of the approval of experts. But a careful reading of the minutes shows that the choice of objects to be submitted for approval to scholarly authorities was in at least some cases market driven. When visitors expressed demand for a particular object, the Craft Advisory Committee often tried to acquire that object and have it placed in the exhibition buildings, since such placement made it suitable for reproduction. For example, in 1938 the committee felt pressed to respond to "constant requests for decanters to complete the set for the cellaret." The antique bottles in the collection at that time were inadequate: "Although the large gin bottle in the bar at the Raleigh Tavern is the correct shape of the period, it is of colored glass, and people who buy the cellarets are desirous of obtaining clear glass bottles." Wishing to accede to consumer demand without appearing to do so, "Mr. [Kenneth] Chorley stated . . . that . . . we should not go out of Williamsburg for something to reproduce which we do not have here," and it was decided "to wait until we procure some of these . . . bottles for use in the exhibition buildings before re-producing these for the cellarets."[20]

This last example returns us to the dance of business and education at Colonial Williamsburg. From the start, any appearance of profiteering was to be avoided. Conventional narratives of the origins and growth of the foundation's business enterprises depict Colonial Williamsburg as responding to public demand rather than creating it. Several people on the foundation's business side explained the growth of the reproductions program in such terms, telling us that tourists have always wanted to buy the objects they see exhibited. As Charles Hosmer noted in his history of historic preservation in America, "the restored buildings . . . had a magnetic effect" on Americans. They bought plans for Wythe House–like buildings, came to Colonial Williamsburg for ideas for furnishings and paint colors, and, because of their apparently insatiable craving for similacra of the colonial, made it hard for Colonial Williamsburg to resist the growing pressures from within to manufacture and market (or at least profit from the licensing of) colonial reproductions.[21] According to Kopper, Rockefeller was opposed to the building of Colonial Williamsburg's second hotel, the Lodge, because "the restoration shouldn't be in the hotel business." Nonetheless, the foundation's trustees approved the project and persuaded Rockefeller that "a modestly priced hotel was necessary" to accommodate the growing numbers of tourists who could not afford the pricy Inn, which the foundation had opened in 1937.[22]

While it is no doubt true that public demand for Williamsburg products was in part self-generated, these representations of the foundation's history downplay the element of economic calculation that was a part of policy making at Colonial Williamsburg from the beginning. Though the public perceived Rockefeller wealth as unlimited, the foundation's officers and advisers knew better. Fiske Kimball, director of the Pennsylvania Museum and a member of Colonial Williamsburg's Advisory Committee of Architects, stated the problem during a 1928 meeting: "It is necessary that the finished town be reasonably self-supporting or the Restoration will be destroyed in fifty years, as no conceivable endowment could be adequate."[23] Rockefeller himself wanted "to enable [Colonial Williamsburg] to stand on its own feet and prosper after he was gone." The hybrid structure of the organization, with its prominent business interests, was designed with an eye to such self-sufficiency. Harr and Johnson reported that in 1949, "the project . . . turned the corner financially, registering . . . an operating profit of $94,000, compared to a loss of $81,000 the preceding year. . . . Junior believed he had taken care of capital needs. . . . And there was hope that, in time, operating profits would begin to take care of future restoration needs as well as maintenance and enrichment."[24] We will return in later chapters to questions concerning the financing of Colonial Williamsburg. For the moment, we emphasize only that profit making has been an integral function of the organization almost from its inception, but great care has always been taken to persuade the various publics that profit is not the foundation's most important product.

The Image of Profit in a Nonprofit Corporation

During our field research, we were fortunate to be able to attend a one-day orientation session for new employees at Colonial Williamsburg. We met in a large meeting room in a temporary warehouse—a huge Quonset hut located in some of the least prestigious, farthest-off-stage acreage controlled by the foundation. During the day we frequently broke into small groups to accomplish, workshop style, some specified task, after which the entire group reconvened. The audience was diverse, including about fifty newly hired workers from every division in the organization. Some had taken positions that would place them in extensive contact with the visiting public, while others would work exclusively backstage; but all, apparently, needed to be taught how properly to see Colonial Williamsburg.

Among the featured topics of the session was the relationship between the foundation's organizational structure and its finances. The facilitator explained: "We're all part of the same program, even though you'll hear different. The hotel side is separate, but we're all under the same umbrella." She went on to lecture us about corporate finances: "How do we get our money? Where do we get our money? What happens to all that money? Do we show a profit?" Answering her own questions while pointing to an organizational chart entitled "Working Together," she explained: "No, we're a nonprofit organization. What happens is—this is very important—you have to make the visitor understand: they view it like Disney World. We're *not* out to make a profit." Of course, she continued, "a lot of people think we're here to make money like a theme park." It is the employee's responsibility to understand and then to convey to the public that the foundation has two sides: "What we have are all the support areas—archaeologists, research to support the education side. These people don't make any money. These people, the hotel side, make money." At the end of the orientation session she repeated: "Any questions about where the money comes from? You got it clear that we're nonprofit? The visitors are always asking how much money the Rockefellers make off this. Those are the smarter questions. They're asking how much of *my* tax dollars goes into this."

As this orientation session shows, Colonial Williamsburg takes great pains to ensure that its employees know, and can teach the visiting public, that the museum is not a profit-making enterprise. The summary description of the foundation appearing on the inside cover of recent annual reports announces the same message to donors: "The Colonial Williamsburg Foundation is the corporate name of the organization founded in 1926 to undertake the preservation and restoration of eighteenth-century Williamsburg. It is a nonprofit, tax-exempt, educational organization completely independent of any other foundation or organization and from all branches of government."[25] On the surface, this brief description is merely a compact statement of fact. But it is also a carefully contrived effort at impression management. The chief audience for the annual report is people who have given money to the foundation and who are encouraged to continue giving, people such as the thousands of patrons who have donated at least twenty-five dollars in that particular year, the hundreds of members of the Raleigh Tavern Society who pledge at least five thousand dollars annually, and the special patrons such as "former diplomat and publisher Walter Annenberg and his wife Leonore," who, in 1989, gave an "unrestricted" five million dollars to the foundation.[26] These are, in a sense, the foundation's shareholders. And the continuing flow of gifts from people like them is what the place has come more and more to depend on to perpetuate itself and grow.

A constant fear among those who work in fund-raising is that potential donors will not give to Colonial Williamsburg because "they think the hotels and restaurants do that, or the Rockefellers have taken care of things," as one fund-raiser told us. As some of his early advisers predicted, Rockefeller was not able to endow the foundation sufficiently to ensure its survival in perpetuity. Carlisle Humelsine, who succeeded Kenneth Chorley as Colonial Williamsburg's president in 1958, and Charles Longsworth, who became chief operating officer in 1977 and then succeeded Humelsine as chief executive officer two years later, had to manage the ongoing institutional transition. Kopper described the situation after Rockefeller Jr.'s death:

> After Mr. Rockefeller's death in 1960, Colonial Williamsburg was on its own in a way it had never been before. The challenge facing Humelsine was to direct its metamorphosis from one man's favorite philanthropy and consuming hobby to an independent institution that could hold its own in the competitive nonprofit world. Now he would have to begin soliciting major financial gifts both to augment the endowment fund and support special projects. . . . In time he hired a development officer, made him a vice president and took his advice on several fronts—including the chartering of the Raleigh Tavern Society. . . . One index of Humelsine's success is that the endowment stood at roughly $50 million when Rockefeller died; when Humelsine retired as chairman of the board in 1985, it was $130 million.[27]

Given Kopper's celebratory rhetoric, it is ironic that by the time we arrived at Colonial Williamsburg the Humelsine era was remembered by most employees old enough to have known it firsthand as a time of unbusinesslike inefficiency. In contrast, Longsworth (who had earned a graduate business degree from Harvard and subsequently served as a development officer at Amherst College and as president of Hampshire College) was viewed rather ambivalently as the man who had been brought onboard to initiate "sound business practices." Some museum-side personnel saw the Longsworth years as a time of degrading commercialization; others averred that the management disciplines he instituted were necessary for the foundation's survival and for the continuing progress of its educational programming. We will return to these divergent assessments in chapter 6. For now, it is enough to state that since Rockefeller's death, Colonial Williamsburg has developed increasingly complex relationships to a growing number of players in the corporate world.

The Good Corporate Neighbor

That visitors from South Dakota would mistake Colonial Williamsburg for a theme park is hardly surprising given what surrounds it. Colonial Williamsburg is a major local economic concern in a small university town in a relatively rural county in tidewater Virginia, but it does not stand alone on the landscape. Over the years the backwater college town of Williamsburg has blossomed into a burgeoning tourist destination in large part because of

Colonial Williamsburg's presence. Many people who patronize Colonial Williamsburg also come to Williamsburg to shop. They may go to the Pottery—a thrillingly chaotic and now venerable jumble of low warehouses selling, at cut-rate prices, lawn ornaments, toys, clothing, shoes, lamps and lampshades, plates, glasses, oriental rugs, kitchen items, food, coffee, spices, baskets, dried flowers, mirrors, picture frames, plants, purses, leather products, ashtrays, and decorative suits of armor, life-size. The Pottery is a family business that grew into a multimillion-dollar operation in a trajectory that paralleled Colonial Williamsburg's expansion. It began as a kiln (hence its name) producing saltware reproductions for Colonial Williamsburg's shops. But nowadays its low-rent appearance is an embarrassment to many who work at the foundation. The Pottery is a giant yard sale, the quintessence of kitsch. It is also the prototype for import emporia such as Pier One and for factory outlet shopping malls, and it is these latter retailing innovations that have lately set up shop alongside the Pottery on one of the major highways leading into Williamsburg.

The Pottery is likely counted among those businesses the foundation sometimes characterizes as "parasitic." Parasitic businesses use their proximity to Colonial Williamsburg to sell products that might tarnish the foundation's reputation. In 1969, in an effort to control exactly the kind of economic parasitism the Pottery represents, to provide working capital, and to broaden the tax base of the largely rural and relatively poor county by attracting "responsible corporate neighbors," Colonial Williamsburg sold a large tract of land to the Anheuser-Busch Corporation.

The foundation had acquired this land—mainly forest—when it bought, with a Rockefeller family gift, Carter's Grove Plantation. At the time there was some internal disagreement at high levels concerning the acquisition of the plantation. According to Kopper, President Chorley, for example, worried that the plantation would be a financial albatross, but he was overruled.[28] The foundation got a plantation and hundreds of acres of land, most of which it did not need. Later, it was able to sell this land to Anheuser-Busch while retaining a forested right-of-way to Carter's Grove.

To many, the decision to sell the land to Anheuser-Busch seemed to be a typical business deal, although Colonial Williamsburg tried to assure its public that it was not selling the land strictly because of the bottom line. To explain its decision, the foundation published a pamphlet entitled . . . *Planning for the Long Term,* which began with some personal reflections by the then president, Carlisle Humelsine. Humelsine noted that several distinguished friends of Colonial Williamsburg had asked him "questions ranging from, 'Why are you allowing commercial interests to destroy the environment of Williamsburg?' to, 'Why are you in the real estate business?' " These friends had, he reported, told him that the foundation and Anheuser-Busch "appear to be strange bedfellows." Humelsine had to distance Colonial Williamsburg from mere bottom-line concerns; he had to reiterate the foundation's claim to a higher morality. He did so by asserting that Colonial Williamsburg had acted according to a pragmatic altruism. The foundation was concerned with the overall economic health of the (at the time) very poor county in which it happened to be the largest employer and taxpayer. The county needed tax revenues, and its inhabitants needed good places to work, so Colonial Williamsburg, by bringing Anheuser-Busch into the neighborhood, was helping the county. As a result, the county would not be as tempted to attract businesses that might damage the "unique Williamsburg setting and the future of this area's environment."[29]

The decision to sell land to Anheuser-Busch changed the landscape in which Colonial Williamsburg operated and made it more likely, perhaps, that the city-museum would come to be perceived as a theme park. Anheuser-Busch set up not only a brewing facility but also Busch Gardens, an amusement park with thrill rides in various modern disguises located in ethnic theme communities, or "hamlets." The hamlets are meant to typify rural life in bygone eras in what Busch Gardens refers to as "the Old Country"— places modeled after England, Italy, Germany, and France. As one television advertisement we heard during our fieldwork described it, visitors are transported to the Old Country "without leaving the new country" by interacting with employees dressed in period or ethnic costumes in "a clean family-type setting."

Colonial Williamsburg also agreed to let Anheuser-Busch use a large portion of the land for residential real estate development, in the hope, some insiders suggested to us, that the upscale enclave community (Kingsmill) Anheuser-Busch planned to create on it would provide a stable local market for the services Colonial Williamsburg offers. Recently, other real estate developments have sprung up in the fertile ground that proximity to the reconstructed colonial city seems to provide. One such community is Ford's Colony, whose architecture echoes that of such Williamsburg landmarks as the Governor's Palace and the George Wythe House. A publicity packet tells prospective customers that "among the best reasons to live at Ford's Colony, one of America's finest planned communities, is its proximity to one of America's *first* planned communities, Colonial Williamsburg. . . . You'll not only see the colonial influence in our architecture. You'll see the colonial ideal of gracious living everywhere you turn."[30] Ford's Colony describes itself in much the same terms in a full-page advertisement that appears in *Colonial Williamsburg,* the foundation's quarterly journal for donors: at Ford's Colony "successful achievers like yourself" can enjoy a private piece of "Virginia's woodlands and wetlands" in a planned community that has won awards for its golf course, wine list and country club.[31]

That Colonial Williamsburg sells advertising space to Ford's Colony reveals that the relationship is perceived as symbiotic, at least potentially, rather than parasitic, even though the foundation never actively sought out an association with this corporate neighbor. As they borrow Colonial Williamsburg's prestige or the theme of history as tourist attraction, enterprises like Busch Gardens and Ford's Colony refashion what that community means to many Americans, transforming as a result the pedagogical environment in which the foundation's researchers and frontline employees must work. Similar refashionings of Colonial Williamsburg occur in the electronic and print media—for example, in the tourist press that churns out articles about Williamsburg as a vacation destination. Consider as an example an article in the December 1992 issue of *Better Homes and Gardens* entitled "Christmas in Williamsburg," by George Bush. Such articles have appeared regularly since the museum's inception in a range of periodicals—*Reader's Digest, Look, McCalls, American Home, National Geographic, Holiday, House Beautiful, Antique Monthly, Time,* and the travel sections of major newspapers, for example. Such publications both reflect and shape what might broadly be called middle-class values. Like the promotional literature of Ford's Colony, "Christmas in Williamsburg" presents upscale nostalgia: "No neon glare disrupts the mood of yesteryear, and Christmas in Williamsburg is devoid of . . . gaudy baubles. . . . You'll enjoy scenes from period plays, plus candlelight concerts and baronial balls reenacted to duplicate the past."[32]

Articles like "Christmas in Williamsburg" are often written with the help of Colonial Williamsburg's public relations and marketing staff. Nevertheless, like the images and built environments real-estate developers create, such images are not entirely under the foundation's control. The airbrushed landscapes they depict become a part of the image of Colonial Williamsburg that the public is thought to cherish—and such "cherished images" become, in turn, part of the cultural context that constrains what the foundation does or thinks it can do. Christmas at Colonial Williamsburg is historically inaccurate, and the public, by and large, knows this. "To be technical," as Bush put it, "many of the lovely decorations are not historically authentic."[33] In fact, the pure-as-driven-snow world the pageant evokes is anathema to the museum's critical social historians. Nevertheless, Christmas will continue to be a major event on the hybrid corporation's calendar as it tries to entertain and educate a public whose desire for a nostalgic past ceaselessly colors the artifactual landscape the foundation works to realize.

The nostalgic Williamsburg that the tourist press creates dovetails with the upscale Williamsburg that Ford's Colony markets and the entertaining Williamsburg that Busch Gardens provides. It is obvious that corporations such as Ford's Colony and Anheuser-Busch trade on their association with Williamsburg. But Colonial Williamsburg's managers admitted that it is hard to tell whether or not their efforts at creating marketing synergies have worked to the foundation's benefit. Will the people who buy Ford's Colony's description of Colonial Williamsburg as a "storybook community" appreciate the foundation's turn toward an antinostalgic social history?[34] Will the people who engage in an entertaining conversation with a costumed employee at the Festhaus in the German village at Busch Gardens see that interaction as being like a discussion with a first-person interpreter at Colonial Williamsburg portraying George Wythe, an Enlightenment renaissance man who tutored Thomas Jefferson and signed the Declaration of Independence? Does Busch Gardens attract tourists to an area they would not otherwise visit? Or does it lure away the families who should crowd the Duke of Gloucester Street in summertime?

Needless to say, such questions are discussed and debated by Colonial Williamsburg employees and officers, and many of them believe that entities such as Ford's Colony and even the good corporate neighbor, Anheuser-Busch, have become the foundation's sorcerer's apprentice. Reflecting on the Anheuser-Busch transaction, one vice president on the business side summarized for us the "schizophrenic thoughts," as he put it, that the foundation has had, in hindsight, about its decision. Stating the perceived negative repercussions first, he explained, "We've had some second thoughts from time to time. I say 'we' corporately. . . . To the extent that people start to think of Williamsburg as where Busch Gardens is, or the Water Country [a water-slide amusement park], or the Williamsburg Pottery, or whatever else comes along next, then we are diminished by that. We've become less what people came to see."

Perhaps this vice president's thoughts were "schizophrenic" because he did not want to admit that the foundation had made a mistake, and that the business side had somehow gotten out of hand by inviting Anheuser-Busch in. So, not content to leave the matter there, he went on to reaffirm the foundation's 1969 decision: "But I would tell you today that Anheuser-Busch is one of the best things that ever happened to Colonial Williamsburg and to this community. They are responsible corporate neighbors. They care. . . . You could rethink it a hundred times . . . [but] this is probably still the best way to develop that property."

Schizophrenic thoughts are the obverse of schizophrenic action. When the foundation acts like a business, it often does so in ways that are perceived to backfire in terms of education. Thus, not only must the foundation's educational programs be constantly strengthened to keep pace with its increasingly sophisticated marketing, its very image as an educational institution must continually be refurbished as well.

Credibility Armor

It is not only rubes from Toledo who look at Colonial Williamsburg and see a theme park.[35] In the same month that *Better Homes* celebrated "a Williamsburg Christmas season" that "is one of the most beguiling holidays your family is likely to experience,"[36] an organ of America's highbrow press, the *New York Review of Books,* published an article denigrating Colonial Williamsburg. The essay, an attack on contemporary architecture by critic Ada Louise Huxtable, opened with a tirade against Colonial Williamsburg, which Huxtable saw as "predating and preparing the way for the new world order of Disney Enterprises," an order that systematically fosters "the replacement of reality with selective fantasy." According to Huxtable, Colonial Williamsburg "has perverted the way we think," for it has "taught" Americans "to prefer—and believe in—a sanitized and selective version of the past, to deny the diversity and eloquence of change and continuity, to ignore the actual deposits of history and humanity that make our cities vehicles of a special kind of art and experience, the gritty accumulations of the best and worst we have produced. This record has the wonder and distinction of being the real thing."[37]

Huxtable's remarks epitomize an enduring critique of Colonial Williamsburg. Many of the museum's critics have said that it is literally too clean (Huxtable's "sanitized" is the favorite word), that it does not include the filth and stench that would have been commonplace in an eighteenth-century colonial town. Many critics go further than Huxtable and imply that Colonial Williamsburg is also metaphorically too clean—that it avoids historical unpleasantness like slavery, disease, and class oppression in favor of a rosy picture of an elegant, harmonious past. As one such critic, Michael Wallace, put it, Colonial Williamsburg "is a corporate world; planned, orderly, tidy, with no dirt, no smell, no visible signs of exploitation. Intelligent and genteel patrician elites preside over it; respectable craftsmen run production paternalistically and harmoniously; ladies run well-ordered households with well-ordered families in homes filled with tasteful precious objects."[38] This, of course, is exactly what similarly positioned critics say of Disneyland.[39] In this view, Disneyland and Colonial Williamsburg produce the kinds of tidied up, oversanitized products they do because they are big, middle-of-the-road "corporate worlds" whose ultimate purpose is profit making.

Moreover, that Colonial Williamsburg is too clean means ultimately that it is fake. If authenticity is what Colonial Williamsburg sells to its public, it is also the point of greatest vulnerability. This is especially true for the foundation's professional intelligentsia—its historians, curators, and the like—for they are in many senses peers of Wallace, Huxtable, and others who take critical potshots at them from the high ground of the ivory tower. But the too-clean critique also comes from the public at large, and the defense against this critique thus becomes the business of the institution as a whole; and this defense is undertaken at a variety of sites of image production.

Every day thousands of people visit Colonial Williamsburg, an institution whose mission is to show the public what colonial Virginia "was really like." The foundation staff knows that in every crowd there are individuals, invisible and unknown Wallaces and Huxtables, casting a cold and critical eye on the museum's claim to present that reality. Authenticity, in brief, becomes as much a question of creating and maintaining the right appearance as the truth itself. As one interpreter put it, "It is important to discuss facts because each facility wants to be accurate and to present to our customers and visitors the best historical interpretation possible and to retain its authentic reputation."

Reputation is something that pertains to the self or to the institution as a corporate personality, yet it is made and maintained vis-à-vis others. As the Colonial Williamsburg staff see it, the museum's reputation for authenticity is on the line every day, and every one of the myriad historical details that the museum collects and exhibits is both a witness to institutional authenticity and a window of vulnerability. When we asked a manager who was working on increasing the accuracy of the museum's costumes to explain the "educational payoff" of attention to historical detail, he responded by talking about reputation rather than pedagogy: "The clothing is just as important as creating an accurate interior, creating any sort of accuracy. Any time you have a break in your credibility, then everything that is credible is lost, or it's called into question. If you have someone who comes in, and they happen to see plastic buttons, or someone wearing obvious knee socks, instead of proper hosiery, then to me that's saying, well, that's not accurate. I wonder if the way that tea service is laid out is accurate? I wonder if the fact that that garden's laid out the way it is, I wonder if that's accurate? You start to lose it. That's why it's so important that our interpreters have the ability to take things that are less than accurate and get people to start thinking beyond them. And catching people, anticipating problems of credibility. Now, if we can catch them up, by using better tools, better floor arrangements, better costumes, better gardens, then that's one less chink in our credibility armor that we have to worry about."

Colonial Williamsburg defends its credibility every day on the streets of the reconstructed capital, but its defenses are not perfect. Mistakes happen. Visitors complain. Colonial Williamsburg's corporate archives contain a revealing record of how such complaints are resolved—files containing letters from disappointed visitors, along with the foundation's responses to them. The letters of response record an ongoing effort to put the best spin possible on these criticisms by invoking Colonial Williamsburg's unwavering fidelity to authenticity.

For example, an elderly couple wrote that their most recent visit had turned into "a long disappointing day" because they "found many things that did not fit the Williamsburg we've known over the past twenty years." They complained that the "lovingly truly preserved past of our America" was being marred by the presence of employees with nail polish, plastic earrings, and tennis shoes. President Longsworth replied: "You brought a sharp eye with you on your recent visit to Colonial Williamsburg. You caught a few of our interpretive staff with their authenticity and courtesy down. You may be sure that each of the violations you cite of courtesy standards and 18th-century apparel and appearance is being addressed by the supervisors of the violators. Your standards are ours, and we strive to see them honored by all employees. Being human, we sometimes fail, but our efforts to achieve authenticity and friendliness have been and will continue to be unflagging."[40]

Phrases such as "reputation" and "credibility armor," as well as the image of being caught with one's credibility-pants down, suggest the pervasive insecurity that, apparently, accompanies Colonial Williamsburg's claims to possess the really real. Even the foundation's social historians, those whose philosophy of history leads them to place greater importance on stories and themes than on individual details, experience this embattled concern for reputation.

An architectural historian, for example, told us what he characterized as a humorous story about an encounter with a visitor early in his career at

Display of locks and hinges for sale at Craft House. (photo by Molly Handler)

Williamsburg. The visitor—"some Joe Blow"—approached him and said that Colonial Williamsburg did not have a single padlock on any reconstructed building that was genuinely eighteenth century in design. In response to this criticism, the historian spent a day tracking down information on the locks in the reconstruction. Then he went to a museum famous for its collection of early American artifacts "to study the twenty-four or so eighteenth-century padlocks they had." He made drawings of those. Next, he told us, he "developed a rough typology—I think there were four recognizable styles of padlock, and the visitor was right, none of ours were like these." As a result, the historian wrote the visitor thanking him and promising that while Colonial Williamsburg could not afford to change all the old locks, "on every subsequent project" they would make more faithful reproductions.

The historian prefaced his humorous story by explaining that he and his colleagues sweat the details because they don't want to be "a joke" in the eyes of the public. His humorous portrayal of himself as an insecure ferret let loose on the problem of padlocks, because veracity in every detail is Colonial Williamsburg's hallmark and because he doesn't want to be a joke, reflects an abiding institutional concern. For the "Joe Blow" who points out flaws in the mimetic portrait of the past Colonial Williamsburg professes to create is another stock character in many stories employees tell about their encounters with visitors. He is, one administrator of frontline interpreters told us, "a magpie." A magpie is a bird that weaves odd trinkets—tinfoil, gum wrappers, colored yarn—into its nest. A human magpie at places like Colonial Williamsburg is someone who collects, indeed is obsessed with, a certain category of obscure historical facts.

Frontline employees are, if anything, more sensitive to the threat of the magpie than are the backstage personnel. To those who deal directly with the public, the magpie is an embarrassing nuisance who may be hiding among every flock of tourists, threatening to reveal an interpreter's ignorance (and knock him or her off the storyline) with a pointed query about some object or theme about which the interpreter will have no clue.

Magpies threaten individual reputations during brief encounters at particular sites, but they also threaten institutional reputations. The architectural historian who said that it is a point of honor that Colonial Williamsburg get the details right was protecting both his reputation and the institution's. "Veracity" or "authenticity," or getting the facts right, is an intrinsic value at Colonial Williamsburg, and it has a double quality. People like the architectural historian sweat the details, in part, because they, too, are magpies. The architectural historian told us that he loved the detective work involved in tracking down just such stray facts. But he also got the facts right so he wouldn't be exposed as "a joke" in public. The institution rewards him and others for responding to Joe Blow's trivial or tangential queries because this keeps the "credibility armor" nicely burnished. The concern for authenticity is as much a form of impression management as it is an ultimate value, a never fulfilled but always sought-after goal.

Luckily for the foundation, most visitors to Colonial Williamsburg seem to accept its claims to authenticity, even as some of them pick at the details. This, at least, is what President Humelsine was relieved to discover after he ordered an "image survey" in the 1960s. Humelsine had worried that "some visitors still fail to grasp the fact that they are viewing one of the largest concentrations of original eighteenth-century structures in an American community. And there are some who view the Historic Area as a reconstruction from start to finish, a bulldozing project followed by the erection of new buildings." But, the image survey showed, "nearly all . . . 94.5% of our first time visitors went home with the proper image of Williamsburg in mind as an entire colonial city comprised of original and rebuilt structures." Only 4.2 percent said that Colonial Williamsburg was exclusively "a city of rebuilt structures."[41] The authors of the survey were also "pleased to report" that the majority of its respondents saw the place as nonprofit rather than for profit, although the percentages, 70-plus to 20-plus, could not have been quite as comforting.

Such percentages, "pleasing" though they may be, continue to exercise the foundation to refurbish and restore the proper image of Colonial Williamsburg in the public mind. The "proper image" of Colonial Williamsburg is an entire colonial city which, through private (nongovernmental) philanthropy, has been restored (and to a lesser extent reconstructed) for educational activities. As we've suggested, the task of maintaining the proper image is never-ending because of the contradictions inherent in Colonial Williamsburg's hybrid nature. It is a business. And the public, predisposed to be skeptical of business, cannot help but assume that the business influences the education. Moreover, precisely because it is a popular vacation destination, the images held by the public are never entirely determined by the foundation. Its very popularity has meant that, willy-nilly, Colonial Williamsburg has become entangled in the agendas of other businesses that are its "good corporate neighbors." These corporate entities also produce words and pictures for the public. Just as Ford's Colony borrows from Colonial Williamsburg and shares (and therefore shapes) its local environment, so, too, do descriptions of Colonial Williamsburg put out by the travel industry influence this image, and so, too, do the multiplex desires of the visiting public.[42]

So, it is in the context of a cacophonous collage of images that the foundation tries to construct a coherent picture of itself. To do so, it must get its publics to see past the reality staring them in the face. They must be persuaded to overlook obvious inaccuracies and anachronisms, as well as all the signs of tourism and commercialism that surround and even invade the site. In short, the public must be made to trust in Colonial Williamsburg's intentions. And ultimately, it is in what the museum does with history that those intentions are most clearly displayed.

3 ■ *Why History Changes, or, Two Theories of History Making*

The Patriot's Tour

During the period of our research, Colonial Williamsburg used the Patriot's Tour, a one-hour guided stroll through the city, to provide its visitors with an overview of the museum. The Patriot's Tour was free to all visitors who purchased a Patriot's Pass, Colonial Williamsburg's most expensive ticket, and the one that was said to be "the best value." The tour introduced visitors to the main historical themes they would encounter in greater detail throughout the city. In addition, the guide sketched a history of the reconstruction and described the foundation's corporate structure. The Patriot's Tour was, in short, a kinetic map to Colonial Williamsburg and its work.

This kinetic map was also an official, managed overview of what the foundation is and does. The Patriot's Tour was designed to focus the visitor's attention—to make sure that newcomers, confronted by the complexity and detail of the site, saw what the foundation wanted them to see. Thus, for our purposes, a description of the tour can serve as an introduction to the way the foundation tries to imagine or fashion itself as a coherent project.

In the spring and early summer of 1990, at the outset of our field research, we took several Patriot's Tours. All followed a similar trajectory. They began at the Greenhow Lumber House on the Duke of Gloucester Street, crossed

Street scene. (photo by Eric Gable)

to the Palace green with its two rows of catalpa trees, and passed by Bruton Parish Church (an early eighteenth-century Episcopal church still in use today), the George Wythe House, and the other houses along the green. Turning in front of the Governor's Palace, the tours proceeded to Nicholson Street, then cut through the green lawn of Market Square behind the Courthouse to return to the Duke of Gloucester Street. The tours then moved into the city's business district, where they ended at one of several sites. Thus, visitors who took the tour were oriented both to the residential area of the town, near the Palace and church, and, at the other end of Duke of Gloucester Street, to the political and commercial quarter, terminated by the Capitol.

Interpreters told us in private that they were free, even encouraged, to create their own tours, within certain limits. And, indeed, we noticed that there was some variation in what they emphasized—which buildings they chose to point out and what they chose to say about them. This variation also reflected what particular visitors happened to ask them. There was nonetheless a predictable consistency to all Patriot's Tours. Even visitors' questions were much the same. What follows is a synopsis of the tours we witnessed, with an emphasis on constant themes.

At the outset of most Patriot's Tours, the guide introduced one of the major themes of the social history that had been established at Colonial

Williamsburg during the Longsworth administration—the importance of class distinctions. We were told that "what you need to keep in mind as you walk through Williamsburg is that . . . ninety percent of the people in Virginia were living . . . in one-room shacks with dirt floors and stick-and-mud chimneys." Because the houses we would see on our tours were "not typical of the general populace," we were enjoined to think—as we strolled past the museum's elegant edifices—"about all these people living so wretchedly." The guides also told us that the colonial capital was a planned city; the layout of the streets created vistas to highlight the town's public buildings with their tall cupolas—the Palace, the Capitol, the Wren Building of the College of William and Mary, and the Public Hospital.

Social historians at Colonial Williamsburg emphasize that colonial architecture was about the display of privilege and rank—about illustrating hierarchy, authority, power, and social distinctions.[1] This theme figured in the way interpreters talked about the city and its buildings. On one tour, for example, the interpreter pointed to Bruton Parish Church and explained that "this was a very class-conscious society." By law, he said, everybody had to attend church. In the "seating arrangements" there, the whole community enacted and witnessed the social distinctions that divided it: "The governor is not going to sit with the cobbler. . . . A member of the House of Burgesses is not going to sit with the cabinet maker." And slaves, he said, sat in balconies, among, yet removed from, the rest of the congregation.

Another interpreter used the Wythe House next to the church (and "one of the most copied houses in America") to make much the same point. She noted that "in the eighteenth century an individual who was important would like a person to be able to see his house and know how important he is. It is also important for people walking down the street to know where the important people lived. . . . It's not just a matter of keeping up with the Joneses and bragging about things. . . . It's the conventions of the time." She called our attention to the symmetry of the stately facade, then pointed out the brick outbuildings several feet from the main house. One, she explained, was the kitchen; it was built separate from the main house not only to buffer heat but because "you also have then a separate space for slaves because they're the ones who are doing the work."

Some interpreters used the Wythe House to introduce themes from Colonial Williamsburg's patriotic history. The Wythe House, they explained, was not only "one of the finest examples of colonial architecture," it was also the residence of the first Virginian to sign the Declaration of Independence, a man who was Thomas Jefferson's mentor. Other interpreters made the patriotic message a punchline or a guiding theme for the entire tour. One, for example, concluded her tour by reiterating that what makes Colonial Williamsburg really important is that "Williamsburg, the society, the people, the culture, played a large influence in the forming of our United States government as it is today."

Occasionally interpreters were able to use sites on the Palace green to combine the themes of social history with celebratory stories of "our" collective past. The Brush-Everard House across the green from the Wythe House was more modest, in keeping with its owner's more plebeian station. Everard, we were told, was an orphan who had emigrated from England to the colony, where he rose through the ranks of the colonial bureaucracy. His biography was "the original Horatio Alger story." Moreover, when the Revolutionary War broke out, "he didn't go back to England, and he didn't become a Tory. The neatest thing about him is that he stayed and he had made the transition from being an Englishman to being an American . . . in one person." From orphanage to Palace green on his own initiative, *and* he had chosen to become American—Everard was the archetypical self-made American man.

As the interpreters introduced us to the layout of the colonial city, they also squeezed in brief descriptions of the structure of the Colonial Williamsburg Foundation and its institutional history. They pointed out, for example, that "the museum itself takes up about 173 or 4 acres, and then there are properties . . . that belong to Colonial Williamsburg." They explained that "we have two divisions: we have the museum division which is educational, and we have hotels, restaurants, and retail sales. And those are the people that help with the bills." The crucial points here were that the hotel side was the "money-making division," that the foundation was not subsidized by the government, and that it was a good corporate neighbor paying "tremendous" taxes to "Jamestown, Yorktown, James City County, and Williamsburg."

In talking about the foundation, interpreters emphasized that its work of restoration is "ongoing." One, for example, pointed out that "every year, as funds are available, we do something new." "Right now," the foundation was "very much into Afro-American programs" and had "reconstructed the slave quarters at Carter's Grove." She went on to stress that "we're not standing still," that "the interpretation of history changes [and] we have to change along with it." Another interpreter explained that "this is just a . . . great big educational institution. We're always learning new things."

The interpreter made this last remark as we were clustered around one of

Bird bottles for sale in the Greenhow Store. (photo by Molly Handler)

the small clapboard outbuildings behind the Brush-Everard House. She had just told us that in an earlier era in the museum's history, all the clapboard outbuildings had been kept freshly painted and the woodwork had been of the highest quality. At that time, she explained, "we assumed that every building on the property would be as neat as every other." But now researchers knew better: "Only the front's important, that's your first impression, so buildings out back are going to be rougher." As a result, she continued, outbuildings at locales elsewhere in the museum-city were being painted less frequently and allowed to wear unevenly. As we looked at the crisp, white clapboard in front of us and imagined more shabbily painted outbuildings elsewhere, a visitor asked about an oddly shaped ceramic jug protruding from under the eaves. The interpreter answered, "Those are called bird bottles" and explained that they had been a puzzling artifact until only recently. Archaeologists found them and everybody wondered "why would you build a bottle with a hole in the bottom? It just didn't make sense." But after much research, "textual evidence" was found verifying that they were ceramic birdhouses. When another visitor asked why they'd have been mounted on the houses—for by now we had noticed several more—she explained that because the birds ate bugs, their presence was desirable in a mosquito-ridden place like Williamsburg. Not surprisingly, on nearly every

Bird bottle mounted on a Duke of Gloucester Street building. (photo by Molly Handler)

tour, the bird bottles prompted a spontaneous question and a similarly spontaneous answer about mysteries to be solved and painstaking research. It was after she told us the story of the bird bottle ("they're now available in our gift shops") that our guide explained that Colonial Williamsburg was a "great big educational institution. We're always learning new things."

When the interpreters talked about bird bottles and clapboard siding, an implicit theme was that the restoration required careful attention to details—to getting the pieces of the puzzle, the facts, exactly right. This ethos was evinced in what came across to us as a kind of excessive honesty on the part of the interpreters. As they talked, they'd occasionally slip up—a slip we, the collective "we" of the tour group, would probably not catch—and correct themselves in mid-sentence. One interpreter, for example, remarked of the Carters, whose house faced the Palace green, that "in the course of their marriage [they] had something like nineteen children." But she immediately amended her statement: "No, seventeen, I'm sorry, I exaggerated." The land area covered by the restoration was never described in approximate terms—as a bit less than 200 acres, for example—but always in exact numbers—"173 or 4 acres" or "176 acres"—although those numbers varied. Likewise, there were always exactly "eighty-eight original buildings," no more, no fewer, no round numbers.

Interpreters were also excessively honest in distinguishing original buildings that had been "restored" from those that had been "reconstructed"
from scratch (a restored house, for example, might be accompanied by reconstructed outbuildings that appeared to be the same age). Or they'd call
our attention to an anachronistic original in order to distinguish it from an
original that suited the time period. On one tour, our gaze was directed to a
severely elegant brick building near the courthouse and we were told that
because it was an original nineteenth-century structure, "we let it stay." On
another tour, we passed one of the Historic Area's handful of houses that was
not owned by the foundation and was still lived in by descendants of its
eighteenth-century occupants. This fact excited several people on our tour,
and our guide remarked that while the foundation covets the building for its
originality, "it's going to be hard to ever interpret that building" because
"we're interpreting a time level of . . . 1770 and that house was built in 1788."
A few minutes later we passed through a garden that contained the "oldest
boxwood" in town—a tall, thick-trunked wall of foliage that "dates back to
1790." The guide was careful to explain that in colonial times, the single wall
would have been two rows, with a path (now overgrown and therefore
invisible to us) between them.

The excessive honesty even extended to pointing out the purposeful ar-
tifice of the place. People lived in the Historic Area. No building, as one
interpreter emphasized, went unused, no "building is just sitting around
vacant" as a mere artifact. Some were inhabited by life tenants such as the
elderly widow who lived in the original yet anachronistic Tucker House; others were rented to employees, the more commodious and luxurious going, of
course, to the foundation's president, vice presidents, and senior administrators; and the refurbished outbuildings being occupied by employees at other
levels of the corporate hierarchy. In all such residences, twentieth-century
elements had to be "disguised." "The rules say you can't show anything twentieth century," one interpreter explained. "No anachronisms! That means no
television antennas . . . no Christmas lights." Other interpreters told us that
garages were made to look like stables, central air-conditioning was allowed
because it did not have to be visible, and garbage cans could be hidden
behind hedges.

When we came across these artfully disguised elements, they were duly
pointed out to us. As we paused on one occasion to marvel at two-hundred-
year-old boxwoods, we were reminded that "we also have wonderful things
like fire hydrants, trash cans, and soda machines that we try to hide." As we
continued our stroll beneath budding trees, our guide added, "If you look up

Drinking fountain in a barrel.
(photo by Molly Handler)

in trees this time of year you see things that look like an upside-down bucket, and it's a light. You don't find them in the summer because of the leaves." On another occasion, our guide asked us to gather around what appeared to be an oversized but barely visible manhole cover. "Listen," she said, tilting her head and cupping her ear as if holding a seashell. We tilted our heads and heard a distant rush. "Traffic," she exclaimed, and told us about Goodwin's and Rockefeller's efforts to convince the United States government to construct a highway *under* Colonial Williamsburg so as not to disturb its historic appearance.[2]

Because every interpreter spent so much time calling our attention to what the foundation was effectively disguising—to anachronisms we might not have noticed on our own—we nicknamed the Patriot's Tour the "invisible landscape tour." For us, this attention to the invisible landscape took on the kind of rapid masking, unmasking, remasking juxtapositioning of surface and substance (is it real or is it Memorex, or does it matter?) that is associated with the postmodern. We wondered what the visitors made of it all. And we wondered how this way of "seeing" Williamsburg reflected the way the foundation saw its work.

We arrived at two provisional explanations for the guides' emphasis on the invisible landscape. First, it could be explained as an extension of the foundation's ongoing concern with absolute authenticity. Colonial Williamsburg is about, among other things, the incremental re-creation of the real past, but the foundation knows that such an endeavor can be partial at best, never complete. It advertises this fact, or educates the visitor about it, by calling attention to the otherwise invisible distinctions between the "original," the "reconstructed," and the anachronistic. But to call attention to the invisible landscape is also, as we suggested at the end of the last chapter, to anticipate a prevailing and enduring critique of Colonial Williamsburg's project—that it is fake, a mask, a disguise, not real, not the past.

Recall that every Patriot's Tour began on the Duke of Gloucester Street near the Palace green. This street is a beautiful avenue. Like the other streets in the Historic Area, it is shaded by tall and stately oaks and other deciduous trees. Inevitably, interpreters would call our attention to those beautiful and obviously old trees and remark that they would not have been there in the colonial era. They would go on to explain that the foundation, despite its commitment to accuracy, would never cut down those trees because it had also to consider visitor comfort. Without the shady trees, the streets in the summertime ("when most of our visitors come") would be unbearable. In pointing to the trees, our guide on one occasion enjoined us to "keep in mind that many changes have been made to the town itself, things we have done to make it basically more comfortable for . . . twentieth-century people." As on many tours, he advised us to look past, or through, such anachronisms in order to imagine the real past. It was as if the Patriot's Tour was trying to orient the visitor's appreciation of the landscape in such a way as to confirm that, yes, the town is artificial, but Colonial Williamsburg could not be as accurate as it wished to be because we, the visitors, and our needs precluded it.

This second explanation, to us, was the key to why the interpreters called attention to the invisible landscape. It was a form of damage control, of impression management, that dovetailed neatly with their other discussions of the work of history at Colonial Williamsburg. The Patriot's Tour was a kinetic map of the reconstruction and the foundation's efforts to create a true, if approximate, past. That re-created past, like the museum itself—with its dozens of exhibition buildings as well as institutional departments with differing agendas—was a kind of collage, not a single focused image. In 1990 the Patriot's Tour was designed to orient the visitor to a social history of the town. The guides emphasized that history—that is, the story the foundation tells—"changes," and implied that such changes both depended on deliberate choice—"right now" the foundation was "very much into Afro-American programs"—and were part of an incremental and ongoing process. In that process, the fragmentary mysteries or puzzles of the past were taken as problems to be solved, a task requiring meticulous research. The Patriot's Tour averred that this process was hardly complete and, indeed, never quite could be, but claimed that Colonial Williamsburg was nevertheless doing the best it could to fulfill its mimetic mission and was being open and honest about its present shortcomings and past mistakes.

Two Theories of Why History Changes

The Patriot's Tour, with its curious concern for an invisible landscape, was typical of the way Colonial Williamsburg's staff interpreted the built environment. It sometimes seemed to us that people were less interested in describing the past than in talking about why the foundation's depiction of the past was constantly changing. As a result, one of the questions we asked our interviewees was why, in their view, history changes.

They usually gave one of two answers. The commonest response was that history changes because new facts are found, new information comes to light. Another explanation, less frequently offered but still common, was that history changes depending on the outlooks and interests of the people who write it. These two explanations went beyond the history of Colonial Williamsburg's history. We came to understand them as the reflections of two opposing philosophies of history that coexisted, even as they competed, in all the work of history making that we studied. At all levels of the institution, people deployed these theories rhetorically to buttress their positions on particular questions of interpretive and institutional policy. To understand Colonial Williamsburg as an institution that makes history for the public, then, one must first understand these two theories and the ways people use them.

The first theory, which we call constructionist, stresses that history is more than the sum of the available facts; the construction of history depends on the viewpoint of historians, on the messages or meanings that historians choose (perhaps unconsciously) to convey. History, in short, is a story with a moral, with a meaning that cannot be adduced from the facts alone. The story that Colonial Williamsburg tells changes, in this perspective, either because new historians and educators come to the museum with new ideas about what the history the museum teaches should mean, or because the foundation reacts to collective pressure from its audiences, whose needs and interests have changed. Historians, in short, are part of a contemporary culture, and the history they construct reflects the present in which they live. One of the foundation's historians told us, "We could tell ten thousand stories about the past, but we only tell one hundred." It is such choices—to tell particular stories about a potentially infinite past—that account for the changing of history at Colonial Williamsburg. And change is not gradual but abrupt, the result of what philosophers of science sometimes call a paradigm shift.

The opposing theory of why history changes, which we call realism or objectivism, stresses not abrupt shifts in chosen meanings but the steady discovery and organization of facts. In this account, history making is a progressive process; that is, it comes ever closer to an objectively truthful account of the past. The work of historians is to discover more and better facts in order to render the histories they write ever more faithful to the total reality of the past. And those histories depend not on historians' ideological biases or personal interests—although these may be admitted to play a role— but on the accumulated weight of the evidence.

During our research, we learned that the issue of changing history was a crucial one for many Colonial Williamsburg insiders. They talked about it frequently, and they drew on both of the theories of history making we have just sketched when they told stories about the history of Colonial Williamsburg's history. One way to tell that history is to trace the successive paradigms that have shaped the museum's message in different eras.

Why History Changes

The Constructionist Version

In the second year of our fieldwork, Cary Carson, Colonial Williamsburg's vice president for research, published an essay in celebration of history museums and local historical societies. In it, he argued that an important part of Colonial Williamsburg's ameliorative work is to "dispel the popular notion that students of history merely add up incontrovertible facts to arrive at the true sum of their meaning." Carson emphasized that historians' ideologies "influence their choice of research topics and the conclusions they reached." Carson's views were echoed by other researchers in key positions in the organization, like architectural historian Edward Chappell, who wrote that "historians and curators who suggest that their responsibility is the simple and objective presentation of facts often use that position to reinforce traditional views of reality. This is conservatism, not objectivity."[3]

The new social history advocated by Carson, Chappell, and their colleagues was a story, and explicitly a story, designed to replace past versions of "the Williamsburg story" that the museum had told its audience. The social historians promulgated this view about what history is and why it changes in a 1985 document entitled *Teaching History at Colonial Williamsburg,* a fifty-two-page booklet intended to be a public charter for the history the museum was to teach over the next ten years. In the first pages of *Teaching History,* the social historians explained the idea that history is a theme-driven construct by contrasting such a view to a naive objectivism: "Colonial Williamsburg has few rivals as a history teacher today [because of] . . . its completeness, the human scale of its buildings, gardens, streets, and lanes, its many pleasing sights, sounds, and smells. . . . This particularity of detail, this rich offering of objects and information, is not, however, sufficient by itself to make the past comprehensible." The "facts," they continued, are essentially inert, meaningless. Objective facts "need a plot, the history a conceptual framework." This conceptual framework would be the assumptions of social history itself, a new paradigm supplying a new theme. "A theme," they emphasized, "helps educational planners write coherent storylines, set priorities, and select sites and programs. . . . [It] helps interpreters choose what to say and what to leave out. . . . A common theme also gives direction to research. It sets the agenda of questions to be asked and helps historians select appropriate methods to be employed in answering them."[4]

To say that history needs a theme that "sets the agenda" is to recognize that history is more than just the facts. In this view, themes and agendas— paradigms, conceptual frameworks—guide historians to choose particular facts and to use them in particular ways. Themes and agendas also make it possible for historians to be unconcerned with facts that have no bearing on the issues that excite them, or even to overlook them altogether.

When people at Colonial Williamsburg drew on this constructionist model, they identified four major paradigms that have guided the museum's work from its inception to the present. People recognized the "Colonial Revival" paradigm of the 1930s, the "Cold War" or "Patriotic" paradigm of the 1950s, the "Six Appeals" theme of the 1960s, and the "Social History" of the 1980s. Though they tended to associate these paradigms or themes with particular decades, they also recognized that the themes overlapped: the symbolisms, rhetoric, and stories associated primarily with any one of them often preceded the decade of that particular paradigm's greatest prominence and may well have endured long after its demise had been officially or informally recognized. Moreover, people rarely told the history of Colonial Williamsburg's history as a single narrative of neatly successive paradigms; rather, they tended to invoke particular paradigms to explain particular features of the museum; as, for example, one interpreter leading a tour of the gardens did: "These gardens have since been termed colonial revival gardens. . . . [T]hey are . . . essentially a 1930s interpretation of what a colonial garden looked like."*

Today, foundation employees see the first phase of the institution's history as a period driven by an overblown aesthetic they call, following common practice among scholars of the decorative arts, "the colonial revival." Documents written at that time can easily be read to support this appraisal. The emphasis is on "style" and "beauty," and on saving style and beauty from "destruction and neglect." At the end of 1935, the foundation could announce the successful completion of the project "as to form, although it will continue as to detail."[5] It had reproduced gardens and grand buildings, like the Palace and the Capitol, that had long since been "razed to the ground" or "denatured." The reconstructed buildings were "milestones in the history of American style." The Palace garden was perhaps "the most beautiful in America."[6]

From the perspective of those who managed the restoration during the colonial revival era, it ultimately mattered less that Williamsburg was one of America's cradles of revolution than that it was a lost artistic masterpiece. It was a cultural capital, and it was this culture—in danger of being "denatured" by neglect and time's entropy—that motivated the restoration. By saving "culture" the restoration would also restore a built environment that reflected the Revolution, but this was, in a sense, a secondary benefit. As William Graves Perry, one of the chief architects of the project, put it in a 1935 report: "The fortunate thing is that American history (the revolutionary part of it) was enacted in the Georgian scene. It is reasonably certain that Mr. Rockefeller would not have felt the interest which led him to include the

---

*A summary account of names and dates drawn from Colonial Williamsburg's institutional history may help the reader to follow the discussions below. The first president, Colonel Arthur Woods, managed the emerging Rockefeller enterprise from before the time of its public incorporation, in 1928, to 1935; he was almost never mentioned in the stories people told. The name of Kenneth Chorley, president from 1935 to 1958, was well known, but we heard few stories about him. Long-term employees spoke frequently of Carlisle Humelsine, president from 1958 to 1979; his administration constituted the "past" by reference to which many insiders defined the museum's present, under Charles Longsworth. Longsworth came to the foundation in 1977 and succeeded Humelsine in 1979. Longsworth was succeeded in 1992 by Robert Wilburn, but we have not studied the museum under his administration.

Restoration of Williamsburg among his many educational philanthropies, had not the important events of our history taken place in Williamsburg during the premierships of Pitt, Fox and North rather than during those of Disraeli and Gladstone."[7]

Reproducing a culture (of a particularly pleasing era) was the strongest motivating force in the 1930s. And this culture, this era (the Georgian), was pleasing in large part because it was a preindustrial one. Thus, working craftsmen were introduced into the museum in that period in an effort to guarantee, as Winthrop Rockefeller later wrote, "that fundamental techniques, drawn from the spirit of the American past, will not disappear in the rugged modern competition with assembly lines and mass production." The Revolutionary-era culture in Williamsburg was also, perhaps, a culture unpolluted in a broader sense, for "nowhere in the English colonies did the transplanted cutting from the mother tree . . . flourish more vigorously than in Virginia."[8] It was a Virginia of two-hundred-year-old boxwoods, Chelsea porcelain, and Hepplewhite furniture. In sum, the early reconstruction era reflected (as it later was explained) the personal tastes of a very rich man who was also a product of a particular time and sensibility.

Colonial Williamsburg began to focus more explicitly on its patriotic message during the Second World War, when the Rockefellers hosted the visits of some 100,000 service personnel from nearby military bases. The message the foundation hoped to convey is captured in a story that President Chorley frequently told: "He was a GI . . . a soldier from Fort Eustis . . . who'd come up with the rest of his unit to tour Williamsburg. Part of our wartime program. I saw this boy in the Clerk's office at the Capitol. He'd become separated from his buddies, and he was standing all alone in front of that Peale portrait of Washington. Suddenly I heard him mutter, 'You got it for us General. And, by God, we're going to keep it.' And he saluted. . . . You know, I told that story to Mr. Rockefeller a few weeks later. When I'd finished, he looked up at me, and there were tears in his eyes, and he said quietly, 'Then it was all worth while.' "[9]

After the war, the leaders of Colonial Williamsburg perceived that the United States faced a new peril, and the cold war message of the museum took shape. According to the report of the 1977 Curriculum Committee, chaired by Cary Carson, "Colonial Williamsburg hammered out the terms of its first and only comprehensive definition of purpose in 1945–46" in a series of letters exchanged between John D. Rockefeller Jr., John Rockefeller III (chairman of Colonial Williamsburg's board at the time), President Kenneth Chorley, and "members of the staff." These people "agreed that it was the

Foundation's fundamental duty to teach the principles of liberty, the ideals of democratic government, and the contribution of colonial Virginians to American culture."[10]

Mass tourism and the family vacation took off after the war, and Colonial Williamsburg strove to provide its growing audience with programs that would both attract and educate them. In 1948 President Chorley, announcing a "new public relations program," asserted that Colonial Williamsburg "must be more than a bricks-and-mortar physical reconstruction" and "more than one of America's outstanding travel attractions." Chorley proclaimed that the museum would become "a symbol of democracy in the troubled world to-day."[11] Accordingly, in 1951, a new *Guidebook* was issued containing an explicit statement (lacking in earlier guidebooks) of the values that Colonial Williamsburg stood for: "the integrity of the individual," "responsible leadership," "self-government," "individual liberties," and "opportunity."[12]

The foundation tried to convey those values to the public through a range of programs that both reflected and spoke to cold war sensibilities. The Powder Magazine was opened to the public in 1949, and the Fifes and Drums, a Revolutionary War–era marching band, was formed in the mid-1950s. In 1957 Colonial Williamsburg began showing its famous orientation film, *Williamsburg—The Story of a Patriot,* a color film that dramatized the Revolution in terms of the individual choices made by Williamsburg patriots. In 1952 the foundation inaugurated "Prelude to Independence," a program that ran from mid-May to the Fourth of July with special events to commemorate the Declaration of Independence. Included in the 1952 festivities was "a graphic exhibit depicting man's struggle for individual liberty," which featured "artifacts ranging from jurors' ballots used in ancient Greece to a ballot box used in 1951 in the first general elections in India." Also included as part of the 1952 "Prelude" was the staging of the Williamsburg Declaration, in which fifty "exiled leaders" of central European countries pledged "the restoration of human rights and political liberties when the Communist governments of these lands are overthrown." The Williamsburg Declaration, "signed into history here on June 12," as the *Colonial Williamsburg News* put it, was promptly put on exhibit among the other artifacts and documents depicting liberty "from the fourth century B.C. to the present day."[13]

That President Chorley unveiled a major interpretive thrust as part of a new public relations program testifies to the intertwining of business and education at Colonial Williamsburg—or perhaps to the ingenuousness with which their interconnection was accepted at that time. Several people explained to us that the creation of new programs served not only to sharpen the educational focus of the museum but also to boost attendance, especially during slack seasons.[14] The annual Garden Symposium, begun in 1947, and the Antiques Forum, begun in 1949, continue to this day to attract visitors with a taste for Colonial Williamsburg's version of colonial American aesthetics and culture. Two long-running though now defunct annual programs were the International Assembly, begun in 1957, and the Student Burgesses, begun in 1958, which brought students together to discuss problems of democracy. Programs such as these brought to life the patriotic and cultural ideals of the museum's two most prominent founders, Rockefeller and Goodwin. They were also popular. Patriotism and the colonial aesthetic sold well during the 1950s, and continue to sell today.

Nonetheless, at least according to insiders' accounts about the museum's turn to social history, Colonial Williamsburg's cold war message began to wear thin by the middle 1960s. The record of the foundation's programs at that time indicates timid efforts to adapt patriotic programs to speak to the rising tide of social protest in the United States. Thus, for example, the 1966 meeting of the Student Burgesses convened under the theme "Protest: A Right and Responsibility" to discuss "civil rights, the draft, Vietnam, the Peace Corps and other current controversial topics." Noam Chomsky spoke at the 1968 International Assembly. Perhaps as a balance, William F. Buckley was the keynote speaker the next year, when the theme was "Order and Disorder in American Society."[15] The *Colonial Williamsburg News* continued to publish patriotic letters from visitors (including those stationed in Vietnam or related to service personnel there), but foundation literature of the time suggests that the museum was losing its patriotic focus.[16]

It was in this context that Colonial Williamsburg began to take its own organizational structure as the content of its message, which became known as "the six appeals." We can trace the emergence of this theme in the foundation's annual reports. The report for 1958, the first one written by Carlisle Humelsine and his staff, differed markedly in style from the previous reports produced under Kenneth Chorley (1951–57), who tended to dwell on the patriotic significance of Williamsburg. Humelsine, by contrast, used annual reports to present "behind-the-scenes" descriptions of various aspects and departments of Colonial Williamsburg, such as archaeology, architecture, or the taverns of Williamsburg.[17]

The culmination of this strategy was the President's Report for 1964, which picked out the word "appeal" from Rockefeller's most famous statement about his motives for restoring the town. In 1937, Rockefeller had written: "The restoration of Williamsburg . . . offered an opportunity to restore a complete area and free it entirely from alien and inharmonious surroundings. . . . Thus, it made a unique and irresistible appeal."[18] In his 1964 report, President Humelsine elaborated on Williamsburg's multifaceted—"many things to many people"—appeal. He listed (though without enumerating) "architecture . . . and town plan," "collections of English and American furniture," "gardens," "archaeology," "our handicraft program," and "the events of the Revolutionary era so important in the birth of our nation." Within two years, "the six appeals" was standard public relations fare, though the precise description of each category was subject to change— archaeology could be more broadly termed "preservation/restoration" or "preservation research," and the sixth appeal, history, could be termed "historic heritage."[19]

These topics corresponded, roughly speaking, to important divisions within Colonial Williamsburg's organizational structure, and "the six appeals" can be read as a kind of shorthand description of institutional fiefdoms struggling to assert their relative importance. As the Curriculum Committee of 1977 described it, "Each of the 'Six Appeals' . . . has acquired its own staff, programs, budget, friends and benefactors, and consequently its own self-justification," resulting in "a bureaucracy whose very organization . . . colors the history we teach." The six appeals were symptomatic of what the committee called the "aimlessness" and "malaise" that, as they saw it, characterized the museum in the late 1960s and early 1970s.[20] From their perspective, Colonial Williamsburg had become educationally moribund, and it was the committee's job to revitalize it.

The social historians who came to Colonial Williamsburg during the Longsworth regime envisioned a new history for the institution, one explicitly different from both the six appeals and cold war patriotism. Like their predecessors of the 1940s and 1950s, they say the museum as an ameliorative institution whose effectiveness depended on the coherence of its message. But they differed from their predecessors in the content of the message they advocated and in the historical personages they wanted to bring to life. For the young Turks, Colonial Williamsburg's new history needed to go beyond political history to consider the social and economic context of the events of the Revolutionary period. They envisioned a museum that would be explicit about the structure of society, especially about relations of authority and power, and inclusive of all members of the society.

This new story was to be explicitly "democratic" and "egalitarian." It would reject, as Carson was to put it, "the traditional notion that rulers are more important than ruled, that might confers the right to be remembered, or that money does all the talking historians need listen to."[21] The new social history would no longer focus exclusively on the "silk-pants patriots" with their refined tastes, but would now include the "other half" (African Americans, both slave and free) and the "middling sort." The new history, social historians believed, would teach visitors to become social critics. Carson stated the intent clearly in a published interview: "I want [the public] to go away disturbed. I see this museum as a device to make Americans look at aspects of both the past and the present that they may not want to see."[22]

Carson and his colleagues also envisioned a new didactic orientation for the museum: the reconstructed environment of Colonial Williamsburg was to be treated as a "laboratory" in which to examine social relationships rather than "as a storehouse of moral precepts." In short, social science was to replace ideology as the ameliorative motor of the museum.[23]

The Curriculum Committee of 1977 recommended that the new Williamsburg story be organized in terms of three themes: "Choosing Revolution," "Becoming Americans," and "The New Consumers." "Choosing Revolution" would revise the museum's version of the American Revolution to emphasize the economic reasons that pushed the colonists to choose independence from England. According to the committee, the earlier history, as represented in the 1957 film *Williamsburg—The Story of a Patriot,* focused on individuals and their choice "to support the American cause." In doing so, it emphasized the timelessness of the principles of that cause and thereby encouraged visitors to rededicate themselves to those principles.

By contrast, the 1977 Curriculum Committee proposed a new story showing that economic self-interest had motivated Virginia's colonial elites to choose revolution, that they had "turned to rebellion as the only solution to repeated economic crises that were undermining their financial and political independence." Told in this way, the story would teach the public how people in particular historical and cultural circumstances rationalized their world; by analyzing rather than celebrating past choices, the museum would help visitors to be better citizens of the modern world: "Understanding how patriots and loyalists reached their different points of view has greater educational value than approving or disapproving of the decisions they made. Learning to make informed, reasoned judgments in matters concerning public policy has become, in our view, more important to a sane, planned future than merely reaffirming our assent to the principles of self-government."[24]

The museum as a laboratory, then, would teach social scientific analysis rather than ideology. Moreover, it would do so through analogies, not anachronisms. Visitors would not be asked "to extort from the eighteenth century ill-fitting parallels to twentieth-century situations." Rather, they would be taught "a framework of ideas and the analytical skills they need to ask how any community works."[25]

The second theme, "Becoming Americans," would use the social scientific concept of a working community to address the issue of the diversity of the American experience and its portrayal in history museums. The committee pointed out that Colonial Williamsburg had been striving to become more inclusive for some time, to extend its representations beyond the elites to consider "Williamsburg's invisible majority. . . . As a result, guests today . . . find slaves, women, children, and just plain ordinary people more conspicuous than they used to be in the Williamsburg story." But adding "multiplicity," the committee argued, was not enough: "Professional historians understand social history in another sense. To them it means the history of society: the groups that form its parts, their organization, and the ways and reasons that that organization and those relationships have changed over time. . . . To make sense of Chesapeake society is to explain how two immigrant cultures—one European, the other African—became indigenous cultures, separate and highly unequal to be sure, but both decidedly American by 1750."[26]

As in the rationale for the first theme, the emphasis would be on teaching visitors to understand the workings of society itself—in particular, the structured inequality of relationships between blacks and whites. The committee envisioned a museum that would show how "the rich got richer"; that is, it would make clear that the elite which Colonial Williamsburg had traditionally enshrined depended for its existence on the coerced labor of African slaves. The future museum would also re-create the mechanisms of authority that allowed this social system to perpetuate itself: "Authority was exercised . . . in an elaborate system of face-to-face exchanges, which an outdoor history museum can reenact to dramatize a way of life that modern Americans know nothing of. Militia musters, elections, court proceedings, cock fights, quarter horse races, and general hell-raising typical of tavern life were all community ceremonies that served as formal and informal institutions of social control. Some of them, if presented in the manner of the Fifes and Drums, but with more thought given to making their social implications explicit, could greatly enliven our interpretation of the magazine, the courthouse, and the taverns."[27]

The proposal to use the Fifes and Drums, a beloved emblem of Colonial Williamsburg the patriotic shrine, to teach about social inequality suggests the radical possibilities of social history. The family, too, was to be presented in terms of the structure of the social relationships it entailed: "Family life was the playing out of roles between various members of a household—parents, children, in-laws, servants, and slaves." Moreover, presenting family life would further the trend toward a more inclusive museum, for "subjects such as child rearing, education, work routines . . . [and] caring for the elderly" would bring onto the stage women as well as men, the young and the elderly as well as adults, and—given that slaves, too, were members of the "household"—blacks as well as whites.[28]

The "Becoming Americans" theme would make a significant place for African Americans at Colonial Williamsburg. First, it would show that they, like their Euro-American counterparts, developed an indigenous American culture: "An initial population of African-born male immigrants gradually became a homogeneous, Afro-American people." Second, it would present "a positive interpretation of the Black experience" by acknowledging "the contribution that all slaves made by their labor." The committee suggested that a portrayal of the work that African Americans did, and the social organization of that work, would teach visitors about "the inner workings of society itself."[29] This argument returns us to the social scientific analysis of economic and political arrangements. We should note that such an analysis has the potential to lead beyond a "positive interpretation" of slavery to a negative one—that is, to an explicit critique of the oppression and exploitation fundamental to a slave-based labor system. Significantly, such an elaboration of the "Becoming Americans" theme is left implicit in the 1977 document (we return to this issue in the next two chapters).

Just as "Choosing Revolution" proposed a social scientific analysis of ideologies, so the final theme, "The New Consumers," recommended a new twist on one of the museum's traditional appeals: the collection and display of antiques. *Teaching History* argued that Colonial Williamsburg's objects and furnishings could be used to explore the emergence of consumer capitalism, a revolutionary social transformation that occurred in the time period, broadly construed, that the museum depicts. The objects in which Goodwin and Rockefeller saw the elegant, dignified cultural sensibilities of the colonial elite were now to teach about conspicuous consumption, that is, about the uses of material objects to signify social status. Moreover, because social historians argued that emergent capitalism made more and more goods available more and more cheaply, "The New Consumers," like "Becoming Americans," would allow Colonial Williamsburg to be more inclusive: "Despite the fact that Chesapeake society was highly stratified, most of the 'middling sort' and even many poorer folks participated in the new consumer culture so far as their assets allowed." Moreover, the committee argued, portraying the "portentous frenzy" of eighteenth-century consumption would allow visitors to think critically about the materialism of their own world.[30]

As we noted above, the advocated replacement of patriotic ideology by social science is a striking feature of the 1977 document. But social science—or science in general—can itself be considered an ideology, as much recent scholarship argues. And social science as an ideology, with its rhetoric of laboratories, experiments, and the progress of research, fit easily into an ethos that had been part of Colonial Williamsburg's culture from the beginning: a faith that ongoing historical research would uncover more and more facts, and make possible an ever more complete and accurate re-creation of the past.

Progressive Realism, or Mimesis

According to the second theory explaining history making at Colonial Williamsburg, history changes because new facts are found, that is, because historians continually gain new knowledge that allows them to write histories better than those that were written before—"better" in the sense of more accurate, closer to the truth of the past as it really was. This was the more commonly stated view, especially when interpreters talked to visitors about why and how the history Colonial Williamsburg tells had changed over time.

Early in our research, we began to use the term *mimesis* to refer to such realist or objectivist approaches to history making at Colonial Williamsburg. For us, mimesis refers to Colonial Williamsburg's avowed mission to re-create a colonial American city as it existed in the mid-eighteenth century. Starting with as many "original" buildings and objects as can be obtained, the goal is to produce and "bring to life" a literal or completely realistic re-creation of that time and place—a facsimile of it. Colonial Williamsburg insiders did not use the term *mimesis*, but they spoke routinely of authenticity and accuracy, of faithful or truthful restoration.[31]

When it is told as the progress of mimetic realism, the history of Colonial Williamsburg's history making relies on two extended metaphors. In the first, the past is seen as a shattered object whose surviving pieces must be put back together like a puzzle. To put the puzzle of the past back together requires the problem-solving skills of a detective searching out mysteries and hunting through minutiae for clues. A puzzle can also be envisioned in two-dimensional terms as a fragmented picture. To put back together such a puzzle one starts with the surviving fragments and fills in the gaps between them in order to re-create a complete portrait of Williamsburg in the eighteenth century.[32]

The second extended metaphor is "to make the past come alive." As important as they are, the colonial buildings by themselves are lifeless, an empty shell or stage setting that must be animated by living people or by stories that suggest them. From the perspective of mimetic realism, the history of the restoration after the initial phases of physical reconstruction is a story of ongoing research into every facet of life in colonial Virginia. Such research, it is thought, will enable Colonial Williamsburg to add the details and activities that will re-create a complete facsimile of the past and bring it to life.

Both extended metaphors have been used by foundation staff since the beginning of the restoration. When architect Perry introduced Colonial Williamsburg to an important audience in the pages of the *Architectural Record* in 1935, he wrote that "the persistent pilgrim" would reach "the goal of authenticity" through painstaking research that would solve the problems posed by an incompletely known past. For Perry, those pilgrims were also " 'detectives' . . . to whom superimposed foundations, fragmentary corners, heterogeneous brick sizes and bonds, varying mortars and manners of workmanship, areas of complete destruction of previous work, became only more puzzles to be measured, weighed, compared."[33] Or, as President Chorley put it, describing the foundation's ongoing restoration sixteen years later, "No Sherlock Holmes seeking to deduce the character of a man from a cigar ash ever pursued more thoroughly and relentlessly all of the evidences which would reveal the character of the restored and reconstructed area of Colonial Williamsburg. From the foundations of the restored area, archaeologists sifted over a hundred tons of artifacts giving indications of the life and customs of the 18th-century inhabitants of Williamsburg. From many sources in this country and abroad information was assembled by researchers digging through archives and libraries, and probing old deeds and letters, old wills and inventories, and old insurance policies."[34]

The social historians who arrived at the beginning of the Longsworth administration also resorted to the puzzle-solving metaphor to explain their program to Colonial Williamsburg's donors: "If a Jackson Pollack puzzle is your idea of an ultimate brain teaser, consider this. Imagine a puzzle 900,000 pieces large. Thousands more are missing. The rest are jumbled together in one enormous barrel. You, the puzzle solver, have as your assignment to pick through the barrel one piece at a time until you fit together enough of them to guess the subject of a picture that can never be completed." This seemingly impossible task, this search for "precious puzzle pieces," was, according to the article, what historians at Williamsburg did every day.[35]

The puzzle metaphor, which recurs in foundation rhetoric from the 1930s to the present day, is enshrined in the exhibition buildings themselves. For instance, a permanent archaeological exhibit in the Anderson House on the Duke of Gloucester Street contains glass cases of fragmented artifacts in conjunction with photographs of whole objects—a pottery shard, a plate. And these glass cases are juxtaposed to a reconstructed tableau—a room with a table, bed, plates, bottles, candles, and so forth. The exhibit bears an explanatory label: "The purpose of archaeology in Williamsburg is to assist in reconstructing the environment in which both the great and small events of Virginia history took place. Excavated artifacts are pieces in the jigsaw puzzle of the past. Here eighty-eight objects removed from the earth of Williamsburg provide precedents for virtually everything seen in this recreated colonial bedroom."

The display is a compact argument for and explanation of the work the foundation imagines itself to be doing. Fragments of a real past, like pieces of a broken jug, clay pipe, or plate, are glued together, and these restored but nonetheless "real" objects become precedents for spruced-up or re-created copies that in turn are assembled into tableaus like the "recreated colonial bedroom." Note that to make such a display out of "eighty-eight objects" (no more, no fewer) is to echo or allude to a similar process ostensibly occurring, if on a vastly grander scale, in the reconstruction of the entire Historic Area. Recall that on the Patriot's Tour interpreters emphasized that there are eighty-eight original buildings on the site. In the foundation's descriptions of its work, "original" buildings provide a framework or anchor for buildings that are "reconstructed." Like the shattered plate on display, some of the pieces of the original (Williamsburg the eighteenth-century city) are missing, and a wholly new piece (but, in the scheme of things, a small piece) must be created to link together the original fragments, thereby restoring their obvious coherence, their original totality. Putting together a puzzle may be a tedious process. But the pieces—88 or 900,000—are nevertheless empirically given, not the result of a historian's imagination.

The metaphor of bringing the Historic Area to life is as venerable as the puzzle-solving imagery. While the first two decades of restoration work at Colonial Williamsburg (until about 1950) were primarily devoted to reconstructing buildings and their grounds, the foundation was concerned from the beginning, as the minutes of architects' meetings show, with making the site a "living breathing picture." Because "animals would enliven the general appearance of the town," it was decided that there "would be horses and horse drawn vehicles and farm animals such as cows and sheep pastured wherever possible and in view." More important, people would be encouraged to use the buildings because "part of the spirit of the city is derived from the activity resulting from the life in it."[36]

Colonial Williamsburg populated the Historic Area in a variety of ways. Some of the houses in the Historic Area continued to be homes for the families who had always lived in them, the foundation having hit on a policy of life tenancy by which residents could remain in their homes after they had been deeded to the restoration.* Other buildings, not intended to be open to the public, were used for offices; still others became residences for foundation staff.

More important to the question of mimetic accuracy, Colonial Williamsburg experimented almost from the outset with ways to people the Historic Area with presences representing its eighteenth-century inhabitants. Costumed "hostesses" were introduced in 1935. Kopper's celebratory history of Colonial Williamsburg credits that program to Rutherfoord Goodwin, son of Dr. Goodwin and one of the restoration's early specialists in interpretive programming: "It was Rutherfoord who hit upon the idea of recruiting hostesses from among the region's gentlewomen and training them in matters of history and Restoration philosophy. He also had them dress in colonial clothes so that they could be identified by (and distinguished from) the visitors who started arriving in ever greater numbers once the Raleigh Tavern opened in 1932." An interpreter whom we interviewed in 1991 told a somewhat different story: "My understanding is that Mrs. Rockefeller decided that it would be nice for people to dress up, and it was . . . let's give the southern people some nice clothes so they'll look good in these nice buildings my husband is building."[37]

Despite their differences, both accounts suggest that the recruitment of

---

*In explicating the metaphor of bringing the museum to life, it is important to realize that the foundation depopulated the Historic Area in order to create the museum, which it then wanted to animate. Andrea Foster (1993: 179–187) has described how race and class affected the treatment of various Williamsburg residents who were bought out by the restoration: "Whites, more frequently than African-Americans, received new housing, were assisted in finding a residence, or were resettled in newly restored houses. Life tenure agreements were granted mostly for whites." An apparently intended effect of the expropriation process was to remove African Americans from the area, resulting in a city much more highly segregated after the restoration than before. As is to be expected, Kopper's account (1986: 164) is more benign.

hostesses from among the local people was an early strategy to breathe something of the native life of the region into the newly restored buildings. If the regional accents and manners of the first hostesses seemed quaint and authentic to the Yankee administrators who managed Colonial Williamsburg, costuming those ladies was intended to further the impression of historical realism. The craft program was another effort to re-create the living past in Colonial Williamsburg's buildings. The first worker, a blacksmith, was installed in the Historic Area in 1936; the program was rationalized and enlarged following World War II.

As Colonial Williamsburg's interpretive programs developed and diversified in the 1950s and 1960s, there was an effort to introduce more "life-on-the-scene" into the museum: sheep, oxcarts, scarecrows, beehives, and crafts demonstrations were all intended to make the Historic Area "come alive." A typical newspaper item of the time explained, "Additional woodpiles . . . are appearing in the Historic Area as spring approaches. It's not that colder weather is anticipated. . . . [It's] just another attempt to give the area a more 'lived-in' appearance."[38]

Visitors, too, wanted the site to be more lifelike and made their desires known to the foundation. For example, a 1981 letter to the president of Colonial Williamsburg from a Florida man advised the museum to "create olifactory [*sic*] detail. In the palace, for instance, sprinkle liquid smoke . . . in the smoke house so that when people lean in to see the hams, etc., they can actually smell them. The same could be done in the cellar. Empty beer on the floor of the beer cask room and wine into the packing of the wine storage room. (The stables smell is taking care of things naturally!)" To which a museum vice president responded understandingly: "We have recently introduced actual wood smoking in the smokehouses with the hope that the smell would linger, and we have had some improvement in that presentation. We achieve an aroma in the wine cellar by placing a few apples in a concealed bucket. They add a fermented cider smell that has been quite effective."[39]

At the end of the 1970s, "life-on-the-scene" was absorbed into a more comprehensive strategy called "living history," one to which more and more American museums have turned.[40] Living history means different things in different museums, but at Colonial Williamsburg the term refers particularly to first-person "character interpreters," as they were called during the period of our research. Character interpreters wore period costume, as did other interpreters, but they "stayed in the first person," that is, they impersonated or played the role of eighteenth-century inhabitants of Williamsburg. During our research, programs involving character interpreters were often prefaced by an announcement that the actors based their roles on meticulous research into the details of daily life. Consider the following explanation from the back cover of an issue of the *Visitor's Companion:* "With the assistance of the Colonial Williamsburg Research Department, character interpreters study the personalities and life histories of the eighteenth-century people they will become. They also acquire a vast amount of knowledge about the eighteenth century as it relates to their reconstructed characters." Grounded in this sort of "knowledge," the life that character interpreters brought to the scene was meant to be faithful to the past. Indeed, some people claimed that character interpreters were able *to become* people of the past, or at least to express themselves as their prototypes would have done. The *Visitor's Companion* explanation continued: "Character interpreters are not actors; they have no script. Every character is prepared to converse freely on a variety of topics from politics to childbearing. A visit with these character interpreters provides the opportunity to learn about the past from the personal viewpoints of the people who lived it. It is a way for the visitor to talk with the past."[41] With the museum thus brought to life, visitors were said to be able to experience the past as it really was, and Colonial Williamsburg as a whole was seen as taking one more step toward total authenticity.

In general, even in the earliest discussions of craftworkers, costumed interpreters, and animals we find people accepting the idea that the goal of authenticity required that the complete life of the past be re-created in the Historic Area. To bring their city to life, Colonial Williamsburg planners have relied on animals, myriad "lifelike touches," and a growing force of costumed employees who engage, to varying degrees, in eighteenth-century activities. They have also relied on persistent and ongoing research into every facet, however obscure, of the life of eighteenth-century Williamsburg. It is worth noting that the goal of total authenticity merges easily with the desire of the social historians of the Longsworth years to make the museum inclusive of all levels of colonial society. Though the ideological and cultural agenda of the first generations of administrators differed from those who came later, all have agreed that accuracy demands the representation of society in toto.[42]

Ultimately, the quest for mimetic realism is imagined or portrayed as a kind of historical progress. Lifelike touches are added, the town is peopled, and the result is an ever more accurate and complete picture of the past. In this view, the museum-city was first populated with what now are referred to somewhat disparagingly as the silk-pants patriots. Next came the craftspeople. By 1968 there were more than a hundred workers practicing more than forty trades in the Historic Area. As the President's Report for 1954 put it, their presence ensured "that society may be seen as not only the gifted, the articulate, the famous, but as men and women who lived useful daily lives, who scolded their children, who knew illness and good fun, toil, ambition and sorrow."[43]

To many employed by the foundation at the time of our research, the new social history was the culmination in the ever progressing work of repopulating the restored city. Social history had added to the living portrait by finding a place in the Historic Area for the "other half"—the roughly 50 percent of Williamsburg's population who were not silk-pants patriots, nor even "middling sort" shopkeepers and craftspeople, but black slaves. Just as the historians of other eras had filled in the gaps of the city by restoring or reconstructing buildings like the Powder Magazine and sites for the practice of handskills, so did social history add structures like the Carter's Grove slave quarter to Colonial Williamsburg's built environment.

In general, the quest for mimetic accuracy privileges a piecemeal accumulation of the accurate and a piecemeal discarding of the inaccurate or inauthentic. Ironically, to say that history changes because new facts are found or because the museum is becoming ever more authentic is profoundly ahistorical, for in this history of history, progress is a constant, historians' motivations are unchanging, and only one significant event—the discovery of new evidence—occurs again and again. A frontline employee at the Wythe House kitchen explained that "they're constantly doing research. And in fact a lot of things that we thought were true last summer, have been proven different—not wrong, but just, you know, we found more information on it." She pointed out that they used to think that sweetbreads were "the brain," but a careful perusal of documents had revealed that sweetbreads were "actually a gland." Her description of why and how history changes typified the interpretive practice of many employees, who tended to focus on the changing of particular details rather than on changes in the overall configuration of the museum: "The fence you see, the split-rail fence, we used to have it only three rails high, but our research showed that it was actually five to six rails."

What is also ironic, but perhaps not surprising, is that the rhetoric of mimetic realism meshes well with a description of the erroneous histories of the past (or of histories written by other people) as being paradigm driven. In other words, when they look back, present-day staff can identify the paradigms said to have prevailed in the past, or those (usually characterized as "preconceptions" or "myths") said to continue to prevail in the present among a public the foundation desires to educate. In this scenario, the mis-

leading paradigms of earlier generations of historians or of a distant "they"—
the public—are opposed to the strict adherence to fact that is taken to
characterize present-day work. We heard many staff members explain Colonial Williamsburg's changing history in terms of the limitations, errors, and
ideological biases of others' interpretations; but they almost always presented the foundation's current research as nonideological, non–paradigm
driven, based solely on known facts and concern for accuracy. To return to
the example taken from the Garden Tour in which the interpreter explained
that many Williamsburg gardens are "colonial revival," not colonial: "You
have a lot more formal gardens in Williamsburg than [there] would have been
200 years ago. . . . So what we're doing is research. And when we come
across how a site was actually used, we will change the garden accordingly,
and interpret the other gardens as colonial revival gardens." In this example,
so punctilious is the foundation with respect to accuracy that even recognized errors will not be corrected until hard facts ("how a site was actually
used") guarantee that any changes will lead to greater veracity.

Not surprisingly, this rhetorical strategy was already in place at the foundation's beginning and became an integral part of the way it portrayed its work
to the public. The 1935 architects' report, for example, explained that the
restoration had to struggle against "the visitor's preconception" of how the
town should look—for example, "erroneous" notions "of long avenues
heavily shaded against a hot sun." Another such preconception was "the log
cabin myth," which the foundation's landscape architect wrote a book to
demolish. Like Colonial Williamsburg staff members today, those architectural historians—"who spent during the first three years of the Restoration
every available hour in exploration, measurement and photography"—portrayed themselves as researching the facts in order to counter past and prevailing misconceptions about colonial America. It was only later generations
of researchers who would see the work of those architects as misconceived,
as "colonial revival."[44]

The coupling of a past-tense paradigm-driven history and a present-tense
factual history reinforces one of the principal implications of mimetic realism—the notion of history making as a progressive process. Errors are relegated to the past, beyond which we who make history in the present can be
said to have progressed, precisely through the ongoing work of discovering
new facts. In a sense, then, mimetic realism has built into it an assertion of its
superiority, as a theory of why history changes, over constructionist versions
of history making. But that is only part of the story, as the next chapter
shows.

4 ▪ *Just the Facts*

We have already said that the historians who came to Colonial Williamsburg during the 1970s and 1980s wanted to change the foundation's message in two ways. First, they wanted to change the content of the Williamsburg story. By focusing more on "the other half" and the dispossessed, and less on the silk-pants patriots, the upper crust, they wanted to tell a story that was more critical than celebratory. But they also wanted to emphasize that history itself is a construct—a selective and willed account of a past that draws moral and political lessons that are shaped by current preoccupations and agendas.

In chapter 3 we described an institution that has, in a variety of ways, constructed itself as a monument to mimetic history but is also fertile terrain for a constructionist paradigm. In this chapter we explore what was happening to the constructionist message of the new history during the period of our field research. We will argue that in the daily workings of the museum, the constructionist view of history is largely overcome and obscured by a notion that history is a simple accounting of "just the facts," and that this, in turn, erodes the message of the new social history.

As an initial, brief example, consider the significance of "the other half," the term the foundation used as an emblem for its efforts to bring African

American history to Colonial Williamsburg. As our colleague, Anna Lawson, has noted, "the other half" is a paradoxical term.[1] On the one hand, halves are by definition equal; the term thus suggests that the Euro-American and African American stories are of equal value. At the same time, however, the African American half is "other," which at least implies some sort of inequality vis-à-vis the unmarked "mainstream" category. When people used the term, we often heard its egalitarian overtones drowning out the implications of inequality, especially when the terminology of quantification (halves) dovetailed with the rhetoric of objectivist history making. Thus, for example, a highly placed foundation educator parried our questions about the ideological content of the museum's African American history by falling back on the rhetoric of mimetic totality: "We have to try to portray the full history of what happened here in the eighteenth century. If we ask ourselves how are we doing, there's one obvious subject matter that's conspicuous by its absence. So you don't start out saying we're going to commit ourselves to the African American story any more than you say we're going to commit ourselves to the gentry story or any other story. We say we're going to tell the story the best we know how and we're going to keep filling in all the blanks we got, and that's a big blank so we're putting a lot of resources in there." In this response there is no acknowledgment of the publicly asserted ideological commitments of Colonial Williamsburg's social historians; rather, the turn to African American history is presented as ideologically neutral—a function of the foundation's unchanging dedication to the facts.

As a second example, this time from the front line, consider a typical tour guide's discussion of the foundation's orientation film, *Williamsburg—The Story of a Patriot*. Recall that the Curriculum Committee of 1977, led by newly hired social historians, had singled out the film as embodying a message or theme—patriotic history—they wanted to replace. Even Philip Kopper, in his celebratory history of Colonial Williamsburg, described the film as "jingoistic."[2] Yet, despite the film's reputation as a cold war icon, interpreters generally told the public that it is merely factually (but not thematically) out of date. As one historic interpreter at Wetherburn's Tavern explained during her tour, "there are a couple of things in there that aren't quite right" as revealed by "later research." As examples, she mentioned that the slaves in church are on the wrong side of the balcony and that a gentleman appears in public without a wig. Nonetheless, she continued, "it's such a good movie" that the foundation continues to show it. Absent from her account was any discussion of the significance of the 1957 film compared with the stories Colonial Williamsburg tells in the 1990s. In other words, an interpretive difference that was crucial for the foundation's leading historians was not habitually discussed on the front line, was not part of the institution's public culture.

The Salted Mine: Documented Facts and Interpretive Training

It is not accidental that guides explain history making to the public in terms of the discovery of new facts, for that view of history is built into their training.[3] When we attended a three-week, in-house training course in 1990, we noted a recurring feature of the relationship between what was understood as factual material (including documents and artifacts) and what was understood as interpretation. Prepackaged ensembles of artifacts or texts—whether in the form of exhibits, stories to be told, or training manuals combining administrative and historical documents—were treated as if they were themselves an undifferentiated, primary reality; in short, "just the facts." Interpreters were trained to use such documents to create their public interpretations. During training sessions these ensembles were implicitly treated as though they were "primary" facts, while the behind-the-scenes interpretive work that went into their selection and packaging was erased. Indeed, trainees were allowed to believe that their use of such materials to discover historical significance replicated the scholarly practices of curators and historians.

We found many examples of the conflation of prepackaged ensembles and primary facts in training sessions for Colonial Williamsburg interpreters—most insidiously, perhaps, when elements of the constructed environment were treated as artifacts that became the factual basis for subsequent interpretations. In 1990, the outbuildings at the Wythe House were furnished to tell a particular story about slavery chosen by the foundation's historians. In that story, cooks were said to be at or near the top of the slave hierarchy because of their skills and their control of the master's food and well-being. To illustrate the cook's status, curators had furnished her private room in the Wythe House outbuildings with a bed, quilt, dresser, curtains, and some chipped ceramics. A book lay open on the bed. By contrast, the other slave quarters were more spartan and contained fewer artifacts.

During a training session for the Wythe House, trainees were told to investigate the slave quarters, which they explored for about fifteen minutes. On reconvening, they were asked to figure out who lived in each room and what their lives were like. In response to leading questions from the trainers, these trainees "discovered" historical truth by induction from the artifacts. But they were never reminded that the rooms had been set up by historians and curators to tell precisely the story they had discovered. In other words, in this training session deduction was masked as induction, as trainees mimicked professional scholars and thereby learned that such experts arrive at the stories they tell by an objective process of induction from the facts at hand.

The practice of treating a constructed ensemble of objects as a primary reality from which, via inductive reasoning, one arrives at a fact-based interpretation of the past was the modus operandi of training sessions at Colonial Williamsburg. Documentary materials were used in the same way. At the beginning of training sessions that we attended, trainees received thick packets of written materials. The students were enjoined to study those documents on their own, but the materials were also covered in oral presentations by experienced interpreters, members of the museum's research staff, and various middle-level managers. The documents were color-coded to distinguish primary sources—letters, diary excerpts, household inventories, and the like—from historical texts written by foundation employees or academic historians. In addition, there were documents we would call administrative—for example, memoranda concerning interpretive priorities, instructions for handling emergencies, and summaries of interpretive techniques. These documents, as an ensemble, became the starting point of an exercise in which the trainees constructed a thematic framework—chosen by their superiors—for deploying historical facts.

The training process enacted what seemed to be an inductive process. The instructors threw out, apparently for discussion, various questions whose answers seemed to arise out of the data given in the training packets. When the trainees provided answers to the questions, the instructors listed the answers as interpretive themes on the chalkboard. Inevitably, the list would replicate an official administrative listing of the topics appropriate for the site in question. Probably most of those in attendance knew that such themes and topics were chosen in advance. Yet training sessions were structured to give trainees the apparent experience of drawing historical conclusions, on their own, from the "documented facts" alone.

On Interpretation

Beyond Colonial Williamsburg's training routines, this fundamental confusion about where fact ends and interpretation begins is central to the way the foundation uses what has become one of its most important buzzwords: *interpretation*. Colonial Williamsburg and many other history museums have accomplished the unlikely feat of transforming a word that is central to constructionist history making—*interpretation,* "to interpret the facts"—into one that implicitly but powerfully promotes an objectivist agenda. Consider as an illustration the titles of some programs offered by the Coach and Livestock Department during the time of our research: "Interpretation of How Oxen Were Used," "Interpretation of How Women Traveled and Used Horses," "Interpretation of Cattle and Their Uses," "Interpretation of Horses and Stables," and "Interpretation of Carts and Carting."[4] If the purpose of such titles is to announce a topic, the words "interpretation of" are unnecessary in every case, since titles like "How Oxen Were Used" and "Carts and Carting" are sufficient and clear. What, then, does "interpretation of" add? The answer is that those two words set apart or highlight an exhibit that is already the result of historical interpretation—how oxen were used, for example—as the real thing, the raw historical data. The image conjured up by "Interpretation of How Oxen Are Used" is one of museum staff "interpreting" an eighteenth-century fact to the visitor. In other words, the staged or re-created scene—costumed employees working with oxen—is presented not as a re-creation, an interpretation, but as the real thing, which must be explained or described to the public. The program's title, by announcing that the work of interpretation occurs in commentary on the scene, obscures the fact that the scene itself is already an interpretation.

That much is evident from the semantics of the titles alone. When we spoke to the ox driver, we learned that the behind-the-scenes construction of the authenticity of animals has been even more complicated than that at Colonial Williamsburg. According to our interlocutor, before he became the foundation's ox driver, oxen had been used primarily for "giving little kids rides" in an oxcart full of hay. He and his supervisor decided to devise new ways to use the animals to enhance the authenticity of the museum: "We . . . wanted the oxen to be more involved in the type of activities that you would actually have seen them involved in back then. Doing actual work out there, plowing the fields, logging, hauling stuff from place to place—regular work with them." Such programming has become common at Colonial Williamsburg as the long-standing projects of filling in the gaps and creating life-on-the-scene have dovetailed with the development of the museum's craft programs (officially, "historic trades"). Increasingly, craftworkers produce objects to be used in the museum itself, and this strategy is said to enhance authenticity in two ways: first, when the buildings and objects thus produced are used as exhibits, they are as "authentic"—as true to the eighteenth century—as up-to-the-minute research can make them; and, second, the activities of these workmen are said to make the museum more authentic, for they reproduce the life of the past.

From the ox driver's perspective—and this was typical of craftworkers and of the foundation's attitude toward them—the working oxen combined both kinds of authenticity. Moreover, the ox driver valued the second type of authenticity more than the first, as became clear to us when he began talking about the problem of tourists who interrupted his work around the village: "It's amazing—I can be out there on my way someplace, and I stop just for a minute, and somebody takes a picture or something. And I find, once I stop, it's really hard for me to get moving again, because you can't stop for one person to take a picture. Before they're done, you've got tons of other people coming. . . . I look at it this way. The pictures they take should be pictures of activity, not a posed picture. To me, if I want to take a picture, I want to take a picture of something that's really being done, and not just somebody posing. So sometimes I'll stop and let them take pictures. But my focus, again, is on working. Like sometimes, if I'm really busy, I won't take the time to talk about oxen. Because I could spend all my time talking about oxen and never get anything done." The creation and staging of "Interpretation of How Oxen Were Used," then, occurred against a backdrop of ongoing work that was understood to be doubly real—as authentic eighteenth-century activity and as functional present-day work. In this institutional culture, people tended to see ox work as a fact, not an interpretive re-creation of eighteenth-century realities. And to "interpret" ox work was simply to tell the public about facts that were there for all to see.*

This, of course, is exactly what we saw in Colonial Williamsburg's training sessions. Throughout the museum, prepackaged ensembles or staged reconstructions—which, from our perspective, are the result of the interpretation of historical data—are thought of and presented to the public as if they were objective facts.[5] This practice gives new meaning to terms like *interpretation* and *to interpret*. At Colonial Williamsburg, the rhetoric of interpretation serves to reinforce an objectivism that remains dominant despite the appar-

---

*The story is even more complicated, for visitors tended to see in the oxen yet a third kind of authenticity, that of animals as natural objects. The ox driver complained that it was often difficult to tell visitors how oxen were used because the visitors were interested only in the oxen as animals: "[It's] impossible to keep in the eighteenth-century period when you're talking about oxen, because people are just so fascinated by the animals. Most of the questions I get have nothing to do with the eighteenth century. . . . I might start out talking a little about eighteenth-century transportation. But if I can talk about it for five or ten minutes, I'm doing good, because automatically the people's interest goes back to oxen."

ent goal of today's museum professionals to teach the public that history is always more than just the facts.

How Not to Talk about Miscegenation

To privilege just the facts affects more than Colonial Williamsburg's philosophy of history; it affects the content of the story the institution tries to tell. To put the matter bluntly: an unintended consequence of allowing just-the-facts to dominate a constructionist historiography is that the teeth of critical history are pulled. This is nowhere more apparent than in Colonial Williamsburg's struggle to incorporate African American history into its mainstream story.

During the time of our research, the history of slavery was one of the top priorities of the foundation's social historians. Yet, as we repeatedly observed, both frontline and backstage personnel felt uncomfortable with that topic and consequently tended to avoid or gloss over it. They were able to justify their discomfort, while avoiding the taint of explicit racism, because they believed that black history was, as they often complained, "undocumented"—it verged on fiction; it never quite had the same just-the-facts authenticity as the stories they could tell about the elite white inhabitants of the town.

The epitome of this pattern of discomfort and suspicion was the way the white interpreters avoided the topic of miscegenation. It was during the colonial era that the "black codes," laws prohibiting sexual unions between slaves and free people, were enacted and enforced. Yet, as is well known, such unions continued to occur. To many historians of the colonial period, those laws and their sub rosa violations are a fascinating and fertile terrain for discussing the topic of slavery in general and for linking the history of slavery to the present of a racially polarized society. In many ways, the institution of slavery required that boundaries between the races be created and maintained. The institution of slavery, constructed out of such materials as the black codes, shaped the American system of racial differences.

Miscegenous unions fascinate the general public, as well. In the historical imagination of many Americans, such unions are exemplified by a standard scenario that has become a kind of archetype: an older master takes a younger slave as a mistress and they have a child to whom, as social conventions require, the master pretends to have no substantive connection. The slave mistress and the disenfranchised mulatto become the symbols for the fundamental inequities of slavery itself—or, perhaps, for the seamy side of history, the great man's dirty linen, which the official custodians of his memory will do anything to hide. Either way, the existence (hidden, suspected) of the slave mistress and the mulatto child points to a moral scandal.

Because this scenario has taken on the status of an archetype (and indeed, because such unions occurred), almost every historical site in the American South where the scenario could possibly have been enacted accretes such a story as part of its "public memory," its unofficial history. Thus, for example, at Monticello hardly a day goes by without some visitor voicing some version of the commonly held belief that Thomas Jefferson had a long liaison with a slave named Sally Hemings. Similar stories crop up at Mount Vernon and many other sites. At Colonial Williamsburg, the Wythe House is the site that attracts such a story, for it was George Wythe who, on the death of his wife, freed his slave-cook, Lydia Broadnax, and subsequently continued to live (albeit in Richmond) under her care; and it was George Wythe who, during the same period, took special pains to educate a mulatto boy named Michael Brown, who lived in the same household.

During the period of our research, then, the Wythe House was the site onto which the general theme of miscegenation was projected by some visitors and interpreters. At the same time, other interpreters defended the Wythe House against just that theme, as just-the-facts notions of history exerted their dominating influence.

On a two-hour walking tour called the Other Half Tour, interpreters from the Department of African-American Interpretation and Presentation (AAIP) used the Wythe House as a backdrop for a general discussion of the ways sexual relations and juridical codes about sexual relations were used to dominate and disempower blacks. Their discussions were brutally graphic. Describing the "middle passage," some guides remarked that female slaves were kept on the upper decks for "the pleasure" of white sailors, while male slaves were kept below "as ballast" or to prevent them from attacking the sailors. Describing the stereotypical image of the shuffling, yes-massa black, they reminded visitors that in late eighteenth-century Virginia, if a male slave even looked a white woman directly in the eye he could be legally charged with rape, then castrated for his crime. They also explained that white masters could violate the laws against interracial unions with impunity because female slaves were property and could not testify in court against a white person. Standing in front of the Wythe House, they further explained that one effect of the legal codes was to drive sexual relations underground, allowing masters to continue to have sexual relations with black women without having to recognize as kin the offspring such unions produced.

Like the Patriot's Tour, the Other Half Tour served as a general introduction to the museum-city and its inhabitants. The Other Half Tour, however, used the format of an outdoor stroll to intimate the marginal status of slaves and the "outsider" status of black history itself. Thus, when they used the Wythe House as a backdrop to discuss the sexual politics of slavery, Other Half interpreters sometimes used the seeming censorship of the George Wythe story by white interpreters "inside" the house to exemplify an ongoing censorship of the black story in general. Just as white masters continued to have underground sexual relations with blacks without recognizing the consequences, so, too, was the foundation's white majority continuing to keep such stories out of the public domain. As one guide put it (after asserting that George Wythe lived with Lydia Broadnax, who became his de facto wife, and that they had a child), "You'll never hear them [the white interpreters] tell you about Lydia or Michael Brown *inside* the house [because] they say it's undocumented."

And indeed, the guides inside the Wythe House tried their best not to talk about this issue even though visitors, irritatingly, would sometimes bring it up, asking whether Wythe had a slave mistress or a mulatto son. They asked, perhaps, because they had been prompted to do so by the Other Half tour; or perhaps because they had read or heard about Fawn Brodie's popular biography of Thomas Jefferson, which sets out to prove that Jefferson had a liaison with Sally Hemings and suggests a similar relationship for Wythe and Broadnax;[6] or, as we came to think, perhaps they simply believed that such liaisons must have occurred and that institutions like Colonial Williamsburg would hide or "whitewash" this fact as a matter of course. In short, some visitors asked interpreters in the Wythe House about Wythe's black mistress or mulatto son because they already knew that the answer would not be forthcoming. In return, interpreters took such questions as threats to their credibility and authority and, by and large, refused to recognize them as legitimate. As one interpreter told us when we asked her if she discussed the Broadnax-Wythe relationship, "I don't talk about that, and I don't interpret any ghosts. I do nothing with ghosts. . . . They ask you, 'Do you know about the ghost that's supposed to be in this house?' And I say, 'No, if it's not documented, I don't do things that aren't documented.' 'Oh.' So they go off to somebody else to see if they'll tell them." For this interpreter, the notion that George Wythe had a mulatto child was as fanciful as the stories that populate many of Virginia's historic houses with ghosts—stories promulgated by popular books sold in the gift shops of Colonial Williamsburg,

Monticello, and other historical sites.* Moreover, that visitors would believe such stories, no matter how often they are denied by the experts, simply revealed their stubborn gullibility.

When this interpreter said that visitors would go to someone else to get an expert's confirmation of a story they were bent on believing, she was not referring specifically to AAIP interpreters. But there was a pervasive and often-voiced belief among white interpreters that the AAIP staff did indeed play fast and loose with the facts in order to tell stories motivated by personal and political agendas. Conversely, when the AAIP interpreters said that white interpreters would say that Wythe's relationship to Broadnax "is not documented," they were alluding to an equally pervasive belief among them that white interpreters used the apparent lack of documents to evade the discussion of crucial racial issues.

Miscegenation is considered to be a sensitive topic. But white interpreters, at least in conversations with us, explained that, while some visitors might find the issue "touchy" or "embarrassing," they themselves would be willing to broach it if only they had the facts to back them up. But they had to be facts, as a lead interpreter put it during a workshop with us, "that you actually can tie to here." To her, AAIP staff members were ignoring particular facts in favor of a message: "[They] want to talk about miscegenation at the Wythe House. And they're using a particular example—you know, having an affair with George Wythe, and they produce this slave called Michael Brown. . . . Well, Michael Brown wasn't even born when George Wythe lived there. Michael was a freed slave who was with George Wythe in Richmond. But there's no proof—in fact, the facts, according to [a professional historian in Colonial Williamsburg's Research Department], pretty much [say that] the child was not his."

Another lead interpreter who was present for this conversation added that the historian had offered an alternative example to use. According to her, the historian, who agreed that "miscegenation is an important thing to talk about," "went back to his books and came up with John Custis." Custis had "left something in his will" to a mulatto child, and "the townspeople of the time sort of accepted the fact that Custis had this mulatto child and cared

---

*In *Virginia Ghosts,* Marguerite du Pont Lee (1966) said that the Wythe House is haunted by the ghost of a Lady Skipwith. As we were writing this section we recalled having seen Lee's book on sale in Colonial Williamsburg shops, but when we called to verify our recollection, we learned that though the Visitor Center bookstore carried such titles as *Richmond Ghosts, Williamsburg Ghosts,* and *Tidewater Ghosts,* it did not have *Virginia Ghosts.*

very much for it." The lead interpreter concluded: "That's the story we need to tell if we're telling the story of miscegenation. So I'm not thinking that's an evil thing to do. The story of miscegenation is worth telling. I mean, every newspaper ad you look at talks about mulattoes. They came because of miscegenation. So you've got to talk about the story. But," she went on, "you need something that you can talk about that's"—and she hesitated as she chose her next word—"*fair* to talk about. And the George Wythe story—particularly since Michael Brown wasn't even born until Wythe lived in Richmond—isn't the story to tell." Like the other lead interpreter, however, she realized that the problem with the Custis story, "the better story," was that Custis did not have "a site" at Colonial Williamsburg, so it would be difficult to bring him into an interpretive presentation.

For the most part, white interpreters and the black AAIP staff did not argue directly with one another about how to talk about miscegenation. Instead, they used each other as distant and convenient foils. The AAIP staff could stand outside the Wythe House and allude to their ongoing exclusion from the historical mainstream by referring to the white interpreters inside the house who say there are no documents. Meanwhile, white interpreters could refer to aspersions cast by "outsiders"—whether visitors or, perhaps more obliquely, AAIP staff—to claim a disinterested, if embattled, faithfulness to a just-the-facts accounting of historical truth.

When they did confront one another directly, they all accepted the ultimate veracity of the "documented" but seemed to lose the capacity to critically appraise such documents and the uses people make of them. This is well illustrated by a conversation that took place at a workshop we held for some of the people most involved in the training of interpreters. In this meeting, an AAIP interpreter and several white interpreter trainers were quick to agree that many white interpreters are reluctant to talk about sticky topics like miscegenation because it makes them uncomfortable. But they also agreed that, as the AAIP interpreter put it, "if you can document it, don't feel bad about it." He went on to describe what he saw as a typical scenario at Wetherburn's Tavern, one of the few sites at the time of our research where AAIP staff worked in tandem with (mostly white) historic interpreters. The historic interpreter took the tour group through the building and then directed them to an outbuilding where a "slave" was waiting. There, an AAIP interpreter spoke to the audience as if from the eighteenth century for a few minutes, then "broke frame" and reemerged as a contemporary tour guide to "interpret" the scene the audience and guide had mutually created. The tour group then returned to the tavern, where the historic interpreter was "inundated with questions about some of the things that we talked about." And because the historic interpreters "don't know where to go from there"—that is, they didn't have the facts at their fingertips—they found themselves unable to respond to the visitors' queries.

The AAIP interpreter argued that such a lack of information was the chief reason that black history in general and miscegenation in particular were ignored or skipped over by white guides—they didn't want to appear ignorant in front of an audience. To this he added: "But some people also feel that if they talked about George Wythe and Michael Brown being his son, and even if it was true, that it would be dragging up the dirt, and it would be marring his name in some way. . . . They'd just rather not talk the dirt. They'd rather just talk about all the good things that he did and leave him in that light." One of the white interpreter trainers in the workshop agreed with this assessment but immediately turned the conversation back to the issue of facts: "I know that there are people . . . who don't want to talk about miscegenation, period, because they think it's dirt. But you also have a lot of people who, as members of a museum community, feel compelled to look at the facts. . . . To be honest with you, I wish it was fact. It would make it much easier. But you do have people who want to base their interpretations on facts . . . and they feel it's not true, so they get themselves into a defensive position. Whereas if we could find a place where it was true . . . you'd still have a heck of a lot of people who would not feel comfortable with that, but you would also have people who wouldn't mind talking about it."

At this point the conversation took an interesting turn—or perhaps failed to take such a turn. No one pursued the matter of why white interpreters feel uncomfortable talking about miscegenation, or why they consider the subject of miscegenation to be "dirt." Instead, the AAIP interpreter responded with a question about particular facts: "Who said it had to be Lydia? Isn't there some evidence that one of the rooms in the house was occupied by a female slave?" He was referring to the Wythe House as it was then decorated, with a pallet in one of the upstairs bedrooms next to which were placed several artifacts, including a necklace of African trade beads. During training, interpreters were told that this tableau was meant to suggest the presence of a female slave and to use this tableau to describe the intimacies of domestic life in an upper-class colonial household. But there was no "evidence" for a particular slave sleeping on a particular pallet in a particular room. So when the AAIP interpreter asked about evidence, one of the historic interpreters explained that there wasn't any and that in future re-creations of the Wythe House interior, the pallet might have to be removed.[7] The group then spent several minutes discussing the available documentation for the Wythe household, until the conversation shifted to another topic.

The turn of the conversation, we argue, is significant. Despite their tendency to justify a position with reference to "documented facts," most people at Colonial Williamsburg rarely worked with documents and facts in a critical way. Indeed, the resort to documented facts was frequently a matter of oral tradition, if we may so phrase it, in the museum. Because the lead interpreters at the Wythe House could cite the professional historian who had verbally assured them that there was nothing to the purported liaison between Broadnax and Wythe, they, in turn, could tell the interpreters they trained and supervised that there were "no documents." As a rule, frontline employees accepted—and used in their interpretations—facts on the say-so of colleagues or superiors who told them that such-and-such a tidbit of information was documented. The frontline personnel took many of their facts from snippets of documents in their training manuals, supplemented by reading (sometimes extensive) they did on their own. But relatively few people at Colonial Williamsburg worked critically over extended periods with historical (either primary or secondary) documents. And let us add, lest our analysis be construed as an unfriendly critique aimed solely at the front line, that interpreters' use of information gathered from a variety of sources—both oral (what their colleagues tell them) and written—is perfectly reasonable and defensible; our point is the disjunction between the social construction of knowledge, *through multiplex and ongoing conversations,* on the one hand, and, on the other, the natives' model of what they claim to be doing, which privileges "documented facts" to the exclusion of all other sources of information.

With regard to the facts of the Broadnax-Wythe case, the Colonial Williamsburg staff asserted that "reputable" authorities and biographers had shown that there was no hard evidence to prove a sexual or common-law marital union. Our reading of those sources confirmed that assertion. We also found, however, that those favored writers used documents and facts to confirm their preestablished notions about Wythe's virtuous "character" as well as the ignominy of sexual relations between masters and slaves. In other words, we found that the authorities whom foundation staff believed to be in control of the facts had agendas and biases that clearly influenced their interpretations and their decisions to credit certain documents and discredit others. Yet, in the production of history at Colonial Williamsburg, the status of those authors as masters of facts was never questioned.

When the official biographers make the case against miscegenation, they rely on what to us is obviously an interpretation, not a fact—that is, their understanding of the "character" of George Wythe and, more insidiously, of the moral significance of sexual relations between masters and slaves. Two recent biographers of Wythe, Joyce Blackburn and Imogene Brown, have responded specifically to what Brown calls "the Brodie allegations." Blackburn admits that "no rational person can ignore the all-too-visible evidence of the interbreeding of races." She nonetheless is content to dismiss Brodie's case with an assertion that, admittedly, "proves nothing"—that "at the core of Wythe's personality was an authentic preference for order and moderation . . . as an expression of his innate control over all appetite, including sex."[8]

Brown refutes Brodie more systematically, but because the evidence is not conclusive, she relies in the final analysis, like Blackburn, on her beliefs about Wythe's character: "After a careful study of Wythe's life, one can only conclude, in the absence of any proof to the contrary, that as an old man, in mourning for his wife and in poor health, George Wythe did not suddenly abandon a life-style that had been characterized by the highest order of virtue, morality, and temperance and plunge into a passionate affair with a slave."[9] The excesses of this rhetoric should suggest to us that Brown is basing her arguments on more than just the facts. For one thing, she presumes that a relationship between Wythe and a slave had to involve a "plunge" on his part—a moral descent, apparently, from reason to passion, from virtue to licentiousness, from white to black. She further presumes, without offering documented evidence to support her presumption, that the alleged relationship between Wythe and Broadnax had to have been characterized by this sort of depraved passion; alternative scenarios—for example, of a more sober relationship based on years of domestic intimacy—are not considered. In short, by linking Wythe to reason and Broadnax to passion, Brown uncritically reproduces a core element of racist ideology, one the people of George Wythe's world often advanced as a natural reason for laws against miscegenation.

When people at Colonial Williamsburg refused to consider the possibility that Wythe and Broadnax had a liaison, they said the documentary evidence is against it. Their documentary authorities were such writers as Brown and Blackburn. But few of the people who relied on those documents seemed to have read them critically. To the contrary, most were satisfied, apparently, that the status of those publications as reputable or official biographies guaranteed their veracity. Indeed, Colonial Williamsburg staff, and visitors, too, tended to reproduce the biographers' understanding of miscegenation as morally sullying. As one supervisor of frontline personnel put it, miscegenation "proves that these white people are really not as pure and proper as they think they are."

In general, people at Colonial Williamsburg accepted "the documented" as the true and legitimate, and the undocumented as something to be avoided in public interpretations. They did not, by and large, examine with a critical eye the information that was presented to them as documented fact. As a result, people at Colonial Williamsburg discussed historical facts much more easily and readily than the moral or political implications of the histories they told.

The topic of miscegenation raises disturbing questions about American slavery and its legacy of racism. It can lead to discussions of sexual exploitation, the brutal power that made such exploitation possible, and the moral failings of the master class who used slaves, against their will, for sexual gratification. This way of framing miscegenation also emphasizes that American racial distinctions are built on antagonism. But the topic of miscegenation can lead in another direction—to discussion of the blurring of racial boundaries that can occur in loving relationships between whites and blacks. The AAIP staff discussed both implications of miscegenation with us, although they differed among themselves about which they preferred to emphasize. Some objected to presenting miscegenous unions as loving marriages, for they felt that most such liaisons were violent and power-laden. Others argued that it is good to tell stories about unions between blacks and whites because they show historical personages breaking down the artificial barriers between the races. After all, many of the African American descendants of "great white men" like Jefferson and Washington want to be included and recognized at places such as Monticello and Mount Vernon—and thereby restored to a rightful and honorable place in American history.

In any case, it was obvious to us that the AAIP staff members we spoke with saw miscegenation as a topic that could be used to raise crucial issues about the politics of race in American history and in the present. But it was difficult for them to raise those larger issues in in-house discussions with other staff at Colonial Williamsburg, precisely because the habitual discourse of the place seemed to turn every discussion of interpretive significance into a discussion of "documented facts." After all, in the workshop discussed in the paragraphs above, even the AAIP staff member was deflected from a discussion of the moral or political significance of the miscegenation story to an ultimately arid discussion of particular facts: "Who said it had to be Lydia? Isn't there some evidence that one of the rooms in the house was occupied by a female slave?" This shows, we think, that in the culture of Colonial Williamsburg, talk about facts displaces talk about what particular histories mean.

Fighting with Facts

This kind of displacement occurred again and again at Colonial Williamsburg during the time of our research. Sometimes staff members were aware that just-the-facts history was deflecting them from the story and were disturbed by it. More often, they were less aware of it or not aware at all. The master cooper was both aware of the displacement and disturbed by it. He gave us what amounted to a native's account of the way the selective—he called it "political"—deployment of facts eviscerated the themes of critical history at the site he had, until shortly before our interview with him, been in charge of.

The master cooper was an enthusiastic supporter of the kind of "people's history" that he felt social history represents. He had grown up in a trade which, he reminded us, has a very long history of labor organizing. To him, the new social history embodies what he thought the hand skills program had always been meant to exemplify: history "of the masses, for the masses, by the masses." When the cooper talked about the trades, he kept reminding us that civilization rides on the back of the working man; it depends on "the people," not kings, presidents, and "leaders" in general. When he used the word "leader," the cooper usually appended a proviso: "leaders if we really need leaders" or "leaders—if most of us would ever want to be leaders." As the cooper talked, we heard the voice of blue-collar socialism.

The cooper explained that the social historians' program had largely failed or bogged down, in part because of a failure in leadership, but mainly because of resistance by middle management. A program that should have been implemented in one year had taken ten, "and we're still not finished." The vice president of research "didn't have to come down here waving a flag," but the foundation's top management did have to "tell the managers that this *was* the program and to get to it." As the cooper saw it, middle managers feared the new, thematically centralized programs because they feared losing their authority and even their jobs.

The cooper tried on his own initiative to circumvent the managerial inertia. He instituted a new interpretive program at his shop—a lecture on the commercial history of tidewater Virginia as seen through the production and consumption of barrels. Initially, he tried to squeeze funds for an extra interpreter from management. "I wrote a memo," but "they threw it in the garbage, that's what they did." To keep the program from being axed for lack of money, the cooper got his men to produce more barrels than normal, and they managed to sell about four thousand dollars' worth extra a year through the stores on the Duke of Gloucester Street. In the year when our conversation with the cooper took place, however, the administration decided that the barrels would no longer be sold because they were inauthentic. The wooden staves were not hewn by hand, and the metal hoops were of low-grade machine-tooled steel, not hand-hammered iron. In addition, the wood—cedar rather than oak—was vaguely inauthentic, though the cooper protested: "But I have proof that coopers in the eighteenth century used cedar."

No longer would coopers make barrels for sale in the shops. The cooper was somewhat chagrined, yet he "could live with that as long as we kept with the program. After all, our first job is to educate, not make barrels." But the administration's next decision angered him. To make the barrels the coopers crafted in the shop more authentic, it was decided that hand-hewn wood would be used, and it would be the coopers' responsibility to supply the wood. As a result, he and his workers spent an inordinate amount of time manufacturing raw materials and less time crafting containers. This, the cooper said, is what particularly angered him. The foundation, in order to make the object more authentic, threatened the "identity" and "dignity" of the tradesmen. As the cooper explained it, tradesmen enter a craft and must work and learn to gain the hand skills necessary to practice the craft. There is no limit to the amount of "hand skill" one can acquire, and the more one acquires, the more identity and dignity one gains. One comes to represent, even embody, the whole history of a craft as one gets closer to the pinnacle of knowledge.

When the cooper protested to management that his coopers would waste valuable time producing raw materials and would lose or never acquire "hand skills" as a result, he was told that this was actually not a bad thing. "They explained that a master cooper like me—trained in London, able to make the finest barrels—simply would not exist out here on the frontier. So that it would not be appropriate to train apprentices to my level. They said that it would be good if they were 'deskilled.'" The cooper allowed that he probably was "inauthentic" because he was too skillful for the eighteenth-century colonial context, but he asserted that all such arguments were essentially being used "politically": people reluctant to institute the "Becoming Americans" program had found a way, cloaked in the sacred mantle of authenticity, to diminish the "identity" and "dignity" of the craftworkers and thus to keep the voices of the masses silent. Eighteenth-century coopers, after all, did not chop and hew their own staves. They bought them wholesale, just as he had done when he was manufacturing barrels for the retail trade in the reconstructed shops of Colonial Williamsburg. Moreover, while it might be true that eighteenth-century coopers had less skill than he did, he doubted they had less "dignity." To "deskill" the coopers in the name of mimetic authenticity was to hide contempt for the working masses under the cloak of historical truth.

Because the cooper complained so much about these administrative decisions he was purged. He was replaced as master of the shop (at Colonial Williamsburg, masters of the crafts, like their eighteenth-century counterparts, actually manage the sites to which they are assigned) and promoted to something like cooper emeritus.

The master cooper blamed middle-level managers for blocking his efforts to enact the "Becoming Americans" program. Doubtless other actors in this drama would tell alternative versions of the same events. But the point is that people used a piecemeal authenticity politically, and the arguments they used were explicitly grounded in a just-the-facts approach to history. This case shows that the themes of social history were constantly breaking apart in the riptides of conflicts over factual authenticity.

The cooper was not alone in accusing management of using arguments based on just-the-facts history to "deskill" workers. Some members of Colonial Williamsburg's militia told us a similar story of how management used facts politically to eliminate jobs. Late in the summer of 1991, militiamen explained that they and other "Class C" interpreters—the highest-paid category—would in effect be demobilized by the end of the year. If management decided to refill their positions, they would do so with lower-paid workers. According to our interlocutors, management was arguing that the militia had grown too large to portray the militia as it actually was in colonial times. Some managers asserted that a militia didn't even exist in 1770 and were using that fact to justify their decision. But as the militiamen saw it, the "executoids"—"the suits and skirts" who work in "the foundation's bunker," the Goodwin Building—were selectively using historical facts to justify a budgetary agenda.

Three months later, in an interpreters' workshop to which we had been invited as outside experts, we mentioned this example in a discussion of institutional politics. Once again, we were asking interpreters why they thought history changes. The first person to respond said that "all historians have a certain amount of bias. And therefore it [history] is going to be changed."

Another added that in the future, people will "look at the information" and reinterpret the exhibits the current staff had chosen "based on what we know now." A third interpreter saw this ongoing reinterpretation "as a way of growing up. . . . Hopefully, we are bettering ourselves to better the visitor's experience. We don't really mind the change if we think it's for the better."

At this point we asked about the possibility of "changes that are for the worse [and] that are also facts. . . . Do some facts make the story worse?" People quickly acknowledged that this sometimes happens. One man said that he doesn't like it when a fact "contradicts" his interpretation and "ruins" a story he likes to tell. We then asked if he would always accept foundation historians' word that something is false; to which he responded: "You have to be convinced within your own mind. . . . I question all the things that come down to me"—and everyone in the group laughed.

It was at this moment that we brought up the story of the militia. We asked the staff members seated around the table how they would use the "fact" that no militia existed in Williamsburg in 1770. The same man who described himself as questioning "all the things that come down to me" exclaimed, "I don't like it cause I'm [a member] of the militia." When we argued the point, asking him how he could justify the museum's militia if its presence violates historical fact, he responded by using facts similarly to attack another inter- pretive unit, the Fifes and Drums: "I don't think the whole Continental Army had as many fifes and drums as Colonial Williamsburg. But that's the way it's always presented. And everything is for the glory of the Fife and Drum, and who cares about the soldiers who fought the wars and the gen- erals who controlled it? The Fife and Drum makes all the decisions . . . instead of . . . the militia. So the tail's been wagging the dog for years! We'd be satisfied with *a* fifer, *a* drummer, one of each. But we don't need this whole battalion of them. If you've heard one fife and drum song, you've heard 'em all!" To this we responded, "Yes, but [our] question is, it seems that fact dominates so much"—and he interrupted, "only when management wants it to. Management makes the fact do whatever it wants it to do. If we [manage- ment] like it, we will expand on it. If we don't like it, we sort of push it under the rug."

When we later reflected on this conversation, we saw that the militiaman was both wary of management's use of facts to promote its interests and willing to play the same game, using facts selectively to do to the Fifes and Drums what management was possibly going to do to the militia. The mili- tiaman, and the cooper as well, were skeptical, even cynical, about the way management manipulated "authenticity" and deployed just-the-facts rhetoric to support or undercut particular programs. But in defending themselves against such attacks it was all too easy for them, too, to phrase their arguments solely in terms of facts.

In another workshop, this time for the foundation's "educational administrators," one manager called facts "the Colt .45, the great equalizer," of historical argument at Colonial Williamsburg. According to him, everybody, from the corporate vice president to the frontline interpreter, has access to facts and can use them to defend their programs. Yet, as we've seen, in the first workshop discussed in this chapter, the AAIP interpreter essentially lost an important thematic point when he allowed that Lydia Broadnax might not have been the slave sleeping on what turned out to be an entirely hypothetical pallet. We have dwelt on this conversation because we find it typical of the way debates about particular facts often deflect arguments away from their intended purpose. Likewise, both the cooper and the militiaman may have lost the game once they began quibbling about such things as whether coopers chopped wood or a corps of militia was more authentic than a fife-and-drum corps. By not directly questioning management's authority to make economic decisions and cloak them in the rhetoric of authenticity, they had no hope—and they knew it—of arguing as equals.

People fight with facts at Colonial Williamsburg. When they do so, it appears that they are fighting about the same thing, that they are at least communicating with one another. But in a sense they are not, for the premises of any particular disagreement—for example, the perception that white guides won't broach racially touchy topics because of a kind of unconscious racism, or the notion that management is acting according to economic motives while pretending concern for authenticity—are left unsaid, undiscussed. So dominant, then, is the rhetoric of fact at Colonial Williamsburg that it is often difficult to raise the question of what the facts are being made to add up to—of what, that is, particular histories mean.

Fighting with Facts on the Front Line

The tendency of Colonial Williamsburg employees to use facts to attack others in institutional turf wars was present in their interactions with visitors as well. Visitors entertain, and are seen by insiders to entertain, many preconceptions and paradigms—"myths," in the language of museum professionals—that museum staff members believe it is their duty to dispel. Perhaps the

The pillory and the carriage are important props for enacting the narratives of nostalgia and progress. (photos by Eric Gable)

most widespread preconceptions are those we dubbed, early in our research, the narratives of nostalgia and progress, cultural paradigms or themes that go back centuries in European and Euro-American traditions. The narrative of nostalgia looks longingly to a past presumed to be simpler and better than the world of the present; the narrative of progress looks back to a primitive past and celebrates the historical progress that has removed us from it and has led to the civilized world of today.

The streets and buildings of Colonial Williamsburg—and of many other history museums—make an ideal setting for visitors to rehearse both narratives. As we have seen, the foundation is well aware that its tidy colonial city appeals powerfully to visitors seeking a simpler world. The nostalgic view of the past appeals as well to many employees. We often heard interpreters invoke the narrative of nostalgia as they told visitors about everything from the preindustrial ingenuity of colonial craftsmanship to the severe simplicity of eighteenth-century penal codes. But we have also seen that the foundation worries about the inauthenticity of a too-clean setting and often (and increasingly) tries to emphasize, in the name of historical realism, the squalor and poverty of the world of the past. This sort of realism converges, however, with a narrative of progress. Many were the times we heard interpreters raise a chuckle from their audience by pointing out the unhygienic barbarities of eighteenth-century life—rendered sheep fat at the wig-maker's shop, publicly shared toothpicks in Wetherburn's Tavern, uric acid at the printer's press, and the ubiquitous references to the presence of animal droppings "two feet deep."

When we questioned them about it, however, many frontline personnel treated the two narratives as irritating if endemic "myths" and blamed the uninformed visitor for importing them to the site. The craftworkers, in particular, self-consciously set out to puncture visitors' notions about both the superior simplicity and the inferior crudity of the past—perhaps because their work in the history of particular technologies had made them especially sensitive to both the gains and the losses consequent on scientific progress. In discussions with us, two senior members of the Department of Historic Trades intimated that this was a conscious pedagogic strategy. As the first, a blacksmith, put it: "In the Blacksmith Shop, we get people all the time who are into nostalgia, . . . who say, 'Yep, they built everything better back then.' . . . And frequently you'll point out to them that not everything was better back then, but that many of the things that survived into the twentieth century are better. Maybe that's why they survived. . . .

"Then we'll have other people who'll come in, and they'll say, 'Well, how can you produce anything by this technology? It must've all been junk if you made it by hand. They couldn't have made the close tolerances or high quality like we can today.' And we'll reverse that and say, 'There were skilled people, on the other hand, that could produce very high-quality objects. . . . Go down to the Wallace Gallery. There are pocket watches on display. Every single component in that pocket watch is made by hand. But it kept time well, lasted this long, it was high quality.' "

According to the second senior craftsman, he and his colleagues adopted this "back-and-forth" strategy because it "pushes people into critical appraisals" of their preconceptions. In the blacksmith's words, it forces people to "think deeper" about certain "broad generalizations" in light of specific facts: "What we're both saying is that you can use that kind of opposing point of view to provoke the visitor into thinking more and not making such broad generalizations, but making more individual comparisons."

To urge visitors to test their beliefs against documented facts from the history of technology is a useful exercise, but it fails to educate people about the paradigmatic status of the narratives of nostalgia and progress and thus leaves those paradigms essentially intact. In other words, when the craftworkers use facts to pull the rug out from under one narrative, they merely substitute the other in its place. Even if visitors are led to think about which narrative can better account for a particular set of facts, they are not asked to rethink, and possibly reject, both narratives. They are not asked, that is, to see that the two narratives are linked together in the habitual thought of modern Americans—that both constitute a consumer preference test (which is better, the old or the new model?) that people routinely apply to the objects of their world.

We even came to doubt that this can really be considered a pedagogic strategy. Frontline craftspeople had a more cynical take on what this form of deflating visitors' assumptions entailed, for they recognized that it was often a frustrated and somewhat hostile response to what they perceived as visitors' tiresome ignorance. Thus, for example, several craftspeople told us a perhaps apocryphal story of a blacksmith's frustration after an endless series of stupid visitors refused to believe that the blacksmiths at Williamsburg's Anderson Forge produced, "like a factory," thousands upon thousands of nails. When yet another visitor remarked, "I didn't know they had nails back then," the blacksmith replied, "Yeah, and I guess the Romans screwed Jesus to the cross." The visitor, a sanctimonious Christian, complained to Colonial Williamsburg's management, and the blacksmith was, according to the differing versions of the story we heard, either fired or severely reprimanded.

What emerges from the craftsmen's pedagogy, then, is not a better understanding of historical constructionism, but, perhaps, a renewed sense of facts-as-weapons. For, just as Colonial Williamsburg insiders fight with facts in institutional turf wars, so frontline personnel use facts to attack visitors covertly—a theme to which we return in chapter 7.

5 ■ *Social History on the Ground*

Christmas at the Wythe House

On 13 December 1990 we attended a special evening at the Wythe House. The program that night focused on the relationships between slaves and their masters during the Christmas season. We were told by several participants that the presentation was meant to be disturbing. It was meant to highlight the inequities that were part and parcel of the social order that Colonial Williamsburg re-creates. Holding such a program at the Wythe House—a symbol both of Enlightenment culture and of patriotism—during the Christmas season—a favorite time for those visitors who want to see an idealized and pleasant past—was intended to bring the critical themes of social history into the heart of celebratory Williamsburg. An examination of this program, therefore, can help us understand how social history works "on the ground."

As is the case for most evening programs, visitors had to purchase a special ticket to see the Christmas program at the Wythe House. Every half hour, a group of about twenty people was admitted to one of the outbuildings on the Wythe property, where a historic interpreter set the scene for what they were about to witness. On the tour from which the following dialogues are excerpted, our guide began by telling us "a little bit about Mr.

An Other Half Tour stopping in front of the Wythe House. (photo by Molly Handler)

Wythe. . . . He was a gentleman with a brilliant mind, and . . . he was a lawyer, a teacher, a scholar, a revolutionary, and he was a judge." Alluding to the fact that Mr. Wythe would be portrayed by a character interpreter, she described him as visitors might encounter him "during the day . . . walking down the Palace green . . . deep in thought." She also told us that the house was one of Colonial Williamsburg's "eighty-eight original buildings," adding that "the door that you'll exit, the front door, even dates back to the 1750s."

She then introduced us to the main themes of the program, which in her view were slavery and the differences between Christmas then and now: "You'll not only see Mr. and Mrs. Wythe tonight, but you're going to see how Christmas was celebrated by the slaves in the eighteenth century. Because Christmas was entirely different at this time in the eighteenth century." She went on to give an account of how Christmas customs have changed over time—Christmas trees, for example, were not introduced into Williamsburg until the 1840s—and inserted a rousing tribute to "the Christmas spirit": "So tonight in Williamsburg you have the sights, sounds, and the smells of these bonfires, and especially the *spirit* of the Christmas season. . . . So you're going to get just a little treat of Christmas at this time in the eighteenth century, but also you'll see, as I mentioned, how it was celebrated by the slaves, because for them, this was more a time of extra work." She concluded with a synopsis of the upcoming dramatization, including room-by-room directions for us to follow on our "time trip back into the eighteenth century."

Having finished her introduction, the historic interpreter guided us along the walkways of the Wythe property to the laundry, which was dark except for the light from the fireplace. We re-create the scene as we experienced it. Two women, dressed as slaves and sitting on a bench against a wall, are speaking as we crowd into the room and try to make ourselves inconspicuous. They talk in an exaggerated dialect—the slave actors' version of historically authentic speech, which, in this set of skits, contrasts sharply with the Anglified tones the white actors use to bring their characters to life.

> *Slave 1:* . . . But you know, I was sittin' here, just a-wonderin' what Mrs. Wythe is gonna give me for my Christmas gift this year—for my Christmas box, you see. Well, you know, last year she gave me that pretty indigo dress—you know, the one with the bow that fell right off!
>
> *Slave 2* [laughing heartily]: You got t' wear that 'bout three, four times at the gathering, then it split right down at the seams!
>
> *Slave 1:* Right down the seams. But I did get one or two good wearings out of it, though. That's for sure. . . . But you know what, though? The more Christmases I go to, the more I gets to thinkin'—I gets a ill feeling about this whole Christmastime thing, and I just be wondering if we ain't be doing a whole lot of smiling on the outside, but cryin' on the inside.
>
> *Slave 2:* You must be thinking about that slave boy that came here that that Jenkins man was talking about—how he got sold off after Christmas.
>
> *Slave 1:* Well you know, that could have been any one of us! You know, some people think that they slaves is—treat 'em like things instead of like people.
>
> *Slave 2* [fearfully]: You don't think that Mr. and Mrs. Wythe will do something like that Jenkins man did, do you?
>
> *Slave 1:* Well, I tries not to think so, but as I said, the more Christmastimes I go through the more ill feelings I get.

Presently, Charles, a young man, enters, complains of the cold and that he is sick, and remarks in a bitter if resigned tone:

> *Charles:* I been tryin' to get this here Christmas spirit, whatever.
>
> *Slave 2:* Ain't we all? We was just tryin' to get into it.
>
> *Charles:* I don't see what everybody gets so excited about. It seem like they just go back and forth, tryin' to get things for this here person, and

goin' over here tryin' to give this. An African man came through here the other day, talkin' about, he ain't *never* heard 'bout this Christmas thing. He said that they'd celebrate the harvest about the same time of the year. But this here Christmas thing, he ain't never heard of. He said, he thinks it's a trick—to try to get us to do more work. And that Christmas box—I don't want dat thing. They can keep dat.

Slave 2: At least it's sumpin'—some folks don't even get dat, Charles.

The scene ends when Charles leaves and the two women speculate that "sumpin' wrong wit him." We are next ushered into the kitchen outbuilding, where we come upon a young slave woman, Lydia Broadnax, quietly singing a spiritual as she pokes at the embers of a dying fire. She stops singing to recall her grandmother:

Lydia: . . . she sure knew how to cook, too! . . . She had the *longest* fingers. She'd be strokin' my head with that fine horn comb. She'd be singin' 'bout freedom and 'bout heaven. She'd be proud to know I'm doin' what she always wanted me to do. Big Mama used to say, "Lydia, always keep your hands movin' fast. That way you have more time to rest!" [Audience chuckles.] Yeah. I didn't know what she meant then, but I sure know what she mean now.

Lydia begins working at the hearth, and Charles enters.

Charles: Lydia, you in here?

Lydia: Charles?

Charles: Yeah. You got that damn brick for Mrs. Wythe? You know how she get when she ain't got that brick. She say her back start hurtin' . . .

Lydia: Yeah, it's over dere! Mr. and Mrs. Wythe is gettin' *trouble in my mind* with all this special treatment they want. Don't they know this is the time of the year we be workin' the hardest anyhow?

Charles: But what they care? [In a sing-song voice:] They go do this thing over here. They gotta go buy sumpin' for somebody over here, and they gotta go over here and buy sumpin'. They got more spirit than that one they call, ah, Jesus—or whatever was around here.

Lydia: I just be glad when Christmas is over, and I won't have to do so much cookin' and so much bakin'! [Her voice rising in anger:] If Mrs. Wythe come in here one more time tellin' me 'bout some relishes and sumpin', I'm gonna tell her . . . she can come in here and knead this here dough. . . . Charles, what's wrong?

> *Charles:* I wants t' see my family. Been 'bout two 'bacca seasons since
> I seem 'em last. Heard 'bout mah sister bein' ill and all. I wants to go up
> there and see 'em for 'bout a week.
> *Lydia:* Well, why don'tcha go in there and ask Mr. and Mrs. Wythe? I
> mean, deys got de spirit and all—she may letcha go on home.
> *Charles:* Naw, me and the missus, we don't quite see on the same level.
> See, she's too busy worryin' 'bout some Christmas gift that she's sup-
> posed to give, or sumpin'.
> *Lydia:* Well, then, ask Mr. Wythe—he'll listen.
> *Charles:* Naw, see, when I talk to him, he just doesn't pay attention—
> like when you talk to him!
> *Lydia:* You get that brick, and then you come on over to me and let
> me tell you what you need to do. You gots to know how to talk to them
> folks. [She puts her arm around his shoulder and leads him offstage, to
> her bedroom.] Come on in. Let's go on inside. I want you to go inside,
> and I want you to tell him . . . [they exit, conspiring].

We are then led into the main house, and upstairs, where we see Mrs.
Wythe fussing in her bedchamber. She comes out into the upstairs hall and
calls out:

> *Mrs. Wythe:* Charles! Have you my brick?
> *Charles* [businesslike]: Yes ma'am.
> *Mrs. Wythe:* Would you lay it on the hearth?
> *Charles:* Yes ma'am.

He goes into the bedroom, she follows him, instructing him about the fire,
then they return, he coughing.

> *Mrs. Wythe:* That sounds poorly.
> *Charles* [sullenly]: I'm not feeling too well. A bad cough.
> *Mrs. Wythe:* Has a plaster been applied? Perhaps a mustard plaster in
> the morning. If you would go downstairs, please, and clear the table for
> Mr. Wythe and the Reverend Henley. I believe that Mr. Henley is about
> ready to depart.

Charles leaves, and we troop belowstairs and into the parlor, where Mr.
Wythe and Rev. Henley are seated at a table, Charles standing in waiting. The
Reverend Mr. Henley is explaining in great detail the Christmas customs of
his native Devon ("the wassailing of the trees," a "custom immemorial . . .
of pagan origin") and asks Wythe about Christmas in the colonies. Wythe

explains that his grandfather "was a Quaker" and that his mother "was largely imbued with the spirit of the Quakers." As a result, he says:

> *Wythe:* I still tend to celebrate the holidays of Christmas in a rather quiet, meditative mood. I find it a good time to renew my meditations upon the lessons of our religion. Unlike many, I will not beat my head over modes of belief and methods of baptism, but I thank God it is my duty to meditate upon this: that God is love, and that in the exact portion as we love, we are in God.*

Henley and Wythe continue their discussion of religion until Charles, who has been standing silently all the while, catches Mr. Wythe's attention. Charles now speaks in the Anglified accent the others are using:

> *Charles:* Mr. Wythe, sir, I'd like to make a request if this is the correct time to do so, sir.
>
> *Wythe:* You might as well ask.
>
> *Charles:* Sir, I've been longing to see my family now for about two years. I heard of illnesses and the bad humors in the family, sir. I assume you understand my position. I'd like to go to visit my mother and sister in Richmond for a week, sir—with your permission and a passport.
>
> *Wythe:* Well, I see no reason you ought not to go. You may leave tomorrow, and I think you might as well ride Roger. But be sure to get back by a week from tomorrow.
>
> *Charles:* Yes sir. [He exits.]
>
> *Rev. Henley:* I must say, he seems a well-mannered fellow.
>
> *Wythe:* Oh yes, he's very dependable, and quite civil. He's been with me for as long as—well, before I was married. He came from our plantations.
>
> *Rev. Henley:* I was pleased to see that you let him go. After all, I fear that far too many masters are careless of the welfare and the wishes of their people, and rather use them more hardly than you do, sir. I'm also pleased to see—and I must commend you on this, sir—that you regularly brought them to church on Sunday, for instruction. If there is any justification for bringing these people to America, it seems to me it is largely that we have brought them out of a state of barbarism and

---

*This speech is drawn from Brown's biography of Wythe. Brown quoted from an "unsigned manuscript" in which one of Wythe's pupils recorded his teacher's religious beliefs in "Wythe's words": "This opinion very clearly taught by reason . . . that God is love—and that in exact proportion as we grow in love, we grow in His likeness" (I. Brown 1981:88).

ignorance to a land of civility and true religion, for the benefit of their souls. I do not presume that that was the purpose for which they were brought out, but nonetheless we may do them that service, and then, I suppose, we may be somewhat justified.

Wythe: Well, I think, sir, that it had been far better had the institution of slavery never been entered into here in Virginia, or anyplace else, for that matter. But as we have it, and it appears that it will be a great long time before we can find a way to abolish the system, I think it is the least we can do for these people to treat them as humanely as can be, and to introduce them, as you say, to the Christian religion, that they may have the benefit of that enlightened faith.

Rev. Henley: Would that more masters were concerned over their people's souls, sir. But I must admit that I concur with you, and I am pleased to hear your sentiments spoken. For, since I came out in February, I fear I have not yet become accustomed to the notion that a gentleman must needs purchase his servant rather than merely hiring them.

Wythe: And may you never become accustomed to it, sir.

Rev. Henley: Yes, perhaps that would be best as well. It certainly does not rest easy upon me.

Wythe: No, and I find it doesn't rest easy on me.

At this point Wythe asks Henley if "it would please you to see a pamphlet that my great-grandfather wrote," and they retire to the library to find it.

After they left, our guide again spoke: "I hope you've all enjoyed your trip to the eighteenth century." She told us that "Mr. Wythe definitely was against the institution of slavery, so eventually he did free all his slaves." As for the slaves, she remarked, "Lydia Broadnax, and Charles, the slave that you saw bringing the bricks, they were both freed. Charles disappeared from the colony of Virginia, never to be heard from again. But Lydia decided to stay with the Wythes as their cook. And the Reverend Henley, before the eve of the Revolution, he decided to sail back home to England. And Mrs. Wythe passed away after a long illness at the age of forty-five. And Mr. Wythe passed away at the age of eighty, but as I tell in the introduction, he did have a fondness for learning. He was even studying Hebrew until his eightieth year."

Getting the Message

After we witnessed Christmas at the Wythe House, we interviewed at length two of the visitors who had seen the presentation in our group. This was our usual research technique, and it allowed us to get a quick if crude sense of what the public was learning at Colonial Williamsburg. Just as the Christmas program was a unique event yet in many ways illustrative of a general pattern in the way social history was being portrayed, so, too, did the unique comments of Jean and Joyce, two late-middle-aged women from Tennessee, exemplify the range of visitor responses to that portrayal.

When we asked Jean what she thought of the program, she responded that "it was very authentic." To her, the program was "an excellent job" because the actors were not "trying to give you an opinion" but were "trying to say this is the way it was. I think," she added, "it definitely gave the sides of both the slave owner and the slave. I am so happy that Mr. Wythe . . . didn't really relish owning humans. And that he did free his slaves." Wythe, she would add later, embodied "a gracious way of living. A cultured way of living." He was "a very brilliant man, a great man of law." Joyce agreed with Jean that "the main point was that Wythe had the slaves." Prodded by Jean, though, she added that slaveholding "became more against his conscience the way it was presented, because he was a signer of the Declaration of Independence, and how can you sign a document, such as the Declaration of Independence, and be a slaveholder? And in that period of time he released his slaves."

For Jean, Wythe's enlightened paternalism called up her own family history. A southerner herself, her "ancestors were slaveholders." Slaveholding "was the way of the day," but "it wasn't right." She grew up on a farm with tenant farmers, the "most loyal" of whom were black. As a child, she "only had blacks to play with." Her "youngest sister was nursed by a black." Jean, in short, had developed "a real affection for the Negro" but in a context somewhat akin to the antebellum master-slave relationship. Her father "cared for his servants" just as her grandmother "took very good care of her slaves" and just as Mr. Wythe cared for his slaves.

If the portrayal of Wythe both made her "happy" and resonated with her own experience, Jean also felt that the program offered a glimpse of the formation and general outlines of contemporary African American culture as a reaction to the black experience in slave society. "Blacks," she explained, "had a certain understanding that even you and I don't have. It's a bond formed . . . from the years of bondage. And from their tribal life." And, according to Jean, that bond continues "even today. . . . In the ghettoes. They have a bond. Their skin is their bond. The color of their skin. They hate our white skin. They really do . . . because they feel that we are a privileged class. Don't you?" For Jean, it was obvious that whites are a privileged class; she had certainly grown up directly experiencing that sense of privilege. Even though she could assert that blacks "aren't oppressed" in direct ways (suggesting that their hatred might be an exaggerated if understandable response to their past), she admitted that "it's human nature that we *never* want them to reach our level. . . . You always keep the under man just under you. They feel it." Nevertheless—and this is what she thought the program captured so perfectly—the privileged have "a bond" with those whose lives they oversee: "There is a bond between a Negro that is a tenant on your farm, . . . that cares for you as a little toddler, and you *love* that Negro." In brief, you love that Negro because you have a superior attachment to her; blacks hate you because of their socially enforced inferiority.

As both Jean and Joyce noted, there was an undercurrent of these bitter feelings in the slaves' attitudes as depicted in the performance. Joyce emphasized that "they're very disgruntled throughout," and both women admitted that "that bothered" them. Rehashing the plot of the program, Jean remarked that "they were disgruntled because the Christmas season is the time that they work harder. . . . But you know . . . all employees, or almost all employees the world over . . . gripe about what they have to do, they gripe about the boss. . . . And so they're human. And they were finding fault." She went on to explain that "this is human nature, to grumble about your work." But Jean also implied that while this sort of griping may be understandable, it does not necessarily evoke sympathy: "A secretary or a computer operator or a bus driver, you *still* gripe and grumble about what you have to do. . . . That's human nature! We're all the same."

While Jean assimilated the portrayal of slave disgruntlement to the natural gripes of employees "the world over" and seemed to identify with the "boss"—her father, her grandmother, the slave owner, George Wythe—Joyce asserted that employees and slaves were fundamentally different: "I work for the federal government, and I often complain about the judges for whom I work. *But* I'm not owned by them. And . . . the disturbing thing, to me, was thinking of this black man coming in asking if he could go and visit his mother and sister. And, yes, you can go, but be sure to have the landholder with whom you'll be visiting sign your piece of paper. Well, I'm visiting here, but I don't have to have anybody sign my piece of paper."

Jean and Joyce learned slightly different things from Christmas at the Wythe House, but in essence, both were given to identify with Wythe and to participate in a kind of joyful relief that he acted humanely toward his slaves and recognized that slavery was wrong. And while they were unambivalent in their sympathy for him, their attitudes toward the slaves were more complex. We think that this reaction is hardly an accident of Jean's and Joyce's biographies but is predictable given the plot line and content of the story. The Christmas program at the Wythe House sandwiched its depiction of slavery from the slaves' perspective between an introduction and conclusion that celebrated George Wythe. Recall that the program began with our third-person guide introducing us to Wythe—"a gentleman with a brilliant mind . . . a lawyer, a teacher, a scholar, a revolutionary." More important, the program ended with Wythe and Henley engaged in a long discussion of the inequities of slavery, with each gentleman concluding that the system "does not rest easy upon me." And then, as a coda, the guide regained her voice to tell us not only that Wythe freed his slaves but also, as the last word, that "he did have a fondness for learning. He was even studying Hebrew until his eightieth year." In sum, it was not the slaves but George Wythe who was the hero of this tale (which, indeed, was announced to the public in the *Visitor's Companion* simply as "Candlelit Evening at the Wythe House").[1]

The slaves nonetheless figured prominently in the program. From their critical perspective we learned of the hypocrisies of the masters' culture. For the masters—especially Mrs. Wythe (and one might wonder about the misogyny implicit in the contrast between the depiction of her character and that of her husband)—Christmas had become less a time of spiritual renewal than of material gratification. They gave cheap gifts to their slaves and tried to squeeze more work out of them during the busy holiday season. And we learned something of what it must have been like to be treated as property (the slaves are fearful of being "sold off") and to be constantly at the beck and call of others, with little personal freedom.

The Wythe House Christmas program also gave the audience a positive glimpse of the development of an African American culture of resiliency and resistance. Lydia Broadnax reflected on the beauty and wisdom of her grandmother, a democrat and a Christian ("singin' 'bout freedom and 'bout heaven") imbued with a powerful work ethic ("always keep your hands movin' fast"). The slaves were able to see through the ruses of the masters, especially the hypocrisy of Christmas ("a trick—to try to get us to do more work"). And they had developed techniques of resistance, especially in the manipulation of their presentation of self vis-à-vis their masters ("You gots to know how to talk to them folks").

In the end, however, it was Wythe's troubled conscience, his declaration that slavery is wrong, that made the audience happy. The depiction of social injustices was offset by the protagonist's disapproval of them. Indeed, in this depiction, people like Wythe were not even responsible for a system they merely inherited; as Wythe put it, "As we have it [slavery], and it appears that it will be a great long time before we can find a way to abolish the system, I think it is the least we can do for these people to treat them as humanely as can be." The proof of Wythe's benevolence is in the coda: freed, Lydia chose to stay with him as a paid cook (Charles, conveniently, disappeared, "never to be heard from again"). This prompted Jean and Joyce to condemn slavery yet exonerate, even venerate, the slaveholder, who was the hero and focus of the story.

Although slaves had a voice in this program, their actions and words ultimately served to highlight the virtues of George Wythe. This tendency was built into the everyday presentation of the Wythe House, as we learned on touring it several times. No character interpreters portraying slaves were present inside the house during regular tours, so the "presence" of slaves was suggested by artifacts and the ways interpreters chose to talk about them.[2] The Wythe House was depicted at a particular moment in the daily routine ("it is four o'clock in the afternoon"). Visitors were led into the parlor and given an insider's perspective on the teatime activities that, we were told, would have been occurring at that moment. The interpreters singled out "you ladies" and told them they would be joining Mrs. Wythe, who "is having tea with her friends." The mistress of the house, we were told, "has directed the slave to set up the tea table and gather the chairs around. When furniture was not in use in the eighteenth century, it was placed by the slaves around the sides of the room . . . allowing the parlor here to be used as a multipurpose space. . . . And in back you'll see the dining room, where Mr. Wythe [is] finishing up the dinner meal with his friends, but then the table, the leaves on the table [will] be dropped, and then pushed around to the side of the room, allowing the dining room to be used as a second parlor."

Here the furniture is a prop that brings Mrs. Wythe, your hostess, to life. The slaves are not actors but shadowy stagehands—props for props—who are at best "directed" to perform some task, at worst invisible altogether as they evaporate into the passive verbal constructions that allow leaves to "be dropped" and tables "pushed around" to make room for the Wythes and their genteel activities. For complex reasons, then, historical figures such as the Wythes remain the focus at sites such as the Wythe House even as Colonial Williamsburg interpreters try to include "the other half" in the stories they tell.*

*The contrast between an active master class and passive slaves was instilled during the training of interpreters for the Wythe House, as we learned when we participated in a three-week training program. Trainees were given a two-page document (dated March 1990) of "mid-afternoon" scenarios for each room of the house. For example, the synopsis for the

Consider the April 1990 tour of Wetherburn's Tavern, one of the sites singled out by the new social historians for the presentation of "black life."[3] Our guide began by explaining the social stratification of Williamsburg's taverns. He compared Wetherburn's—"the eighteenth-century equivalent of the modern luxury hotel," which catered to "men such as "George Washington, Thomas Jefferson, Patrick Henry, and other members of the legislature"—with lower-class establishments such as Chowning's, "better known for its drunken brawls than for anything else." As we went through the various public and private spaces of the building, the historical interpreter emphasized "the tavern keeper's business" (another topic that was specified for the site).[4] He offered a monetary evaluation of the things we were seeing and the services the tavern offered, and correlated such values with the social status of the taverns' owners, workers, and clientele: "We're not going to stop in this next room, but I'll let you step on in and take a look around. You might especially want to notice the very fine desk and bookcase. Notice all of the silver inside. That tells you certainly how well Henry Wetherburn is doing financially, but also how elegant this tavern and many of its customers were. . . . We can be charged up to one shilling for your basic meals. Drinks are extra. So it begins to add up. These prices do not translate very easily into modern money. But at that time . . . your average middle-class craftsman and many farmers are taking home on average two to two and a half shillings a day."

As we concluded our tour of the building, our guide invited us to look at the outbuildings, where we could learn more "about the slaves who lived and worked on this property." As an introduction to that topic, he explained the differences between our *Gone with the Wind* stereotypes about "nineteenth-century slavery" and "slavery as it was during the colonial period." In the earlier era, "we find that your average slave is fairly expensive, and so the

---

parlor explains that "after dinner the ladies will leave the gentlemen in the dining room with the wine. The gentlemen will later join the ladies for tea or coffee." In the student's room, "a student has been working all morning and has broken for dinner to return at a later time"; in the library, "Mr. Wythe . . . has been working alone"; and in the southeast bedchamber, "Mrs. Wythe was in this room earlier working on the tape loom." In the scenario for the southwest bedchamber, however, the training document makes use of contrasting grammatical constructions to highlight the agency of Mrs. Wythe while muting that of her slave: "Domestic activities of female house slave who lives in a corner of the room; Mrs. Wythe has been sewing and quilting earlier." Indeed, in the parlor synopsis, passive verbal constructions eliminate slaves altogether: "Tea equipage has been placed on one table and a decanter and glasses may be placed on another." Even inanimate objects are given greater agency than slaves: "Sometimes the furniture may still be at rest."

cruelty we hear about is really not as prevalent here in the eighteenth century. Your average slave who has just gotten off the boat from Africa can't speak the language, has no skills, is going to run you about twenty pounds here at the time of the Revolution. And that's about what your average craftsman or farmer is going to make in about a year's time. . . . A slave that has a skill is going to be very highly valued. So when Henry Wetherburn owns twenty-nine slaves, that tells you he has a great deal of money. . . . Most valuable is Caesar, *seventy pounds* he is worth at Henry Wetherburn's death. So that is more than two years' labor for a middle-class craftsman or farmer. That's a lot of money. Caesar is valuable because he's a farrier. . . . So, if he were free, he could certainly command a pretty good wage. . . . Sylvia the cook is valued at fifty pounds, which is still a great deal of money. Cooking is considered a skill, so a slave cook who can cook well is going to be very highly valued. . . . So we are talking about very valuable people—people who have rights as people, but first and foremost they are property."

Although his discussion gave some attention to the slaves' lack of freedom, it focused on morally neutral monetary values and on the comparatively benign form of slavery that existed at the time. Hence the oft-repeated argument that because slaves were expensive, masters could not afford to mistreat them. On another tavern tour, for example, our guide asserted that the most expensive slave of whom there is any record in Williamsburg was valued at one thousand pounds. Asking us if the master would mistreat such a valuable property, he concluded: "No, he'll treat him like an NFL quarterback!"

Not only did the Wetherburn's Tavern tour reassure us about the treatment of slaves, it further mystified slavery as a system of exploitative relationships based on racial differences through its persistent rhetoric of monetary values. To present slavery in terms of the market value of slaves—compared with the annual incomes of various categories of freemen—is to privilege an abstract calculus by which all individuals are judged in the same terms. We thought at the time that such a presentation would make it possible for visitors to think that the highly skilled Caesar, worth seventy pounds, was higher on the socioeconomic ladder than "your average craftsman or farmer," whose yearly income was much less than seventy pounds. That possibility was realized during a tour we took later of the Raleigh Tavern. There the historic interpreter went through a sequence of presentations similar to those we had heard at Wetherburn's. He told us about the cost of meals relative to average salaries, the greater expense of the meals of the wealthy, and the value of the slaves who cooked and served the meals. As he explained that an untrained slave child was worth about twenty-five pounds, a cook fifty, and a hosteler seventy, a woman in the audience interrupted: "Was that in one year?" Before the interpreter had grasped the gist of the question—Is that how much money slaves made in one year?—a man in the audience tersely responded, "They didn't get nothin'."

When slaves were not being objectified by the interpreters in terms of monetary values, they were assimilated, as subjects, into a universalized society of consumers. During a tour at the Wythe House outbuildings, our guide explained why Lydia Broadnax was "one of the most expensive" of the fifteen slaves the Wythes "had on this property": "If there's one person I was going to alienate or displease it wouldn't be the cook. . . . You put a lot of faith in cooks real fast because if they cook well you're okay. If they make a mistake, you get sick, you get real sick. Their knowledge and their skills were important. And because of that they were treated much better than average." We then passed through Lydia's quarters and the guide continued: "We see that Lydia has a few things you might not suspect. We have . . . delftware, some majolica there, a fairly decent bed, and *privacy*—curtains, something you didn't find earlier in the century, . . . so you see even the emergence of a very paltry, but substantial slave material culture. . . . Conditions were changing for everybody."

In general, the overriding effect of these spiels on the value of slaves was to reduce all individuals—slaves, slave owners, and the tavern's socially varied clientele—to the same calculus of monetary value. Despite differences of wealth, all were fundamentally equivalent individuals. All could be evaluated according to what they cost or consumed, and all rose as they acquired skills that others valued. "Your average slave . . . just . . . off the boat from Africa," without language or other skills, seems to be just another aspiring Horatio Alger, ready to begin climbing, if on a lower and cruder ladder.

A Charter for Social History

Colonial Williamsburg repeatedly overwhelmed any sustained discussion of the conflict between masters and slaves by recitations of the benign paternalism of masters, the value of slaves, and even by depictions of slaves as consumers. The Wetherburn's Tavern tour and Christmas at the Wythe House, like many other programs devoted to the presentation of social history, were chartered by the 1985 mission statement, *Teaching History at Colonial Williamsburg*. It is not surprising to learn, then, that the ambivalences and elisions that characterized those tours are built into the charter document meant to guide social history at the foundation between 1985 and 1995.

In chapter 3 we examined an early version of this charter, the report of the Curriculum Committee of 1977. The earlier document proposed to reorganize Colonial Williamsburg's message in terms of three themes: "Choosing Revolution," "Becoming Americans," and "The New Consumers." The final document settles on the second of these as its master theme, one that encompasses (though without naming) the other two: "The Becoming Americans story . . . will be a narrative of nation-making presented in ways that reflect the major findings of recent scholarship. Told as a history of social change, it will start farther back in time [than past versions of the museum's story], will feature a larger cast of characters, will reveal community relationships, and will give familiar political events and personalities a more informative context. Generations of Africans and Europeans, thrown together far from the homes of their forefathers, invented a social system, devised a political philosophy, and selected leaders, thereby laying the groundwork for a flexible and open society that has endured for two hundred years."[5] Here, at least by implication, are most of the proposals of the 1977 document: an emphasis on a social scientific examination of a total social system, which necessarily means a story that includes all members of society, pays particular attention to the cultures of both African and European Americans, and recontextualizes the traditional story of the American Revolution in terms of economic and social history.

Yet, to package the various strands of the 1977 plan into the theme of "Becoming Americans" decisively alters the emphasis of the message to be conveyed. As the 1985 charter puts it, "Becoming Americans" is a story of "nation-making"; that is, it is a new version of Colonial Williamsburg's traditional patriotic and celebratory message. Moreover, "Becoming Americans" is also a story of ethnic assimilation, a story in which both African and European Americans can be treated equally. Such a balanced presentation—both "halves" of colonial society are to be portrayed—certainly creates a far larger place for African Americans than did the museum's previous stories. It tends, however, to downplay the hierarchical relationship (white over black) of the two groups in favor of a type of benign multiculturalism in which group differences are all similar and therefore unthreatening. More generally, it does what American public discourse almost always does: it minimizes a critique of social class in favor of a celebration of individual success.

This is not to say that the 1985 charter is without a critical perspective on social inequality. The American story, we are told, "is a success story," but this is immediately qualified: "at least for those of European stock." For other peoples, "the consequences were not pretty. Success has its price, a price that Europeans had a habit of exacting from others. . . . Slaves built the colony's prosperity, but shared little of it. . . . So our theme also acknowledges that many became Americans against their will and because there was no other way."

But no sooner is this critical perspective given voice in *Teaching History* than it gives way (in the very next paragraph!) to the benign story of ethnic pluralism: "In choosing our theme, we have deliberately used a plural noun; the protagonists in our story became not one American, but Americans of many different stripes. . . . The history we teach . . . must therefore explain how not only English but also African, European, and surviving Indian peoples rebuilt separate yet interdependent societies and how each provided its members with creative opportunities to lead lives worth living even in slavery or under cultural domination."[6]

Here the story is almost exclusively a success story, one in which the protagonists are collectivities—that is, individualized groups. Just as individual immigrants were able to come to Virginia and make their fortunes—even if only a "middling-sort" fortune—so different ethnic groups can be presented as making a place for themselves in the New World. Instead of a story of exploitative interdependence within a larger socioeconomic system, we have a story of the differing "contributions" that Americans of varying origins made to the birth and development of American culture. Instead of a story about whites over blacks, we have a story in which Africans are just another immigrant ethnic group, with chances to make a contribution and develop a distinctive culture that parallel those of any other group.

In a similar way, *Teaching History at Colonial Williamsburg* presents social hierarchy in terms of a universalizing consumerism that elides class differences. Recall that "The New Consumers" was a major theme in the revised history proposed by the 1977 Curriculum Committee. Although consumerism is not retained as a titled theme in the 1985 charter, *Teaching History* argues that a "consumer revolution" paralleled and indeed propelled a political revolution. Colonists became American by consuming.[7] Moreover, in the *Teaching History* version of the mid-eighteenth-century colonial economy, consumption is about making class distinctions: "No longer were the rich content only to own more than the middling planter. New furniture forms were demanded, and up-to-date fashions were the rage." But because consumption was increasingly possible for an increasing number of people, it also facilitated social mobility, at least for those above the lowest classes: "In the end the pursuit of material possessions was not confined to the economic and social elite. We need to emphasize that by the 1750s the middling sort, too, were purchasing amenities. . . . Yet it must be noted that this consumer revolution touched the poor hardly at all and passed right by black Virginians."[8]

Even elites were chasing status, although their consumption patterns reflected the influence of "potent English-inspired ideals of gentility and urbanity." Thus George Wythe would feel the need to purchase scientific instruments such as the air pump (a featured object at the Wythe House) because he had imbibed the culture of the English Enlightenment. Buying the right things became a sign of culture, and thus "the presumption of civility was increasingly conferred on anyone who owned and knew how to use the tremendous variety of portable consumer goods that everywhere became more available and affordable by the middle of the eighteenth century." The upshot is that people consumed in order to increase or maintain their social status. This was to be one of the chief lessons of the history chartered by *Teaching History:* "At Colonial Williamsburg we can vividly demonstrate the importance of food, clothing, speech, and deportment as symbols of people's place within the communal order. It will also be important to point out that, despite its hierarchical structure, the early American community of white Virginians was not a closed system but remained fluid throughout the eighteenth century. Within established social rules, movement up and down the social ladder occurred primarily as a person's access to wealth changed."[9]

The story of colonial consumption, as outlined in the charter, reached Williamsburg's streets and exhibit buildings—via interpreters, special programs, and labels—pretty much intact. Indeed, it became virtually ubiquitous. At the DeWitt Wallace Decorative Arts Gallery, for example, a visitor who admired one of the many masterworks on display—an oak cupboard manufactured about 1670, thick and heavy and almost medieval in appearance—could read in the accompanying label: "Cupboards of this form, ostensibly intended for the storage of dining equipment, often served another function as well. Fully dressed with an array of valuable silver and ceramics and an Indian callico cover, such cupboards were intended as statements of one's personal wealth and social position."

On the street, this essential message, perhaps already too crudely drawn by the social historians, often took on a kind of exaggerated quality that, to us at least, verged on parody. To illustrate our point, consider several Lanthorn Tours we took in 1990. This program, which required a separate, seven-dollar ticket, was announced as "an evening walking tour through the streets of Colonial Williamsburg and into four candlelit craft shops." During the tour, visitors would "explore the social and economic worlds of eighteenth-century craftspeople and look at the products of their trades."[10] On the tours we took, however, this theme was more narrowly construed as a discussion of fashion. As one interpreter put it, the tour on which we were about to embark would convey "a feeling about what it was that people thought was fashionable." Another explained that he would tell us "who set the fashion trends two hundred years ago, [and] we're also going to talk a little bit about the economy, . . . how it differed and at the same time how it was almost exactly the same as our economy today."

Although the Lanthorn Tours varied in the shops each visited, several that we took began at the Wig Shop. There we were told that wigs began as a royal fashion, that this fashion quickly spread among the English elite, and from them to the colony, where "it spread like wildfire." On one of these tours, the interpreter introduced the consumerist theme with a question: "Now, what one reason can you all think of that anyone would want to wear a wig? Think! Why do you all have Reebok shoes?" "It's cool," responded a teenager in the group, and our guide continued: "It's cool, exactly. For the same reason some people drive Cadillacs, other people drive Ferraris, other people drive Lamborghinis, other people drive Volkswagens. You want to show off how much money you have, and so you wear a wig. . . . If you're wealthy enough and you own slaves, you may even have your slaves wearing wigs."

Another guide made many of the same points, although in a different style. She used the wigmaker's account book, a list of the types and prices of wigs: "They run all the way from the royal governor, who paid sixty-five pounds, . . . which was almost as much as what a journeyman, who is the wage-earning person, . . . would make. So his one wig made a big statement. But you could buy a brown bob wig for just over two pounds. . . . Sometimes we know that gentry would buy their slaves horsehair wigs. If you were putting your slave in a wig, you were making a fashion statement, a statement about who you were as well."

Not only did the interpreters reduce wigs to a Veblenesque "fashion statement," they also stressed how much discomfort the eighteenth-century trendsetters had to endure. Wearing a wig required shaving one's head bald as an egg. Holding up the straight razor with which the job was done, one interpreter asked, "You want to see if I can try this on any of you? This thing is so sharp that not only will it take your hair off but if there are any lumps, bumps, or ridges, it'll smooth them right out!" The interpreters played up the absurd grotesqueries of wig wearing. Wig hair was set with "pig fat." "So," as one interpreter put it for effect, "you've got this fat in your hair. Now what happens when you go be-bopping down the street in the summertime, and it's hot? It's going to start running down the back of your neck, all over your silk and satin. So . . . they're going to tie on one of these things to the back of your neck. This is the eighteenth-century version of the rat tail. . . . In the bottom of this black bag [at the end of the rat tail] is corn meal." The guide reminded the visitors that fat goes rancid, stinks, and attracts flies, which are "going to land in your wig and not get off again!" On every Lanthorn Tour we took that stopped at the wigmaker's, the interpreters mentioned the pomade (although sometimes it was bear grease, sometimes "rendered sheep fat—[pause] yeah, sheep fat") and rubbed their visitors noses in it, as it were.

During tours such as these, guides seemed to use the story of consumerism covertly to attack their ostensible guests, the visitors. Several of the male guides seemed particularly eager to single out the women on the tour for special ridicule. After emphasizing the disgusting things one had to do to wear a wig—"to be fashionable . . . because he wanted to impress individuals"—one guide asked, "Ladies, would you do this?" And indicating the wigs on display in the shop, he said, "We have wigs up here for you if you care to do this. How many of you would not do it? Put your hands up high." Most of the "ladies" put their hands up high, enacting a parody of the elementary school classroom. While the "ladies" kept their hands in the air, the guide delivered his punchline: "Those of you ladies that have your hands up, how many of you have ever worn a pair of shoes that hurt your feet? So why'd you wear them? You wore them for fashion. Do you have a pair of jeans at home that are a little too small? Why do you wear them?" Interrupting, a boy in the group said, "I never wear them." The guide responded, "Not you, your sister!"—to which his sister replied, "I don't know." This allowed the guide to mock—"You don't know. You're not going to say in front of Mom!"—and then to conclude: "So we do things today for fashion, the same reason we did them in the seventeen hundreds, for fashion."

The Evisceration of Social History

What are we to make of the content of social history on the ground at Colonial Williamsburg? Consumerism was a salient, even guiding theme in the stories we heard. On the one hand, consumerism was described as a motor for creating class distinctions. With this focus social history became a Veblenesque caricature of itself. Everything could be reduced to "fashion," and fashion, in turn, was reduced to people buying and using things in order to display to others, in qualitative terms, their net worth. On the other hand, consumerism was also portrayed as a universal solvent. Monetary values became an apparently objective measure by which visitors were encouraged glibly to compare the value of slave and master; and consumerism was shown to provide a world of goods by which people of the past all satisfied, according to their individual abilities, their needs and desires.

Moreover, as it was depicted on the streets, the theme of eighteenth-century consumerism often dovetailed with the benign multiculturalism of the "Becoming Americans" theme. Both themes presented the past in terms of the actions of individuals (or ethnic groups, collectivities of individuals) striving to better themselves, to live the good life, to succeed. Though the unevenness of the playing field was occasionally mentioned, the fact that the game was fundamentally unfair was not stressed. To return to our visitors, Jean and Joyce: it is not surprising that they could participate in Christmas at the Wythe House and then conceptualize the distinction between freedom and slavery as abstract social statuses *while at the same time* erasing that distinction by likening the complaints of Wythe's slaves to the griping of working people today. *Teaching History at Colonial Williamsburg* accomplishes the same feat—class exploitation and slavery are critiqued, yet at the same time, African American slaves are portrayed as just another ethnic group whose members have the chance to make good, or to fail, according to their individual merits. In sum, the depiction of slavery at Colonial Williamsburg during the time of our research tended to minimize class exploitation and social conflict while encouraging visitors to celebrate slave individuals as players like any others in "the great procession" of American history.[11]

We are a long way from the original vision of the social historians who ostensibly set the agenda for history making and history teaching at Colonial Williamsburg. They wanted to use the museum to "disturb" complacent Americans about the injustices of the past and, indeed, about the relationship of those injustices to present-day social conflicts. Yet social history on the front line tended to comfort visitors' qualms about social injustice or banish a discussion of it altogether. If guides tried to disturb visitors at all, it was by the type of personal attacks on consumerist taste that we saw exemplified on the Lanthorn Tours.

Why has a critique of social injustice been encompassed by a celebration of the virtues of men like George Wythe? How and why has a class-conscious social history been reduced either to a celebration or (more sporadically) a critique of consumerism? One set of possible answers comes from Colonial

Williamsburg's critics on the cultural left, answers that are very close to our own. And as we have already pointed out, such answers have become a part of the discursive culture of Colonial Williamsburg as members of the staff defend their institution against attacks from the left and as such defenses become a part of the interpretive environment of the reconstructed city.

Scholars such as Michael Wallace, Mark Leone, Camille Wells, Carroll Van West, and Mary Hoffschwelle have all noted that, despite the turn to social history, the museum continues to reproduce the hegemonic perspective of the upper classes. In explaining why this is so, these critics often implicate the foundation's elitist leadership and its upper-class patrons or blame its upper-middle-class audience. As Wells put it, the "Colonial Williamsburg Foundation carefully cultivates its image as an educational institution with broad public appeal, but its true audience is thoroughly upper middle class in purse and sensibility." Because the foundation "relies heavily" on this audience as a source of revenue, she continued, it provides atmosphere and artifacts that are "not only agreeable and informative but desirable to own."[12]

Even as they would admit that Colonial Williamsburg looks like a "Republican Disneyland," members of the foundation's staff read (and dismiss) such critiques as a kind of conspiracy theory of history making. Thus Cary Carson, responding to what we have written elsewhere about Colonial Williamsburg, summed up our argument: "Their rap sounds like this. Capitalist Williamsburg is a slave to 'ticket receipts.' To maximize profits, 'administrators believe that teaching history to a mass audience [must be] as much concerned with "entertainment" as it is with "education." ' " One without the other is 'unpalatable.' Only 'a sanitized version of the nation's past' can be 'sold in the cultural marketplace.' " Carson knows our argument is hogwash because, in his seventeen years at Colonial Williamsburg, not once had he been told "to change my tune or downplay this or that kind of history because somebody upstairs thought it might displease the ticket buyers." He added: "That feeble old jab lands few solid punches on museums today."[13]

We agree with Carson. Colonial Williamsburg does not censor its story on the orders of "somebody upstairs." Nor is the rub-your-nose-in-it story of consumerism something the visitors demand in order to have an enjoyable experience of their visit to the re-created eighteenth century. Throughout the period of our research, our interlocutors among the social historians and among the middle-level managers of particular sites constantly told us not only how much freedom they had to produce the history they wished, but also how little control they had over their frontline employees. Managers claimed that "they" (the frontline workers) finally made the stories, as often as not in ways "we" would be ashamed of or would disapprove of had "we" only known. This, coupled with avowals that businessmen were merely "convenient scapegoats," was the standard, and plausible, defense against critiques coming from the academy that Colonial Williamsburg was run by a Republican cabal. It could take the form of a complaint or an apology—usually, "the interpreters are more conservative than we are," or "they're resisting what we want them to do. They're a bunch of southern matrons or southern matron wannabes, so what do you expect?" Or the defense could take the form of a celebration: "We're a museum dedicated to the founding of democracy, so we run our programs that way too. Particular stories, in practice, are a popular compromise."

That employees made up their own tours was a standard line among employees as well—in a sense, part of the PR of the place; thus the remark, often incorporated into the Patriot's Tour, that each interpreter is free to make up his or her own tour. Some employees, however, were more cynical about their freedom. When we asked one of the interpreters at the Wythe House how much guidance interpreters got from the professional historians as they worked on remaking the interpretive program, she pointed up the long path leading from the house to the garden: "See that arbor over there? They sit there quietly in the shade while we work here in the sun." Interpreters were free alright—free because they were left to their own devices. Or they were free (remember the cooper's tale), but left without resources. Or they were not free—someone was always looking over their shoulders.

Yet, in this chapter we've intimated that whatever freedom the interpreters have is insignificant as far as history making goes. Social history "on the ground" is much the same as social history "on the page" in the foundation's official pronouncements. Interpreters say pretty much what *Teaching History* tells them to say. We—and other critics in the academy—have been accused of suggesting that the new social history at the old museum is the product of a conspiracy. Obviously, that conspiracy is not a simple one. Much of the history that is delivered on the ground cannot be explained as carefully planned ruling-class propaganda, for, as the Lanthorn Tours suggest, Colonial Williamsburg's interpreters often use the messages of the new social history to insult the very audience the critics of the foundation assert that it courts. After all, do you encourage people to buy your upscale knick-nacks by rubbing their noses in the absurdities of eighteenth- and twentieth-century consumerism?

In the next chapters we will describe the social and cultural settings in which it seems plausible that frontline employees would feel free—or, perhaps, compelled—to insult their patrons in this way. We will explore manager-employee relations in order to suggest that the corporate production of a certain kind of freedom puts a straitjacket on the kind of past the foundation can loose on its public.

6 ■ *The Company Line: Aspects of Corporate Culture at Colonial Williamsburg*

The Company Line: Selling It, Buying It, Ignoring It, Resisting It

At the end of our first year of field research, an essay entitled "Passing on the Quality Spirit" appeared in the *Colonial Williamsburg News*. It was written by Steve Elliott, who was at that time the foundation's vice president in charge of administration. Following the trend in the corporate world in the 1980s, Colonial Williamsburg had made "quality" a central theme in internally directed corporate discourses. In 1987 President Longsworth established "a specific portfolio for *quality performance* and place[d] it in the hands of Steve Elliott"—hence Elliott's regular discussions of quality in the pages of the *News* during the period of our research.[1]

"Passing on the Quality Spirit" was written in celebration of thirty-three employees who had attained twenty-five years of service in the foundation and, consequently, had been presented with silver bowls at an annual ceremony. In the essay, Elliott reflected on two clichés frequently heard on such occasions:

> The first comment goes something like this: "Mary's the best; they just don't come any better." To younger and still-learning folks, our

"old hands" are walking legends. We view them as somehow having achieved as-close-as-humanly-possible perfection. . . .

But, in fact, the best and the longest are quick to point out that you get good and stay good by always trying to do better. Trying new ways and striving to do it better (and quicker and at less cost) keeps the job interesting and makes the organization stronger, which benefits all of us.

Secondly, we've all said or heard that "no one can ever replace John." And in many respects that's true. Each of us is unique and approaches our job as the individual he or she is.

But Lord help us if we mean that "no one is going to be able to do this job as well as John can." Think about it. That would mean mankind is on a continuous downhill slide!

The challenge to each of us . . . is to leave a place better because we were there.

The challenge to managers and each excellent and long-service employee is not only to keep getting better—but to have prepared at least one, and preferably several, up-and-comers who can *keep* building on his or her successes.

Think of *that!* That's a formula for upward progress far into the future.[2]

In this five-hundred-word editorial we find many of the themes that dominated corporate discourse during the period of our research. There are, first, the narratives of nostalgia and progress that, as we have already seen, were paradigmatic in the Historic Area. In Elliott's essay, long-service employees are in a sense representative of an earlier era or an earlier generation. He suggests that when we view them from our present-day perspective, they seem to be "walking legends," exemplars of a "perfection" we ourselves will never attain. On the other hand, to subscribe too exclusively to such a perspective would deny the fact and necessity of corporate progress. It is axiomatic, in Elliott's view, that Colonial Williamsburg will be "better" than it was before, that there will be "upward progress far into the future."

The dilemma of nostalgia and progress is solved by another central strand of corporate discourse, the appeal to individual effort. Individuals are unique as personalities (and we may celebrate them, nostalgically, in personal terms, as we do at ceremonies honoring retirees); but in the corporate world they are part of a team, and the significance of their work lies in their contributions toward "mak[ing] the organization stronger, which benefits all of us." Moreover, as we shall see, images of team (and the related metaphor of

Entrance and courtyard of the Goodwin Building, dedicated in 1941 as the foundation's corporate headquarters. It is absent from most official Colonial Williamsburg guidebooks and maps. (photo by Molly Handler)

family) and the insistence on mutual benefit function also to mystify (the old Marxian term hardly seems too strong) the class hierarchies and antagonisms that are endemic in the corporate world of Colonial Williamsburg.

Elliott's essay is certainly not unique. During our research, we came across literally hundreds of texts like it in the pages of foundation publications like the *Colonial Williamsburg News,* the annual reports, and the dozen or so "desk-top publications" put out by various organizational units within the foundation; and in memos, brochures, and advertisements. Most of these publications were written for audiences within the foundation. If American corporations are, as anthropologist Dan Rose has claimed, "infinitely extended structures of persuasion," it is worth pointing out that the work of persuasion is directed inward, to employees, just as relentlessly as it is sent outward, to potential customers.[3] Customers, of course, must be persuaded to buy the products a corporation sells. Employees, similarly, must be persuaded to buy the company line on everything from corporate identity to corporate discipline.

Like customers, employees often resist or ignore corporate messages. Indeed, that the same messages were repeated ad nauseum in Colonial Williamsburg's media of "internal communications" suggests that management expected people routinely to tune out the corporate line; hence repetition was necessary. Thus it's not surprising that through one of those serendipitous connections of fieldwork, we learned how one employee happened to resist an initial version of Elliott's essay. This person was at the bottom of the managerial hierarchy, but she had worked with Elliott for many years and communicated regularly with him. She told this story of persuading him to alter what he'd written: "The essence [of Elliott's essay] was, nobody's indispensable, and that . . . we've gotta get off the idea that nobody can be replaced. Because if we were like that, we couldn't run. . . . And in there was a sentence that said that it was . . . the *worker's* responsibility to be grooming and training . . . the people that would ultimately succeed them. . . . Well, what he was saying was fine, except he was forgetting one major ingredient. Which was, that person didn't have the power—they were not empowered—to get that staff on board. . . . *Management* was going to have to see that the personnel were provided for grooming, and then the grooming would take place." Accordingly, she said, she called Elliott and urged him to "balanc[e] that statement with the insertion of management as well as the employees." As the final version of Elliott's essay shows, she was successful; she persuaded him to add "another word or two, . . . but it made all the difference, because it was a *shared* responsibility. Whereas until he interjected that shared responsibility—which is *the whole thing we're stressing*—it was one-sided. It was just this poor working slob out here who had to train the next one, with management totally outside the issue."

As we have already noted, Elliott's editorial was part of an ongoing effort to promote quality as a kind of corporate talisman. The quality campaign coincided with some lean years in the attraction industries and, more generally, with a trend in American corporate culture toward what were perceived as Japanese-style management techniques: cost cutting and organizational restructuring. When Elliott's colleague made reference to the newfound emphasis on "shared responsibility," she was referring to still another theme prominent in the foundation's corporate rhetoric at that time: the notion of "empowerment," of creating quality by allowing employees to "take risks" as they attempted (in Elliott's words) "to do it better (and quicker and at less cost)." Elliott's colleague, deeply loyal in her own way to Colonial Williamsburg, nonetheless chafed at slogans that did not do justice, in her estimation, to the reality of a complex workplace.

In this chapter we will examine these and other themes in the foundation's corporate culture. Before beginning, however, two caveats are in order. First, our aim is not to delineate "the" corporate culture of the Colonial Williamsburg Foundation. It seems clear to us that Colonial Williamsburg participates in a wider national, or even international, culture of corporate capitalism, and, consequently, that much of what interests us about its corporate culture is not unique. It is true that we could discuss Colonial Williamsburg as a singular local culture with distinctive traditions—concerning the Rockefellers, for example—and a distinctive history; certainly the natives sometimes talk, though somewhat vaguely, about a distinctive corporate culture in this way. But for our purposes, describing the uniqueness of Colonial Williamsburg's corporate identity is less important than understanding the relationship between corporate discourses and history making.

Second, we have not tried to study the effects of corporate culture on daily routines. Though people talked to us constantly about, for example, "empowering" employees to "take risks," we did not try to measure the impact of such talk on work. We did not, that is, attempt to measure changes in risk-taking behavior among workers and managers. Nor, to take another example, did we try to verify stories about the changing quality of corporate life by making a detailed study of Colonial Williamsburg's corporate organization over the past fifty years. Such a project would have taken us far beyond the scope of this book.

There is, however, one exception, as we will see in chapter 7. We took some pains to analyze the relationship between pervasive corporate discourses and the work of history making on the front line. At that particular work site, we were able to consider at length the ways in which corporate culture inflects not only how history is made and told at Colonial Williamsburg, but the social relationships between the history-making "proletariat" (the front line), their supervisors and managers, and the researchers and upper-echelon managers who supervise the frontline supervisors.

Horseshoe Souvenirs: Nostalgia and Progress in Narratives of Corporate History

For decades people have come to Colonial Williamsburg in search of the tidy and uncomplicated world of an earlier era—a fairytale community of neat houses, cheerful residents, fine craftsmanship, and wholesome, unambiguous values. To some extent, the foundation indulges and encourages this perspective, as it celebrates the virtues of the American Revolutionary period and the founding fathers. On the other hand, as an educational institution dedicated to purging popular misconceptions, Colonial Williamsburg also works to counter overly nostalgic and hence inauthentic views of the past. That long-standing concern has dovetailed with the more recent focus of the social historians on the forgotten history of the uncelebrated unwashed masses. But debunking nostalgia also fits nicely with a narrative of progress: to teach that the past was not tidy and harmonious, but dirty and unjust often reinforces the public's belief in the superiority of the modern world. Indeed, not only the public but also many frontline interpreters and the people who train them are willing to laugh at what they perceive as a primitive past, with its superstitions, unsanitary practices, and quaint customs. On the other hand, those who buy too wholeheartedly into the narrative of progress may find themselves rebuked by a historian, trainer, interpreter, or visitor extolling the virtues of the world of the past. And so it goes: though opposites, the narratives of nostalgia and progress are inextricably linked; each is capable of triggering the other at any moment.

We found a similar interplay of these two narratives when employees at Colonial Williamsburg told us their versions of corporate or institutional history. To our repeated questions about how the foundation as an organization had changed, people responded both with narratives of loss and with narratives of progress. In the narrative of loss, or nostalgia, Colonial Williamsburg was—at some earlier, often unspecified, moment—smaller, friendlier, more humane. Within the corporation people treated one another like family and knew one another by name; visitors, too, were treated in more "personal" ways, and the corporation's products were of higher quality than they are now. That world, that corporate culture, has been lost or diminished by increasing "commercialization" and bureaucratization as the foundation has grown ever larger, added layers of management and administrative protocols, and been forced to compete ever more fiercely in the tourist marketplace.

By contrast, in the narrative of progress the foundation has both steadily grown and steadily improved itself. This tale was most often told with respect to the museum's mimetic mission. As we noted in chapter 3, an objectivist historiography is almost by definition progressivist: history changes because new information is found, which allows the foundation to make "better" history by bringing the site ever closer to authenticity, to exact replication of the past. There is a related narrative concerning the business side of the foundation. That which, in the narrative of nostalgia, is seen as increasing bureaucratization can alternatively be presented as increasing rationalization. "Sound" business and administrative practices make more efficient use of resources and hence make more money available for educational programming; they also create greater opportunities for employees to receive professional training, to be fairly compensated, and to participate in decision-making processes.

As we said above, we will not attempt, in what follows, to assess these narratives for their accuracy. It is clear that Colonial Williamsburg *has* grown; numbers alone tell that story. There were 31,000 visitors in 1934; close to 100,000 in 1936; close to 600,000 in 1952 (of whom more than half were paying customers who purchased tickets to the exhibition buildings); more than 1 million visitors in 1957; 484,648 paying visitors in 1961; 870,000 paying visitors in 1971 (plus 500,000 more who visited without buying tickets); 1.1 million paying visitors in 1973; and 1.2 million paying visitors in 1976 and again in 1988.[4] There were 100 employees in 1931; 200 in 1936; 944 in 1941; 822 in 1946 (the war had caused a retrenchment); 1,133 employees in 1949; 1,327 in 1951; more than 1,800 in 1960; and nearly 3,500 by 1973.[5] The annual income, or operating revenues, was $9.6 million in 1960, $14.2 million in 1965, $25.8 million in 1971, $46.3 million in 1976, $64.4 million in 1981, $97 million in 1986, $119.4 million in 1989, and $136.1 million in 1994.[6]

These numbers indicate growth, but they say nothing of the quality of the growth, nor of changes in corporate structure and culture, not to mention the significance of the growth in the eyes of employees and visitors. Hence the relevance of the narratives of nostalgia and progress: in our view, these readily available narratives render the brute facts of growth and the apparent facts of ever-increasing organizational complexity meaningful for the people who must cope with them. They are paradigms, even myths, that natives (employees, visitors) rehearse with varying degrees of critical awareness and that are powerful enough to absorb all manner of factual evidence. Indeed, if one looks at what people have said about the site in previous decades—going back almost to the beginning—one finds the same two stories of loss and progress. We conclude, therefore, that however great the changes in Colonial Williamsburg's organizational structure and functioning, the linked narratives of nostalgia and progress are not an accurate guide to them—though they are, obviously, a guide to the ways people think about change.

In lieu of charting organizational changes, we turn to an examination of how people use narratives of progress and loss in particular situations. To begin with a simple example: during the period of our research, Colonial Williamsburg had instituted an "eighteenth-century" public auction during summer afternoons as a piece of "living history" to engage the strolling crowds. A manager in the business-side products division—a person responsible for "developing" reproductions to be sold in Historic Area stores—told us the following anecdote: "I was on my way into one of the shops, and I happened to stop at this public auction, and I was standing on the edge of it and there was a couple there. And the man turned to his wife and said, 'Can you believe this? This is like having another retail store out here,' he said. 'Anything to get money!'" The manager was chagrined: "What we thought was something representing the eighteenth century that made everything more authentic, they saw . . . as a way for CW to make more money." In sum, the public auction could be read as evidence both of the foundation's increasing commercialization and of its increasing authenticity—and it's not easy to know which reading is more astute.

More elaborate narratives of corporate history are often ordered chronologically by reference to presidential regimes. "The present" during the period of our research began in 1977 with the arrival of Charles Longsworth; "the past," then, was the previous regime, that of Carlisle Humelsine, or sometimes an indefinite past of "Rockefeller and Chorley and Humelsine," as one person put it. Almost everyone we consulted, whether on the museum side or the business side of the foundation, thought Longsworth had been "brought on board" to get Colonial Williamsburg's financial house in order. Business-side managers told the story—of the transition from Humelsine's regime to Longsworth's—as a Weberian narrative of development from patrimonial caprice to bureaucratic rationality. A common theme in the stories was the budgetary irrationality of the pre-Longsworth years; in the words of one vice president: "At the end of the year they figured out how much money they needed, and they got it from the Rockefeller family. . . . There was no accountability for budgets, in my view." This person spoke in similar fashion of the inefficiency of the pre-Longsworth years: "There were too many people. People weren't busy enough. They had plenty of time for coffee breaks. And I didn't think they were as productive as they could be."

Another vice president emphasized the inconsistent personnel policies Longsworth had to address: "We had no wage and salary program. So . . . you're paying one person this amount, another person this amount, they're doing the same jobs, one's black and one's white, and you get a lawsuit on your case, they go to the EEOC [U.S. Equal Employment Opportunity Commission]. . . . We had favoritism being shown, because there were no standards by which to deal with people. You know, a guy would go [to work] in the King's Arms Tavern drunk and he would get fired. His brother would go in, cause he works at [Christiana] Campbell's [Tavern], drunk, and nothing would happen."

In the narrative of progress, not only did Longsworth address administrative and managerial irrationality, he took the lead in rationalizing the educational programming and its relationship to the foundation's business side. One business-side manager told us a long story about the growth of the crafts program, or historic trades, in the Historic Area and the parallel growth of the foundation's Craft House reproductions merchandising program. In this tale, two serious problems developed during the Humelsine years. First, craftsmen were selling the products they made out of their Historic Area shops. As visitor demand for their handiwork increased, the shops "became production driven, and they had backup shops with all sorts of modern equipment to produce the product that was sold to the public." By the late 1960s, those practices had come to be viewed as crassly commercial: "For example, in the blacksmith shop, you could go and get those little horseshoes with your name stamped on it." To counter this commercialism, or its appearance, and to maintain clearer boundaries between business and education, the foundation opened two Historic Area stores in 1972–73: "A decision was made, so that those shops could more accurately reflect what a craftsman or a tradesman did, to pull the sale of objects out of those [craft shops] and put it into operating stores in the Historic Area."

But a second problem remained: competition between those Historic Area sales outlets and the merchandising program that controlled Craft House (located outside the Historic Area in the Colonial Williamsburg Inn) and the hotel gift shops. Under Longsworth, that problem was solved by putting all the retail outlets together in one administrative unit, under a vice president for business operations. By eliminating internal competition and rationalizing the relationships among the foundation's many product lines, revenues were increased. Not only did this provide more money for educational programming, it made the Historic Area less commercialized and more educational, because it allowed tradesmen to spend their time on research, interpretation, and the accurate depiction of eighteenth-century crafts instead of production for sale.

Those and other related innovations of the Longsworth regime, discussed above in stories of corporate progress, can also be framed by a narrative of loss. In this view, as explained by an administrative assistant to one of the vice presidents, the Humelsine regime may have been "paternalistic," but "the benefits [of paternalism] were that there was, I believe, what we call the more human quality that existed in that era. People were people. We were the family." People throughout the organization made similar statements, claiming that in an earlier era, social relations among employees and between the front line and visitors were warmer, slower paced, and more personable than they had become in the Longsworth years. Sometimes this nostalgic story was told as one of diminishing quality: if, as the foundation claims, quality manifests itself in service to visitors, then Colonial Williamsburg's quality has diminished over the years as it has worked to attract ever larger paying crowds without significantly increasing the resources available to frontline personnel and educational programs. One frontline supervisor told us that, "because we are so busy, we don't have the time to take with people like we used to have. . . . I think we've gotten so structured, especially in the exhibit buildings, because we want to get them in and out, that we're not putting as much personal emphasis on the visitor as we could."

Stories of diminishing service and quality were closely linked to the idea of increasing commercialization. In this view—and contra the optimistic perspective of the business-side manager quoted above—the Longsworth years were ones in which moneymaking and corporate efficiency became the foundation's highest values and education was relegated to a secondary role. As the administrative assistant quoted above explained it, during the paternalistic Humelsine era there was an "organizational mentality of turning back to Rockefeller . . . we need another handout, Dad, could you send more money?" Because Rockefeller money gradually dried up, Longsworth's innovations were necessary, if ultimately drastic: "With the Longsworth era came the so-called 'we can't afford to operate any more like we used to. Now we're going to run it as a business.' Implying that we did not run it as a business before! In that came a lot more commercialism, a lot more . . . attention to the bottom line. We needed that, to a degree. A lot of people had trouble with the extent of the commercialism, particularly in the products area. I mean, we'd sell anything. We'd sell the rug off the floor if somebody'd buy it. We sell things and we put our name on things now that we'd never ever have considered before. Absolute taboos! From T-shirts, sweatshirts—much more into the souvenir stuff. Well, some of that was economic survival, I guess. Times changed. Approaches changed. If you can make a buck off of it, and people want it, and it's not too bad—but somebody tell me, what is educational about a potholder with a picture of the Capitol on it?"

Though a stock narrative, there is an important critical note in this version of it: "Implying that we did not run it as a business before!" This manager recognized that the narrative of progress (from patrimonial inefficiency to bureaucratic rationality) perhaps shortchanged past practices in order to validate present ones. We often heard people catch themselves, as it were, in too-literal rehearsals of the narratives of progress and loss, and then qualify them with reference to other facts or viewpoints the standard stories didn't accommodate. For example, the administrative assistant qualified her story about the familial corporation of the Humelsine years when she described the situation of the foundation's largely African American manual laborers: "I wasn't real close, but of what I knew . . . a lot of those people were really kind of under the thumb of the masters." Similarly, the vice president who told us of pre-Longsworth budgetary irrationalities entertained the possibility that the administrative changes of the Longsworth years had led to a decline in quality, at least from the perspective of frontline workers: "We've put . . . the brakes on spending to such a degree that [it has] . . . reduced the quality of the service the visitor sees. Many employees view it that way. In some cases there's probably truth to that. . . . We don't have the time to do the quality job we used to have. Employees say this. I don't know that *visitors* say this." And the vice president who told us of personnel inconsistencies admitted that the management structures—"what we called, in a positive way, career ladders"—put in place to correct those problems led to new problems in the form of too much bureaucracy: "The downside of career ladders is that it builds levels of supervision. And the next thing you know, we had about twelve levels, from the top all the way down to the bottom."

These interruptions in the narratives of progress and nostalgia never led, as far as we know, to an explicit rejection of either. Just as Historic Area interpreters sometimes pulled the rug out from under visitors by switching from one paradigm to the other, people switched between the two but never subjected either to a sustained critique. If the story of progress broke down under the weight of the evidence, the story of loss could be substituted for it. But by and large, people did not turn to other narratives for the telling of corporate history.

What might an alternative narrative be? From our perspective, it would have to encompass the narratives of nostalgia and progress—that is, an alternative history of Colonial Williamsburg's corporate culture should show the same stories being told generation after generation, almost regardless of the facts of organizational change. To give an example: in the accounts of women who had worked as hostesses (costumed interpreters leading tours through the exhibition buildings) both before and after the Second World War, the postwar development of automobile tourism and the family vacation made the prewar era seem a golden age of leisurely touring and genteel visitors (see chapter 7). Yet today's frontline interpreters, and visitors, too, often look back to the 1950s as a golden age of leisurely touring in comparison with the overcrowded commercialism of the present. Similarly, employees in the 1950s felt that personal relationships within the growing corporation were becoming more impersonal. Even the president of that era,

Kenneth Chorley, recognized it: "It was not many years ago when I knew by name and face every employee of Colonial Williamsburg. I called them all by their first names and was called 'K.C.' by them; but the size of the family has doubled since the war and it is no longer possible for me to keep as much of the close personal touch with all the 1327 employees as formerly."[7] This, of course, is precisely what people told us about the quality of intramural social relationships today in comparison with the more familial atmosphere of the 1950s—which Chorley, at that time, saw as less familial than earlier decades.

In other words, the narrative of loss transcends any facts or statistics (about visitation, staff size, and resources) that might serve as evidence of changes in Colonial Williamsburg's way of doing business. The past can always be seen as a golden age from the perspective of a temporarily disgruntled—or perhaps simply an aging—employee or visitor. Alternatively, the past can easily be seen as a primitive time when the museum was less educational, less accurate, less efficient—as employees might tell an inquisitive outsider who, they sense, is inclined to be critical of the foundation. "Those little horseshoes with your name stamped on it" epitomized, for many people we knew, a cruder, more primitive commercialism that Colonial Williamsburg had outgrown. The business-side manager quoted above mentioned their demise as evidence of educational progress. On the other hand, the administrative assistant quoted in this section was skeptical of today's 'T-shirts and potholders. The point in all of these stories is to emphasize "change" and then to evaluate it—in either of the two ways we've discussed.

But how much *has* Colonial Williamsburg changed? The interview with the administrative assistant took place in the Williamsburg Lodge, one of the foundation's hotels. During a break in which she went for coffee, the interviewer took a moment to browse in the gift shop. There he found two baskets of small black iron horseshoes, stamped with "Colonial Williamsburg" and priced at $5.50 for the larger version and $5.00 for the smaller, which had a key ring attached to it. A sign asserted that they were handcrafted by Colonial Williamsburg blacksmiths.

Silver Bowls

The presence of the horseshoes in the gift shop did not necessarily contradict the story about their removal from the Historic Area. From our visits to their shop, we knew that the blacksmiths were no longer making such items in front of the public. Yet the gift shop sign proclaimed that Colonial Williamsburg blacksmiths had handcrafted them. Assuming the statement was true (or better, assuming it was a deliberate untruth), we have another instance of a fact, like the colonial auction, which could support both narratives, nostalgia and progress: Colonial Williamsburg was becoming ever bolder and crasser in its commercialism; it was more authentic and educational than ever before.

Since the facts alone cannot determine which alternative narrative is more valid, we turn to a different sort of analysis, synchronic rather than historical, to make sense of the foundation's corporate culture. Several things seem clear to us: Colonial Williamsburg has been balancing business and education from the beginning, and therefore, commercial and noncommercial motivations or logics have always competed there; further, as it has grown, it has created new organizational structures and protocols; and, finally, employees situated at particular locations within that ever-mutating organization often make sense of change by rehearsing the two narratives we've analyzed.

This ensemble—the business-education duality, the constant organizational changes, and the standard narratives accounting for them—forms, we might say, a system that hasn't changed much since the advent of mass tourism after the Second World War. Dozens of interviews with employees who told us about how the foundation has changed, and our reading of such sources as the *Colonial Williamsburg News* and the annual reports (from the early 1950s to the early 1990s), have led us to conclude that those aspects of Colonial Williamsburg's corporate culture highlighted in the narratives of nostalgia and progress have changed very little in five decades, despite the natives' sense of ongoing, sometimes momentous changes. *What persists is a fairly rigid organizational hierarchy accompanied by egalitarian discourses that work to persuade people to overlook it.* Our analysis here would be tritely Marxian— "ideology mystifies reality"—except that we are unwilling to insist on the "false consciousness" of the natives. That is, we think that many workers at Colonial Williamsburg have a kind of double consciousness: they simultaneously accept and are critical of both the reality of corporate hierarchy and the unending egalitarian discourses that pretend it doesn't matter—an issue we will revisit below.

For now, let us return to Steve Elliott's essay, in which we find many of the themes that have dominated corporate discourse for the past half century. Let's begin with the "long-service employees" and the annual ceremony honoring them. Almost from its inception, the *Colonial Williamsburg News* has devoted considerable space to listing the accumulated years of service of employees. In 1953, the foundation instituted the policy of awarding a silver bowl to employees who completed twenty-five years on the job. A 1983 article in the *News* explained the origins of the award in these terms: "A gold watch, silver tray, cash, and a medallion with choice of another gift were among the first suggested awards. . . . Later discussions concluded the award should be uniform for all employees, dignified and impressive, significant to Colonial Williamsburg or its period, readily recognizable as a 25-year service award, and meaningful to the employee's family."[8]

That the award "should be uniform for all employees" is crucial: long-term service awards are egalitarian in the sense that the criterion for earning them—the accumulation of passed time—is the same for all employees, no matter what their rank or position within the corporation. Moreover, the time commemorated by the awards is a "homogeneous, empty," and quantified time—time "counting itself," to borrow a phrase from the linguist Benjamin Lee Whorf.[9] The award measures time in exactly the same way for all employees—regardless of the quality of their work time. Thus, though time may well pass differently for indoor workers and outdoor workers, or for manual laborers and executives, the award takes no notice of this; it marks time in the abstract. The award, then, treats all employees as equals, despite great differences in authority, remuneration, and responsibility—hence the imperative that the award be the same for all.

The silver bowls are awarded to twenty-five-year employees at an annual dinner. On that occasion, a high-ranking executive reads a personalized vignette about each awardee. We interviewed the administrator responsible for concocting those vignettes, and she explained that she started with the employee's personnel file, extracting and feeding enough background information to the executive to enable him to develop "rapport" with the employee during a half-hour interview. The executive took notes during the interview, then returned to his office to dictate a narrative about the employee, which his secretary transcribed. The administrative assistant retrieved the transcription in order to "edit it down to some pablum that we can do in two minutes" at the award ceremony. She added that "the most important thing we're striving for is the personal." Not only were the two-minute versions read at the ceremony, condensed versions of them were published in the *Colonial Williamsburg News* with a photographic portrait of each awardee.

Those photo galleries suggest a line of analysis that the texts accompanying the pictures work to obscure. The portraits make obvious the correlation of race and gender with the structural inequalities that separate long-service employees within the corporate hierarchy. The most spectacular success stories are those of white males; for example, the man who came to the foundation in 1966 as a staff writer and by 1983 had become the vice president of communications and government relations. African American men and women, and white men and women in working-class jobs, tend to stay in the same or similar jobs throughout their careers, with promotions being narrowly circumscribed within work domains like restaurants or stockrooms. A black woman, for example, worked in the dining room of the Williamsburg Lodge for twenty-five years; a black man "spent the past 25 years working as a kitchen helper, bus boy, houseman, gardener, waiter and utility man." Middle-level managers are predominantly white, and women especially seem to move laterally from one administrative position or unit to another, only rarely becoming executives or administrative officers.[10]

These published portrait galleries and our behind-the-scenes glimpse of how the texts accompanying them are constructed suggest two different but closely related strands in the corporation's egalitarian discourse. The first strand we might call contractual and functional: it asserts that employees form a team who have agreed to work together for the common good, and that their goal is achieved when each individual accomplishes his or her specialized task within the complex organization of Colonial Williamsburg. This is organic solidarity with no mention of hierarchy. The second strand (which, as we shall see in chapter 7, is crucial to social interactions on the front line) we might call personal or personalized: it asserts that despite the size of the organization, Colonial Williamsburg employees should know one another personally and strive to treat one another familiarly, even familially. These two strands are often interwoven in corporate discourse, though we will treat each in turn.

The Seven-Year Plan: An Egalitarian Social Contract

In 1977, when Charles Longsworth was brought in to head the Colonial Williamsburg Foundation, many insiders felt the institution was aimless and floundering. Four years later, President Longsworth published an essay in the annual report in which he explained that "financial uncertainties" and "increased demands for justification of philosophy and mission" made it imperative for each of "America's museums and cultural organizations" to reexamine "its purposes, how well it serve[d] these purposes, and how well it [was] reaching its intended public." President Longsworth went on to discuss the "brilliant report" of the 1977 Curriculum Committee (see chapter 3, "Why History Changes: The Constructionist Version") and to reflect on how history was changing at Colonial Williamsburg.[11]

As we have seen, the 1977 curriculum report eventuated in a public document, *Teaching History at Colonial Williamsburg,* that was intended to guide the museum's interpretive work from 1985 to 1995. While the social historians who produced that report worked to revise the Colonial Williamsburg story, President Longsworth and his staff worked to remake its corporate culture. Their work eventually led to a seven-year plan, which was being vigorously promoted by management during the time of our field research. The plan established seven objectives for the foundation to focus on during the period 1989–95:[12]

1. To exceed visitor expectations
2. To strengthen the educational program
3. To intensify preservation and maintenance
4. To be the best place to work
5. To improve support services
6. To enlarge financial resources
7. To be a leader in protecting the quality of the environment in the Williamsburg area

During the spring of 1990, President Longsworth held several open question-and-answer sessions to explain the seven-year plan to employees and to give them a chance to ask questions about it. We were able to attend one such session, which was held in a large, modern auditorium. Occupying center stage, Longsworth used an overhead projector and microphone to broadcast his message to the 130 or so people we counted in the audience. A polished and dignified speaker who spoke extemporaneously in complete sentences, Longsworth began on an egalitarian note with an appeal for "conversation" and a "sharing" of "ideas, criticisms, suggestions—whatever's on your mind."

The main portion of Longsworth's presentation—before the open question period—consisted of a review of each of the seven-year objectives. He explained the first, to exceed visitor expectations, in the following terms: "To . . . do everything we can, to make sure that a visitor leaves here saying 'that was even better than I thought it would be. That exceeded my expectations.' . . . And that's what we individually and collectively can assure by our hospitality, by our courtesy, by understanding our visitors' expectations and needs, by developing programs that are responsive, by making this an important place in their lives. And it's the one [of the seven-year objectives] we absolutely have to succeed at, because visitors are the ones who provide the means for us to go on." The theme of hospitality and courtesy—the emphasis on good interpersonal relationships—will be considered at length below, but for now we want to focus on the president's assertion that not only success but the institution's very survival depend on everyone doing their utmost to satisfy Colonial Williamsburg's visitors. This was perhaps the least challenged axiom of corporate culture that we heard people express at Colonial Williamsburg—and we heard it again and again. Management has been repeating this message for the past half century (it is one of those unchanging elements of corporate culture),[13] and it was often deployed as an argument against criticism, discontent, and any idea or maneuver (such as the campaign for better wages organized by the hotel and restaurant workers' union during the winter of 1990–91) of which management didn't approve. It was the "bottom line," as it were, and most employees seemed to accept it: if we don't do our jobs well, they would say, the customers won't come, and then we won't have jobs. President Longsworth hammered on this theme in his regular columns in the *Colonial Williamsburg News*: "Let me remind you that the surest way to work our way out of the recession and to protect your job is to work together and *exceed every visitor's expectations*." "We're here so the visitors can be out there; they do not come to Williamsburg so we can have jobs. They come to enjoy and learn. . . . If they do, we will have . . . jobs."[14]

This discourse is egalitarian in the sense that everyone in the corporation, from the highest to the lowest, is portrayed as facing the same conditions of economic competition, and, further, in the claim that each person's survival depends on the work of every other person in the organization. In the question-and-answer session, Longsworth returned to those ideas when he discussed the fourth of the seven-year objectives: "What makes a place the best place to work? Lots of things. The attitudes: fellow workers to each other, management to you, you to me. I feel that we work together and, sure, I'm the president, and that's a lofty, responsible position. But I can't do my job if you don't do yours, and that works the other way around, too." Here, again, is the contractual and functional strand of corporate egalitarianism, and not only that, but also an explicit statement of the dominance of equality over hierarchy: we all do different jobs, all those tasks are functionally necessary to corporate survival, hence we are all equally dependent on each other, despite differences in rank.

Closely related to this functional egalitarianism is the idea that business depends on customers, who, in corporate discourses, replace management as the ultimate seat of authority. This argument, or imagery, is implicit in much of the trendy management literature on which Colonial Williamsburg executives were drawing at the time of our research. The authors people mentioned to us most frequently were John Kotter and Tom Peters. In his best-selling book *In Search of Excellence,* Peters argued that the success of the most successful companies is due to their relentless attention to their customers' needs. This is nothing more than a refurbished formulation of "the customer is always right"—something that employees at the foundation had been told for at least fifty years.[15] One result of Peters's popularity at the time of our research was that people throughout Colonial Williamsburg wavered between the terms *visitor* and *customer.* Moreover, management preached the idea of "internal customers"—that is, that all the functionally different positions within a corporation are customers for one another's services. The egalitarian implications of this are obvious: to portray everyone within a corporation, regardless of rank, as a customer of everyone else is to render all, equally, buyers and sellers. All participate equally in a marketplace, working together yet acting as individual consumers do, choosing goods and services and making decisions about how to allocate resources.

We heard the most striking example of this rhetoric from a manager of one of Colonial Williamsburg's restaurants: "We're obviously here for the guests. Our guest is our boss, is our supervisor, okay? But as a manager, the first thing you have to remember is that you lose the opportunity that, let's say, the waitperson has, of greeting our guests, making—I can't do it directly. I have to do it indirectly. And how do you do it? You do it through your employees." At this point, the interviewer asked the manager if he could interact with guests if he wished, to which he responded: "Oh, I do all the time. But, see, I'm no longer in the front of the house all the time. I have a lot of administrative work. . . . You know, I used to wait on tables. I used to be a bartender. You interact constantly. And I don't have that. . . . But I don't mind it, because I can do it indirectly now. . . . A lot of people don't realize, you know, that a *dishwasher* works directly with the guests, because they give that guest a *clean plate,* a clean fork, a clean glass. That is very, very important to them. And see, sometimes they don't realize how important that job is, or they work actually indirectly by making sure that the people upstairs, who are serving the guests, have clean dishes so they can serve—so they're working directly and indirectly with them. So, my job is to make sure they're happy. Make sure they're taken care of, and they enjoy their work, and they *feel* like they're part of that whole thing."

In this explanation of a manager's work, the guest is the boss—the customer is always right—and all the workers within the organization are equally involved in satisfying the boss-guest's needs. Managers are in a sense less privileged than front-of-the-house employees, who interact directly with the boss-guest. But managers are compensated for this loss of privilege by getting to coordinate the work of the entire employee team. In this sense, managers work "indirectly" with the boss-guest, exactly as a dishwasher and other behind-the-scenes employees do. It is the manager's particular responsibility to make sure that dishwashers understand how important they are— understand that they and their managers are equally involved in serving the boss-guest as well as those internal customers, the other employees in the restaurant whose work depends on the availability of clean plates. If the manager succeeds in convincing the dishwasher of his or her integral role in the operation—"make sure . . . they *feel* like they're part of that whole thing"— the dishwasher will be happy and will work hard to make the boss-guest happy.

Climbing the Corporate Ladder

As the preceding examples show, management projects a vision of the corporation in which all employees work together and are equally integral to the success, even the survival, of the whole. But since a corporation is almost by definition—and certainly in most people's commonsense understanding of it—hierarchical, and since there is a chain of command that all employees experience in their daily work, the reality of "lofty" positions juxtaposed to lowly ones can never be overlooked. At Colonial Williamsburg, as in American culture generally, the egalitarian ethos is preserved, despite the obvious differences of wealth and power that separate people, by the belief that success and upward mobility depend on individual effort.

The administrative assistant whom we quoted above told us that in reviewing the personnel files of silver bowl recipients, she had noticed "two types" of career history: "You have the person . . . [who has] been in one job, and never done one other thing. We had two waiters this year who were like that. . . . And they have been happy . . . to do that one thing, and that's all they've ever done. Then you've got the people who move around a lot. And you can see a twenty-five-year work history where they've zigzagged through twelve different positions." As we continued our conversation with this woman, it became clear that she did not account for the difference between the two types of people in social terms; rather, her assumption was that different career patterns reflect differences in ambition and motivation: "The ones who stay [in one position] are fairly contented with it. They are more contented than the person who's moving around, who obviously chose to move out of whatever they were doing. It may be that they were not as aggressive, . . . not a go-getter." Particularly ironic is the fact that this same manager told us a rather harrowing story of her own failure to advance within the organization. It seemed clear to us that her career pattern had been shaped by a complex interplay of class, gender, personal choices, and circumstances. Yet she attributed her failure—"I haven't gone anywhere in twenty-five years"—to her lack of "guts," to her choice not "to change" her situation but to "wallow in it."

A disenchanted employee may blame herself for her failure to advance,[16] but this was not the usual story that managers told about employees—too much emphasis on failure is inconvenient for the upbeat egalitarian stories of corporate rhetoric. Rather, if long-service employees stayed in one menial position for twenty-five years, it was because they were happy with that situation—they were successes at what they did, not failures. People used the waiter as the prototype of this sort of person. The restaurant manager quoted above and a manager of one of the foundation's hotels contrasted their own desire to climb the corporate ladder with the ambitions of waiters. Waiters, both told us, are "professionals." They "enjoy the people . . . they serve [and] also the people that they work with." Their hours are "flexible," they don't have "huge pressures," and waiting tables can be quite "lucrative." (Indeed, one vice president told us that it was common knowledge that waiters at the foundation's most elegant restaurant, the Regency Dining Room at the Williamsburg Inn, had incomes that rivaled those of the vice presidents, earning as much as $80,000 annually!)* In sum, waiters are success stories. As the hotel manager explained it to us, "the people who've always been waiters and don't want to be anything but that, . . . it's not a sign of failure. They're very successful, they're professionals, they do a great job, I wish I could be as good a waiter as they are."

We can think of two reasons why the waiter is the stock figure of the successful and contented menial. First, waiters are good figures for egalitarian tales because many managers and executives in the hotel and restaurant industry—indeed, many Americans of any profession who have spent four years in college—have themselves waited tables. Both the restaurant manager and the hotel manager quoted above were college educated, and both had started their careers in the hotel and restaurant business as waiters. But they attributed their upward mobility to their own drive, just as they attributed their wait staff's lack of mobility to personal choices. The restaurant manager had been hired by Colonial Williamsburg after completing a

---

*By contrast, wait staff we spoke to estimated that the most successful waiters and waitresses in foundation establishments made no more than $25,000 annually.

university degree in hotel and restaurant administration. When he told his story, he said that he had worked his way up in "the industry," beginning as a dishwasher, waiter, and bartender in his college days. He came to the foundation as a management trainee and worked in various positions in the hotel and restaurant subsidiary. The career histories of managers such as these exaggerate, we think, the possibility of upward mobility, because they fail to take account of the differences between a "management track" job and that of an ordinary waiter. It is one thing to wait tables in college (and then, retrospectively, to see that as the beginning of a "career") and quite another to do it because that is the only opportunity for work that one has. No wonder, then, that in the career histories (as summarized in the pages of the *Colonial Williamsburg News*) of long-service African American employees at Colonial Williamsburg, waiters "work their way up" to be headwaiters or dining room captains or even assistant managers. They do not, however, become general managers or vice presidents.

A second reason that may account for the use of the waiter in egalitarian discourses is the fact that waiters' incomes include tips and are therefore not officially defined or publicly known. By contrast, the pay scales for most other jobs below the level of the top executives in the foundation are publicly announced in job descriptions and advertisements. Given such public knowledge, it would be difficult to tell the success story of, for example, laborers in terms of how "lucrative" such positions are—though one can fudge the issue by calling waiters and all other nonmanagement employees "professionals." The salaries of those at the other extreme of the corporate hierarchy are not publicized—perhaps, as some frontline employees suspected, to hide the wide gap between executives and everyone else. The same vice president who told us about the Inn waiters became indignant when we pointed out that annual salaries or hourly wages for all but the top executives of the foundation are publicly announced. Not only did he refuse to discuss his salary, he argued that to do so by giving us even ballpark figures for the salaries of his fellow vice presidents would be an invasion of their privacy. Ironically, he was more than willing to tell us the salaries of "VIP" waiters, even though he later admitted that the figure he gave us with such self-assurance was only a guess—a figure he'd heard mentioned. In sum, if waiters can conveniently be presented as financial success stories in the discourse of egalitarianism executives, by contrast, must be presented as just like every other employee; hence their salaries, which belie this representation, remain undiscussed.

Another aspect of the egalitarian strand in corporate discourses about wages is the notion that people should be paid "competitively." In his question-and-answer session, President Longsworth spoke of management's efforts to revise and update the foundation's wage and salary structure as part of making Colonial Williamsburg "the best place to work": "We need to pay you competitively. For the most part we do, and in some cases we don't." He went on to explain that the Human Resources Division was conducting surveys to determine which employees were not "paid fairly competitively according to the marketplace," and he promised to rectify inequities.

The idea that pay should be competitive within an industry—that is, that waiters or accountants or vice presidents at one corporation should earn about the same as their counterparts in other companies—deflects attention away from the question of why salaries differ so greatly within a particular corporation. Why, that is, should executives make ten, twenty, fifty, or two hundred times what manual laborers make? The standard answer is that the higher-paid positions are functionally more important, and that the "talent" to fill them is harder to find and takes longer to develop, than is the case for more menial positions, which, it is assumed, can be filled by anybody. But to discuss salary structures in terms of narrow functional criteria presupposes, first, that such criteria are rational or objectively derived rather than cultural or political; and, second, that talent and individual initiative, rather than other structural and cultural factors (race, class, and gender again), explain why individuals "end up" where they do. Again, in the egalitarian ethos, the system is fair, and everyone has a chance and a choice as to how far he or she will advance.[17]

Quality Teams and Employee Empowerment

We have already noted that the works of John Kotter and Tom Peters, management gurus of the 1980s, were read and admired by Colonial Williamsburg executives. Preaching creative leadership rather than bureaucratic management, near fanatical devotion to customers' needs, and a renewed commitment to quality and excellence, these authors seemed to offer solutions to American businesses floundering in the new conditions of global, multinational capitalism. Quality teams and employee empowerment, two ideas drawn from this larger trend in management theory, were especially important at Colonial Williamsburg during the period of our research.

Founded as it was by Rockefeller money, Colonial Williamsburg has always considered itself a top-quality organization. When, on the verge of retirement in 1979, Carlisle Humelsine was asked what his epitaph should be, he responded: "I think the most I want to be remembered for is the development of an organization that represents quality. I think that's the hallmark of Colonial Williamsburg."[18] Despite Humelsine's sense of his legacy—despite, that is, the foundation's long-standing self-identity as a quality organization—the Longsworth regime embarked on a comprehensive campaign to improve quality at Colonial Williamsburg. This was announced in the annual report for 1987, which features, on the front cover, the word "quality" in large letters superimposed on the foundation's motto: "That the future may learn from the past."

In the copies of the report made available to employees, a cover letter from Longsworth announced that "Colonial Williamsburg has adhered to quality as a basic trademark. In 1987 we set the stage for a renewal and strengthening of our commitment to quality of service, of products, and of operations." Inside, in his "Report from the President," Longsworth explained the reasons behind this renewed commitment to quality: "Colonial Williamsburg, with its mission of preservation, history education, and service and hospitality, operates in an increasingly competitive world. We offer our visitors and guests a learning experience as well as the amenities they enjoy, but we exist on the discretionary side of the family budget where the range of choices is constantly increasing. In our highly competitive world Colonial Williamsburg's best strategy is delivering and exceeding the quality and value visitors have come to expect." With the need for quality having thus been explained in terms of a hostile marketplace, an appeal to employees' dedication to their work follows as a matter of course: "Colonial Williamsburg is an organization where each employee, in his or her own way, contributes. . . . It is the quality commitment and involvement of good people that will attract visitors."[19] Here the linkage between quality and the contractual egalitarianism of corporate discourses is clear.

But what, substantively, is quality? The foldout front cover of the report features fifteen illustrations (most of them sumptuous color photographs) of the highlighted text, "Quality is our hallmark." The first images equate quality and mimetic authenticity by juxtaposing the foundation's objects and interiors with eighteenth-century illustrations to show how similar the reproductions are to the originals. Photographs of tradesmen at work show "dedicated" employees creating those reproductions—that is, putting the quality of authenticity into them. Photographs of visitors touring the Historic Area show them "receiv[ing] quality experiences" from museum interpreters. Finally, photographs of a hotel room, a restaurant dining room, a golf course, and Craft House show that "Colonial Williamsburg quality extends far beyond the highly visible costumed staff—from shopping and dining to accommodations, sports, maintenance, and office support."[20]

Inside, in his "Report from the President," Longsworth defined quality in somewhat different terms. As in much of the foundation's official discourse, his essay deftly conflates American history and the history of Colonial Williamsburg. It begins with a lengthy quotation from a modern historian's work on "tobacco culture" in tidewater Virginia at the time of the Revolutionary War. The quotation features an internal quotation from an eighteenth-century English traveler testifying to the high quality of Virginia tobacco and explaining that planters trademarked their products and, due to their reputation for quality, received higher prices for them. Next, Longsworth described the "tooled bead" of the weatherboards of Williamsburg's eighteenth-century buildings: "The extra handwork helped shed the rain . . . improved the appearance . . . [and] made the building better." These vignettes of eighteenth-century "quality and craftsmanship" lead, in Longsworth's narrative, to the quality of the modern-day foundation: inspired by the past, Goodwin and Rockefeller "marked" their "enterprise," the restoration, with "their adherence to authenticity" and "their insistence on quality." There follow several stories of the heroic pursuit of authenticity in the early years of the restoration—stock stories with a wide circulation at Colonial Williamsburg.[21]

Having provided Colonial Williamsburg's commitment to quality with a documented pedigree—from Virginia's planter elite to Goodwin and Rockefeller—Longsworth was at last ready to define it: "I think of quality in two ways. First, it is meeting our visitors' expectations. For Colonial Williamsburg, with its tradition of excellence, it is *exceeding* them. Second, I believe quality is the result of each employee's commitment to do his or her best, reflecting personal commitment to the organization and its mission."[22] Thus the craftsmanship of the past merges with loyalty to the modern-day corporation, both being understood in terms of individual effort and market competition. In this context, quality is exceeding visitor expectations, that is, serving the boss-guest individually and as an egalitarian team in order to ensure the survival of the team and each of its members.

The quality campaign announced in the *1987 Annual Report* had been taking shape since the early 1980s, when the corporation began organizing "quality circles" (which, by the time of our research, were called "quality teams"). Quality circles owed much to late-1970s notions about Japanese management style—in particular, to the idea that "empowering" employees to "solve problems" and develop more efficient ways of doing their work was a key component in maintaining a firm's competitive edge. The vice president whom we quoted above concerning "career ladders" explained that the works of such writers as Peters and Kotter had convinced Colonial Williamsburg's top management that they had to "streamline" and "flatten the organization." This meant, in part, eliminating management positions, but it also entailed empowering employees. In the words of a hotel manager: "It's called pushing problems down to be solved where they should be solved. Looking for ways to do things at a lower level in the work hierarchy." Not only would this give workers a greater stake in their work, it would free managers from attempting to solve problems about which they weren't knowledgeable.*

The biggest success story that we heard about a quality team concerned workers at the laundry: "Their main problem . . . was heat. You know, that's the nature of laundry. You can't wash and dry with cold. It's *heat.* And they said, you've got to give us relief: it's 120 degrees in here. And so, okay, let's form a quality team of your employees, and they put together about eight of them. And they researched on the various ways of possibly cooling that facility to make it more comfortable. . . . So they went around and they visited different places. And coming back on an airplane—there were a couple of them that were visiting I forget where it was . . . and they reached up for that little thing, for air, and they said, hey, how about that?! And so they came up with a system where they could cool the person at the work station instead of cooling the building. And they gave a presentation to . . . the director of hotel services . . . [and he] costed it out, it's going to cost about sixty thousand dollars—they did it!" The vice president who told us this story added that some of the members of the laundry quality team were illiterate. In sum, stories like this show the lowest and humblest as decision makers, as problem solvers and successes in their own right. They are the dedicated workers whom management envisions as part of a team contributing equally to the overall success of Colonial Williamsburg.

When we heard the story of the laundry, we asked why the facility wasn't air-conditioned, to which the vice president responded that it couldn't be done "efficiently." That word suggests a rational calculation that forestalls further discussion; but one could well ask who at the Colonial Williamsburg laundry is charged with calculating efficiency, and by what scale of values do

---

*An added benefit not so explicitly stated was that flattening the hierarchy dovetailed with corporate downsizing. Low-level employees could be empowered without, however, having their salaries raised. Recall our discussions with craft employees in chapter 4.

they determine how much money should be spent on worker safety and comfort? Quality teams and employee empowerment were not meant to let workers in on those sorts of decisions.

Indeed, as far as we could tell, quality teams and the employee empowerment they generated were never intended to help workers challenge management's exclusive right to establish organizational priorities. Rather, the arena for problem solving in which such teams functioned was narrowly confined to the shop floor, the front line, the work station—that is, to sites where employees could indeed be allowed to figure out how to do things "better and quicker and at less cost" while never being invited to ask or answer larger questions. Thus, when the *Colonial Williamsburg News* noted the results of quality teams and "employee involvement," the list was dominated by items such as reorganized tool sheds, new lightweight vacuum cleaners, and redecorated or reorganized work spaces.[23] Such innovations may indeed have improved the working conditions and the efficiency of employees, but they did not empower workers in the sense of changing the existing power structure of the foundation.

Corporate Communications

Contractual egalitarianism in Colonial Williamsburg's corporate discourses is intertwined with a second variety of egalitarianism, which we call the personal or personalized. In the presentation of the twenty-five-year service awards, for example, the reading of biographical sketches of the silver bowl recipients was intended as a "personal" touch. As we have seen, an upper-level executive armed with facts gleaned from personnel files interviewed long-service employees. The administrator responsible for briefing the executive before the interviews told us that sometimes she provided the interviewer with the employee's ID photo, so that "if he's going into a work site, maybe a kitchen, or housekeeping, . . . where he wouldn't perhaps really know this person by face, it helps him to spot the person. And that makes a big difference, if he can walk up to somebody and say, hello, how are you, and it takes the edge off." The result, according to our interlocutor, was "almost an army out there of folks who have that firsthand opportunity to feel like they know him a little bit."

As the last phrase suggests, what seems to be important here is a charade of the personal. Executives do not deceive themselves into believing they have personal relationships with each of the hundreds of employees under them, just as workers do not believe that presidents and vice presidents know them personally in any meaningful way. Nonetheless, everyone wants to act as though relationships they know to be impersonal are in fact personal: what is crucial is the appearance of a personal connection and the resulting camaraderie which that appearance allows people to enact. And let us add right away that we do not criticize—as a sign of "inauthenticity"—the importance that Colonial Williamsburg insiders place on the appearance of the personal; the appearance of the personal is culturally central ("authentic") in this world, as our discussion of frontline work in the next chapter will show.

The appearance of a personal connection between management and workers was a central theme of President Longsworth's question-and-answer session. Such sessions were designed to be "conversations" that gave workers one-on-one access to management. Longsworth mentioned "a regular monthly employee lunch" he had instituted. "If you haven't been invited," he added, "it's not cause I don't like you. It's because the computer selects the names and your name hasn't come up." In this example, to avoid the personal in the form of favoritism, invitations to lunch with the president are selected randomly by a machine; this also avoids an opposite form of the personal, dislike. We are left with an image of an executive who likes all employees equally, one who has, at least potentially, a personalized relationship with each of them and who actualizes as many of those potential relationships as time and the computer permit.

Longsworth's question-and-answer session and the one-on-one executive interviews with long-service employees were part of a larger trend at Colonial Williamsburg during the time of our research. Management had embarked on a campaign to improve "corporate communications." That effort was closely linked to the drives to improve quality and to "flatten" the corporate hierarchy. If inefficiency was in part a function of overmanagement and needless organizational complexity, one way to improve the situation, it was argued, was to break down the barriers between organizational units. Such barriers were often conceptualized in terms of a lack of communication and cooperation between individuals. Thus, for example, one employee complained to President Longsworth (during the session we've been discussing) that "we all seem to work in our own little departments instead of one great big team for the visitor." To which the president responded: "It's a very tough problem to address. And it has its roots in history: this organization grew up with vertical lines flowing up. And it didn't matter so much what you did with the guy next door as long as you satisfied the president. We're trying to squash that down . . . but it doesn't just happen overnight. One of the subjects that we debate quite a lot in the management committee is just this: how to encourage greater interdivisional . . . cooperation." At this point, one of the president's lieutenants chimed in with some announcements of upcoming events that he felt were relevant to the issue at hand—picnics and recreational programs that, he explained, were "designed to . . . develop cameraderie . . . that crosses all divisional lines. We're working on trying to communicate better."[24]

That management felt the need for better communications to be acute is suggested by the fact that three programs were being established at the time of our research to enable employees to feel comfortable questioning their superiors. "Speak Out!" was explained by President Longsworth in these terms: "Speak Out!' will enable you to address a question or concern in writing to a single person. Only you and that one person (who is yet to be named) will know what you have written. The person will direct your inquiry, compliment, or complaint to the person at Colonial Williamsburg who can best give you an answer. The person answering will not know who you are unless you want him or her to know."[25]

The other two programs were an ongoing employee opinion survey and something called "skip-level interviews," a program designed to allow employees "to ask their boss's boss questions," as one of the executives interested in the program told us. He went on to explain that the combination of openness and anonymity that marked all three programs was designed to allay employee fears: "There was a lot of comment out of the employee survey about anonymity, protection, and retribution. And it's hard in an environment where employees don't trust their managers . . . to provide those upward communication opportunities without stepping on the chain of command, which is an important part of the organizational structure."

This remark led the interviewer to ask the executive about trust: "How could employees ever trust managers—since managers hold the power to fire them?" He went on to speculate that this would always be the case in a hierarchical business organization, an argument the executive denied. In the view of this vice president, the problem was personal, not structural; it was a question of faulty communication between individuals: "It's people not being willing to give the benefit of the doubt to someone else. They'd rather ascribe a motive to someone—if somebody does something, oh, they're sure it was because of this. As a matter of fact, it may be that person just sees things differently. But they never confront each other and resolve their differences. . . . Whether it's co-workers, or managers and bosses, they're not putting it on the table and saying, what's bothering you today?"

When managers talked to us about the need for communication and its promise, they rarely commented on the possibility that people who occupy hierarchically different positions within the corporation may "see things" so "differently" that no amount of dialogue will resolve their differences. Instead, they made statements such as the one above, reflecting a pluralistic egalitarianism—nodding to a kind of interpersonal relativism. You, the employee, have your viewpoint; you see things with a different subjectivity based on your distinct personality. I, the manager, have my (equally valid) viewpoint. Once we learn to listen to one another because we trust one another—eureka!—we discover deep similarities and resolve our differences by a kind of mutuality even if you are an employee and I am a manager. Egalitarian pluralism and interpersonal relativism lead to a kind of universalism, in which, it is assumed, everyone shares the same values and interests. Hierarchy—the fact that differences are usually resolved because inferiors must sacrifice their values and interests to those of their superiors—is never a topic.

We Make Money, They Spend It

At Colonial Williamsburg (as in other institutional settings) the possibility that even two ostensible equals—two managers or administrators in separate departments—may never resolve their differences is usually papered over in practice. Usually, this is accomplished when people invoke slogans that seem specific enough to serve as mission statements (e.g., "to exceed visitor expectations," "to be the best place to work," "that the future may learn from the past," "authenticity," "quality," and so on) but are also sufficiently oracular to allow for a great deal of dispute in the name of consensus. In this way, mission statements can serve as umbrella values that seem to encompass particular differences, much as interpersonal pluralism ultimately gives way to a deeper interpersonal universalism.

But differences are not always easy to deny or overlook, and this was especially the case when administrators and managers talked about the problem of communication between the two sides of the hybrid corporation. When we asked how the two sides worked together, managers, executives, and employees all responded in similar ways. As an administrator on the education side put it, "They're the revenue guys. . . . The hotel folks are the revenue dudes." By way of contrast, he cheerfully asserted that "we educators can always spend more than anyone can make." Or as a business-side vice president explained, those on "the museum side" look on their business-side counterparts as "moneymongers," while "on the business side, they go, oh, those museum guys, they know how to spend money like it's going through a sieve."

The pervasive and rarely challenged assumption that one side makes money while the other spends it made mistrust and misunderstanding inevitable. Quoting the business-side vice president again: "The hotel people are looking to get the most money out of something, which they turn over to museums. I think it frustrates them that the museums spend it so quickly and freely. The museum [people] don't have the appreciation the hotel people do of how hard it is to make that dollar." On the other hand, to education-side employees, making money was often talked of as a kind of perversion or pollution of the corporation's larger mission. The "real" mission of the place, they'd joke, was no longer "that the future may learn from the past," but "that the future may *earn* from the past." And they often assumed a fundamental incompatibility between learning and earning.

But even those who could point out instances where making money meant a trade-off with education tended to defer to the moneymaking expertise of the "corporate types" and to recognize the tremendous financial resources necessary to the long-term mission of the institution—to "preserve" the past for future generations. To give an extended example of this deference, consider again the case of the third golf course. Many managers on the education side were critical of the foundation's decision to incur a large corporate debt to build a new golf course because monies spent on that project would be unavailable, they thought, for educational programs. The destruction of forest and the modification of the terrain bordering the Historic Area meant that valuable archaeological information, not to mention potential future reconstruction sites, would be lost. Some on the museum side went so far as to talk of corporate fission. Having a hugely costly (if profitable) business side made the public think the foundation, with its $120-million-a-year budget, was bigger and more financially sound than it really was, so why not sell off the for-profit side? Without a business side, they ventured, the museum side would be better positioned to pursue donors and beef up its endowment.

Yet people rarely took seriously, or pursued to its logical conclusion, the notion of completely severing the business side of the foundation from the museum side. Consider the following scenario, sketched for our benefit by a museum-side administrator: "If you ask [President Longsworth] why a golf course, he'll tell you conferences. If you ask him why conferences . . . he says that's what's necessary to hotels. And then you say, why hotels? And then you're really getting to the heart of the issue. But given the structure of the organization, it would be radical in the extreme to conceive of an alternative. That's not to say it's impossible, but our hotels are very profitable." Hotels were "very profitable," he went on, because their proximity to the Historic Area allowed them to charge exorbitant rates (" 'Rapacious' probably overstates the case, but they're high"). But, he continued, the problem was that Colonial Williamsburg hotels did not have a monopoly on this selling feature. "Kingsmill now advertises their conference center by 'right next to the Historic Area. Only a ten-minute bus ride away.' They don't have to maintain the Historic Area, but they can have the benefit of 'Come to Williamsburg.' " Thus "they can trade on the name" while also offering "waterfront, golf courses, Busch Gardens, free beer at the brewery."

The view of this museum administrator was not that the foundation should get out of the hotel business, but that the decision to build a third golf course was justified due to competition from resort-conference centers such as Kingsmill. He accepted this decision—and the notion that hotels support education at Colonial Williamsburg—despite recognizing that the hotels and restaurants would not have eager customers without the Historic Area to entice them there. In sum, he realized (as he put it) that the relationship between the two sides was "symbiotic," but he tended to treat the input of the education side as if it were merely raw material—a found object like the Historic Area itself—which the business people packaged and sold. So he deferred to them the ultimate authority to make decisions about how best to make (and divide) profits, even while recognizing that the business side had made poor decisions in the past. It was they, after all, who had sold the land (at a bargain price) to Anheuser-Busch without anticipating that the new neighbor would become a competitor for conference customers. That he could continue to have faith in the proposition that the pursuit of profits made a new golf course a necessity if the experts, "the finance gurus," said so reflected a fundamental faith that the business side made the money while the education side merely spent it. In this, he echoed the common corporate wisdom—a paradigm for how the two sides worked together that was reiterated at all levels of the organization and in all kinds of media.

Sometimes it was admitted that the museum side made some of the money it spent. In the annual reports, for example, the education side was portrayed as generating some revenue—through ticket sales—but not enough to cover the cost of running the museum. Hotels and restaurants took in more than they spent, but not enough to cover the museum side's losses. Ultimately, those pie-charted documents showed, the shortfall was covered by capital gains and dividends realized on the foundation's endowment.

If the Historic Area could be said to "make money," then it did so through ticket sales. Yet, even this revenue-generating capacity of the museum side tended to disappear as people talked about profit or as they figured income and expenses in interdepartmental budget meetings. Thus an administrator in the Visitor Center (where the tickets are sold) could make the following argument to us without feeling that he was shortchanging anyone. He was trying to convince us that his department, rather than "Hotels," was in fact the most profitable in the entire corporation. His budget, he said, was only $3.5 million, yet his employees generated "$20-plus million in ticket sales" that went to support "educational programs"—which to him counted only as an "operating cost" with which the entire foundation was saddled. In this accounting, it was the clerks who sold tickets who made money, not the workers in the Historic Area where the show was provided. Our conversation with this man brought home to us how arbitrary—and undiscussed—are the commonplace notions about who makes money and who spends it at Colonial Williamsburg.

Earning Is Learning

If education types sometimes talked of the conversation across the boundary as a zero-sum game in which education sacrificed potential pedagogic gains in order to preserve or maintain long-term economic viability, business types tended to talk in terms of both sides gaining. For them, the ultimate business of Colonial Williamsburg was indeed learning, and they were quick to assert that learning and earning were not incompatible, even as they were proud to emphasize the degree to which they had been able to convince educators of that fact. To them, considerable progress had been made because educators, under President Longsworth's tutelage, were learning to "speak the language" of business; they were beginning to understand that if one wants to educate, one must learn to be more "responsive" to the needs and desires of customers.

Business-side managers and administrators were more sanguine than were their education-side counterparts that the two sides could work together without painful trade-offs. While they recognized that the relationship had in the past been adversarial, and that educators still on occasion dug in their heels when faced with inevitable and market-driven changes, they generally talked of the present efforts at communicating across the hybrid corporation's internal border in more glowing terms. A common theme was that communication worked so smoothly precisely because they deferred to the education side's ultimate authority. It was, after all, Colonial Williamsburg's status as "a nonprofit" that allowed them to produce something more uplifting than "razor blades," as one executive put it. What made their work at Colonial Williamsburg so fulfilling was, as another executive explained, "working for an organization that has some greater vision than making money."

A director in one of the departments responsible for Colonial Williamsburg's products and reproductions offered us what he felt was the epitome of this achieved harmony: the new (1989) *Williamsburg Reproductions* catalog. Since its inception in 1937, the reproductions program has generated institutional tensions, as curators and historians on the Products Review Committee have sought to hold in check the tendency of business-side marketers to promote the reproduction of objects that (from the educators' point of view) are not authentic to Colonial Williamsburg. The products director with whom we spoke is the same man who described the progress the foundation had made under President Longsworth in rationalizing the relationship between its two sides. According to our interlocutor, he and his staff had always accepted the primacy of the foundation's educational mission. In the reproductions program, he said, "we're educational and we're saying that we developed these products so that we can interest and inform our customers about the eighteenth century through the decorative arts. . . . Educational basis first, income for the foundation second. And if you've read our goals and our policy statement—first is education because we're an educational institution, and our products activities have to support that."

As this man explained it, the working relationship between his department and the curators and historians had improved markedly in the recent past. For one thing, curatorial mission and marketing success had been brought together through a program whereby the curators received a percentage of the reproductions royalties to use in acquisitions. "Curators love to collect," he explained. "The heart of a museum is the fact that you can acquire objects." But "they need money to do it," and after the Rockefeller era, money became increasingly hard to find. The new program linking acquisitions to reproductions provided, at last, a direct "incentive for the curators to work with the money guys."

When it came time to redo their catalog, his department, building on this new linkage of the curators and marketers, worked closely with the educators to turn a simple catalog into an affordable illustrated history book that wouldn't look out of place on a coffee table. The curators were persuaded to write pedagogically productive (scholarly) sections on the decorative arts, and the foundation's chief education officer wrote an introduction outlining the role of the decorative arts in the colonial era and in the developing historiography of that era. The idea was that these essays would tell much the same story as that conveyed by the museum itself. This, according to the marketing executive, was the story of a "tradesman who wasn't just a little old shoemaker doing things because he loved to do them" but was instead a close analogue to the modern manufacturer who provides Colonial Williamsburg's reproductions—a man "responding to patronage," that is, to consumer desire. The resultant catalog was "a million-dollar production"—100,000 copies went on sale to the public at $19.95 each.

The curators we interviewed seemed equally pleased. They had come to recognize that their audience of consumer-students were not purists. "We have two types of consumers," one curator told us. "Some who want to buy an occasional Williamsburg object and put it in a modern home, and others who want to re-create the Wythe House! And in the products/selling side of that, we're just acknowledging that, and trying to educate them—making them know what is the background of the object that they buy." Curators also agreed that the new catalog was an educational advance on the old one. The new catalog had "fifty pages of educational content out of three hundred-and-some pages . . . probably ten times what was in the predecessor." Also because educational content "was one of the selling points of the catalog," the curators had agreed not to act on the idea of "extracting those pages as a pamphlet, that we could sell as a Wallace Gallery brochure." To have done so would have lessened the marketability of the vastly more profitable (if equally educational) coffee table catalog of Williamsburg reproductions.

In conversations such as these, we always felt a gap between our perceptions and the spoken perceptions of our interlocutors. For us, it was as if, in the act of communicating across the boundaries of culture and capital, administrators had learned a certain fluency in the vocabulary of their counterparts but had also, as a result, managed to evacuate specific meaning or content from ostensibly key symbols such as "learning" and "education." For example, it was clear that the "money guy" was less interested in educational content than he was in using educational form—scholarly essays—to produce a product that would make money and act as an advertisement as well. It also seemed clear to us that the educational content of the essays in the reproductions catalog was of dubious merit; in sum, the essays provided a way of "naturalizing" consumer desire by providing an upscale pedigree for it (the silk-stocking patriots were avid consumers just like you).

Given this, the cynic's appraisal of Colonial Williamsburg's real mission—
"that the future may earn from the past"—seems to be correct. Such a view
dovetails with a wider (and long-standing) critique of business-culture hybridity, which, put bluntly, is that whenever profit becomes an institutional
bottom line, education becomes just another product. Rather than an alliance between separate but equal partners, a hierarchical relationship de-
velops in which business takes priority over education. In such an analysis, it
might be said that the emphasis on communicating across the corporate
boundary, the emphasis on the place's "educational mission," is little more
than propaganda—a convenient party line that business types, especially,
know is something they have to pay lip service to in public but privately
recognize as window dressing.

The problem with this scenario, however, is that it implies a kind of
conspiracy—a theory that is all too much a part of our particular cultural
landscape, and therefore something we should be skeptical of. Moreover, to
prove a conspiracy one would need more than circumstantial evidence. One
would need to have an insider admit that business types are putting out one
story for public consumption while keeping private what really motivates
them. One exposes a conspiracy only with the help of an insider informant.

We never had such a conversation at Colonial Williamsburg. If the business types were paying lip service to education, then they did so with disciplined consistency. Of course, this may simply reflect the limits of our research. Anthropologists generally promise *their* public (that is, you, the
reader) a unique glimpse into a native way of life by offering to share the
results of what we call "participant observation." We imply that we have
come to know our natives intimately—that we have encountered them in
ways that go beyond the superficial or the touristic; that we have interacted
with them in private as well as in public. But at Colonial Williamsburg, this
anthropological ideal eluded us (if, indeed, it's ever anything more than a
convenient advertisement for disciplinary uniqueness). When we talked with
officials on the business side, we encountered them in their offices. We sat on
one side of the desk, they on the other. Our tape recorder or open notepad
marked the boundary between us and defined the encounter as a public
one—something "for the record." To a manager—a person "trained in how
to manage people," as one vice president phrased it—an interview is just one
more in a series of public presentations. Even if a conspiracy existed, it is
unlikely that anyone would have confessed it in such public encounters.
What we heard instead was something far more fascinating.

We had conversations such as the following, in which it was impossible to determine whether the speaker was deluding us (and any "public") with lip service or revealing an ongoing process of self-delusion. We were talking to one of the foundation's chief marketers. We were not tape-recording because he was more comfortable without the recorder running. He was telling us about the many ways that Colonial Williamsburg was making itself more of an "attraction" to visitors. "Attraction" was, he knew, a word with bad connotations because it harkened to "amusement parks," to Disney World and Busch Gardens. But he didn't "mind the word 'attraction,'" because there was nothing wrong with admitting that most visitors came to Colonial Williamsburg "for reasons other than to be educated." To clinch the point, he added, "To me, Monticello is an attraction."

Yet, at the end of a generally upbeat account of how a new media blitz was making Colonial Williamsburg more visible as an "attraction," he abruptly began to criticize a recent decision to let staff on the education side work closely with a doll company. It was his personal opinion, he said, that the administrators in the Historic Area had made a mistake when they welcomed a company that produced a line of expensive dolls called the American Girls Collection, which represented girls from particular periods and regions. The dolls were marketed along with their clothing and clothes for the girls who bought them, and with children's books portraying the dolls' lives and thus teaching something about girlhood in America's past. The company had recently introduced a new doll, Felicity, who was portrayed as an inhabitant of Williamsburg in the colonial era. The company had approached the foundation to arrange a "convention" at Colonial Williamsburg to introduce the doll to its customers. There would be special tours for the hundreds of Felicity girls and their mothers, and a play based on the Felicity books would be performed at a series of tea parties. The foundation had agreed, so for a few days (to our amazement!) the streets of Williamsburg were populated with dozens of living replicas of the dolls, and its hotel lobbies were crowded with company officials and their customers.

The business-side executive commented that the educators who made the decision to allow the convention had "had a point." The alliance would surely be profitable for Colonial Williamsburg, not only because of the business the convention generated but also because the thousands of Felicity fans would "always remember Williamsburg" and "bring their daughters here," just as their mothers had brought them. But he worried that the foundation had sacrificed "credibility for profit," because those customers, however loyal, would associate the place with "a doll, a fake person, a person who never lived." In becoming too closely associated with "a total fantasy," Colonial

Girls with their mothers and American Girls dolls. (photo by Eric Gable)

Williamsburg had, he emphasized, potentially "compromised" its "mission." But when we asked him how, specifically, the mission had been compromised, he responded, "Look at the mobcaps the girls are wearing. They're not our mobcaps, which are made by licensed manufacturers working with the highest standards of authenticity."

It is impossible to tell whether he was ultimately more worried that the doll company's mobcaps were made to lesser standards and were therefore pedagogically adulterated coin, or that the foundation was losing business to a competitor, another of those corporate parasites that borrow Colonial Williamsburg's prestige to sell a product. If the latter is what chiefly preoccupied him, then we might conclude further that what he said at the beginning—that the doll was a fake and therefore a danger to authenticity—was for him merely a convenient rhetorical ploy, an argument he might indeed have used, in camera, as the administrators discussed whether to grant the doll company's request. Perhaps, for him, things would have been fine if a licensed Williamsburg manufacturer had made the doll.

One could also make much of his use of the word "credibility." When Colonial Williamsburg sells an obvious fake, its reputation as a purveyor of truth, the one element that makes the place an "attraction," is put at risk. In the end, then, this businessman was less concerned with the content of that truth than with its appearance—something that translates into a marketable credibility. His job, as he saw it, was to ensure that visitors came to Colonial Williamsburg and to predict how much money could be generated from them to help meet the foundation's cash-flow needs. At the beginning of our conversation, he had remarked about the sophistication of his department's marketing research. By linking what they learned about visitor demographics with surveys on "visitor satisfaction" and comparing shifts in numbers and kinds of visitors with recent rises in ticket prices, his department could, he felt, predict how high ticket prices might be raised before significant numbers of visitors would be driven away. He had managed to make such predictions without even knowing why people came to Colonial Williamsburg in the first place—a great (if ultimately trivial) mystery to him. All he needed to make accurate predictions was a reasonable faith that people would continue (for whatever reason) to find Colonial Williamsburg attractive to visit. He trusted others—the educators, the curators, the licensed manufacturers, the people in hotels and restaurants—to produce the attracting product, whatever it was. Ultimately, he had an abiding, if unexamined, faith that this product was in general authentic, of the highest quality, educational.

Corporate Critics

In sketching the themes we found central in Colonial Williamsburg's corporate culture, we have been led to discuss the problem of corporate communications and to describe some of the ways in which disagreement and difference are talked about, or not talked about. But our sketch must raise a question: Did Colonial Williamsburg's employees buy the company line? Clearly, if they bought it hook, line, and sinker, there would be little need for management to reiterate it endlessly, as they did. On the other hand, if the company line had no effect at all on employees, it is conceivable (at least from a functionalist perspective) that the place couldn't survive as a viable organization. The answer, then, lies somewhere between these extremes.

As we gradually learned, there were plenty of native critics of the company line at Colonial Williamsburg. Moreover, even the most sanguine booster, the most eloquent spokesperson for the foundation, could also—in midsentence—act as his or her own critic. In short, Colonial Williamsburg employees exhibited a divided consciousness about the company line. They bought it and they didn't buy it—sometimes in the same breath. What, then, was the true relationship between the complaints and criticisms workers habitually voiced (voices too often elevated by academics to the level of "resistance" or "counterhegemonic discourse") and the company line?

As we wandered Colonial Williamsburg's streets, it sometimes seemed to us that all we had to do was turn on our tape recorder to get yet another worker who'd never met us before to bellyache into our microphone. That we encountered so many employees who wanted to criticize Colonial Williamsburg did not surprise us, for at least two reasons. First, natives tended to assimilate us to the preexisting category of the outside corporate evaluator or the muckraking reporter. Some months before we began our work, a consulting firm had also been interviewing employees, conducting surveys and focus groups pursuant to management's desire to improve corporate communications. The researchers had encouraged the employees to speak frankly about what it felt like to work for a company that aspired to be "the best place to work." Likewise, employees were also familiar with attention from the media; indeed, the reporter digging up dirt is a national icon—and so people are willing to convey "dirt" to inquisitive outsiders.

Second, Colonial Williamsburg (like much of corporate America at the time) was suffering severe economic strain and was responding by firing or laying off employees. In the midst of corporate downsizing, employees were bound to be critical of what appeared to be the hypocrisies of corporate rhetoric.* For whatever reason, then, people who were angry about what the corporation and its leaders were doing would tell us their views, perhaps hoping we would make them public.

A particularly pervasive critique had to do with inequities in pay. Many employees believed that Colonial Williamsburg gave its bosses too much and its workers too little, and that when it came time to trim corporate fat, it was the workers, not the bosses, who had to tighten their belts. One such employee, on meeting us for the first time and hearing that we were writing a book about the place, asserted that it was "the most top-heavy corporation" he knew, noting that in a year when the foundation added four new vice president slots it "let go" twenty-seven people, including a cook-interpreter "who had worked twenty-three years." There was a pervasive belief that the current

---

*A vice president told us that management was learning about these worker complaints through its employee opinion surveys: Colonial Williamsburg, he told us, "is a very tense organization. And while we talk about quality . . . employees frequently will say . . . 'Hey, the audio doesn't match the video—because out of the other side of your mouth you're saying, cut budgets five percent.'" He concluded that "workers distrust managers . . . because of the inconsistency of what they hear versus what they see happening. . . . Morale is not what we would like it to be."

crop of bosses was making consistently bad decisions—investing heavily in another golf course, for example, while cutting back on educational programs. To many employees, such inequities and inefficiencies were a fact of life. Several people told us, for example, that Colonial Williamsburg managers and executives were particularly incompetent precisely because amateurs were playing at being corporate types, or that the place's nonprofit status kept its executives insulated from the rough-and-tumble of the real world. Others said that across the board in American business, "suits" are overcompensated and those who do other kinds of work are undercompensated.

As we listened to these employees, we were fascinated by the way they assimilated or used elements of the company line as they couched their complaints in a language that could perhaps be compelling in that environment. Given that they were using parts of corporate-speak in their critique, and that despite their criticisms they often professed satisfaction with their work and with the company as a whole (or as an abstraction, as a kind of Platonic ideal), we found it hard to evaluate what they were saying.

Typical of the kinds of conversations we had was an interview with a craftsperson on the job, a wheelwright who was enthusiastic about his work and a measured booster of Colonial Williamsburg. The discussion was framed by general questions—what did he like about his work, what were some of its pitfalls?—and he talked in articulate bits and pieces as he continued to work on a wheel and in the quiet moments between visitors. Tradespeople are at the apex of a hierarchy of skills at Colonial Williamsburg. They are recognized as artists and as living embodiments of a certain excellence. Their images and the images of what they produce are icons of the kind of "quality" that corporate rhetoric projects as an ultimate value. Yet, the "tradesmen" (and almost all are men) are also blue-collar workers, and they know it. Like members of skilled trades elsewhere in corporate America, the foundation's craftspeople are particularly sensitive to the paradoxes of skill and compensation that occur as the corporate pie is divided up among the corporate family members. Those paradoxes framed the wheelwright's responses to our questions. He kept circling around the key fact that, as he put it, a vice president "doesn't know how to make a wheel. Anyone can be a museum executive. Those are a dime a dozen. The people that know these skills aren't. And that's . . . the frustrating thing—you point out to these folks that—you know, they say, 'Well, we're going to pay you comparable to a plumber.' Then you put in the next quotient, [which] is, 'Okay, let's say there's only two plumbers in the country—how much would they make?'"

The wheelwright loved his work, so he was willing to put up with such structural inequities. But he wished the foundation would live up to its rhetoric. Given that the top management were constantly extolling the uniqueness of the craftsmen, and given that they wouldn't pay them more, they could at least recognize them for their "special talents." The wheelwright wanted to be treated as a "living treasure," like "they have in Japan." He envisaged being sent around the country to demonstrate his craft: "The recognition would be one way of compensating us that doesn't cost the foundation a dime, and is good publicity. I'm for, you know, helping the company out."

In talking in this way, he could be a team player while also calling attention to the gaps between corporate rhetoric and practice. Thus, while seeming to reiterate the company line that a good part of worker dissatisfaction could be solved by more honest communications, he noted, "They always say, well, we're the pacesetters. . . . [But] then they bring up pay; they say, 'Well, but no museum pays well.' So why don't we be leaders there? set the standard? If they came to me with the books open, saying, 'We're in serious financial trouble,' I'd even be willing to say, well okay, I'll sacrifice this and this and this. But they always do it in a way that's kind of sleazy." Because management was constantly producing rhetorical smokescreens, it had a "credibility problem." The managers were always hiding, for example, the very salary inequities that caused so much worker resentment. This, we discovered, was a common complaint among workers. One employee told us it had been a constant topic at the public meetings held by President Longsworth to improve corporate communications. Supposedly, during one such meeting, after a corporate vice president "drew a circle, a pie like they always draw, and showed how this went to taxes, this to upkeep, this to salary"—the point being to show why they couldn't afford to pay employees more—a woman called out, "We know all that about the pie, but what about the wedge that goes to vice presidents and the wedge that goes to the rest of us?" The vice president in charge of the meeting claimed not to know. Later, in another meeting (according to the same employee), the vice president was summarizing a report by a consulting firm showing that "our wages, our benefits, everything were way lower than average," when another employee asked if the text of the report would be available for all to read. The vice president countered that the report "was paid for" by the foundation and therefore private. "Each department will get a summary relevent to their area."*

---

*Above, we discussed management's aim to pay employees "competitively"—that is, according to the prevailing scales of remuneration in the industry—rather than fairly, as the wheel-

Given this pervasive atmosphere of mistrust and resentment among employees, it is not surprising that among the wheelwright's peers in the historical trades, nearly everyone (according to him) felt that employees in "capital giving" were making way too much money. In his opinion, if the foundation would explain in an open way "that you've got to put out money to make money . . . people around here would understand that, but the problem is that they hide it, so everyone is skeptical."

Talking about worker skepticism and management miscommunication, the wheelwright evinced a certain skepticism himself. On the one hand, he felt that "management was really trying to find out what's wrong," but, on the other hand, he doubted the effectiveness and perhaps the underlying sincerity of its way of eliciting workers' opinions: "If [top management] would just get out of [the] office and come down and talk to people, instead of hiding behind the cloak of this opinion survey, people would talk to [them]. But . . . it just seems that they're out to get middle management. . . . In the last opinion survey, there wasn't anything [like] 'Do you think this is Chuck's [President Longsworth's] fault?' . . . It's all [about the problems] below vice presidents. So the people that are going to get critical assessments are the managers and the directors of departments. . . . And then they set up these touchy-feely little quality teams, but they don't train people in how to lead them. And there's all sorts of things that go awry. [Describing what happened when a group of apprentice and journeyman craftspeople participated in one such quality team:] they were promised the written comments from the man from a company that did the survey. So when we got to our feedback session we didn't have the comments. And we asked . . . the assistant director of the department where they were, and he said, well, we're not going to give them to you. But we were promised them. And a big stink was made of it, and it ended up being purely principle—that we were promised something and we didn't get it. So we finally got it . . . and I was the only one to read it. You know, I felt like I should, because we made such a stink out of it. . . . I don't know why—there wasn't anything in there that was real bad. The really wild thing is that during all this they're talking about . . . our ownership of the company. And we don't even own our comments." These little altercations

---

wright, for example, defined it in his parable of the plumber. Management also insisted that employees' complaints about their pay were grounded in poor corporate communications; the vice president for human resources explained in the *Colonial Williamsburg News* that "the employee opinion survey showed us that there is a very close relationship between the number of employees who said they were satisfied with their pay . . . and those who said they had enough information about how their pay was determined" (quoted in Saylor 1990b:17).

between managers and tradesmen were, according to the wheelwright, "hilarious" both because the rhetoric—you employees own the company, you are empowered by participation in employee surveys and quality teams—was obviously a sham, and because what managers were reluctant to reveal seemed so trivial. Worse, the argument was shown to be an empty exercise because the workers themselves didn't bother to follow through once their demands were met.

Like the wheelwright, employees who wanted to expose the hypocrisies of corporate rhetoric often used President Longsworth as a foil, collapsing a critique of corporate policy with an attack on its leader. Thus, one such employee illustrated what he saw as the emptiness of Longsworth's gestures at "making himself available" to employees as if all were equals by recounting what he claimed was a sharp confrontation at one of the president's town meetings. As he told it, an employee stood up at one of the meetings and asked Longsworth why, if he cared so much about employee relations, they never saw him on the street. According to him, Longsworth replied that he was on the street every day—"He said he rode his bicycle down the DOG street [Duke of Gloucester Street]—he named the bicycle, some fancy brand that cost a thousand dollars—and said he rode the bicycle every morning at six-thirty. Well, the garden crews aren't even out at six-thirty."

That President Longsworth would mention riding such an expensive bicycle proved to this employee that the president was "insensitive." He practically spit as he said it—"insensitive"—and propelled himself immediately into divulging more evidence of the insensitivity of top management. He mentioned a foundation officer who owned a fancy car and "parks it where he wants. Right on the lawn if he wants to. How do you think that makes employees feel?" Equally insensitive, according to the employee, were the wives of top management. He claimed that one of them had wanted to use an eighteenth-century kitchen as a private office (because "it had a wonderful chimney") but wanted it moved from its original site to the backyard of the house supplied to her husband by the foundation—a little task that "an architect told me cost a hundred thousand dollars. They could have rebuilt it for sixty."*

*Parking issues were a frequent source of complaint among employees. One visitor aide wrote to "Speak Up," a column in the *Colonial Williamsburg News,* to explain the impracticalities—and consequent hardships employees experienced—of the rules about who was allowed to park where. She made a point of noting that the vice president who was the chair of the Parking Committee had responded to complaints like hers by noting that the long walks from parking lots to work sites "was good exercise." The vice president blandly responded that the dis-

Whatever the factual basis of such anecdotes, plenty of workers were quick to excoriate President Longsworth and his vice presidents in similar terms. They'd mention someone's fancy car and in the same sentence the fact that he never talked to anyone. The implication always seemed to be that if those in charge were only more sensitive or more genuinely communicative, then Colonial Williamsburg would live up to its promise of being "the best place to work." Thus, in personalizing problems, in making them out to be problems of communication, the internal critics tended to repeat the same underlying themes of the celebratory company line. For example, even though the wheelwright considered much corporate rhetoric to be a counterproductive sham, he continued to have faith in its deeper premises—that if employees could only communicate as individuals, if "Chuck," the president, would only meet face-to-face with the workers, the murk of mutual mistrust would be dispelled.

But the near constant linking of insensitivity to the flaunting of wealth raises a difficult question. Would it have been enough, in the workers' minds, if President Longsworth and others like him had been more careful about hiding their wealth? As we have seen, another common complaint was precisely that salary scales were deliberately hidden from employees so they would be less aware of the specifics of disparities in compensation. Interestingly enough, when Longsworth stepped down as president at the end of the period of our research (he went on to serve as chairman of the foundation's board), his replacement was praised because he drove a beat-up American car and went out of his way to talk to everyone. The new president is paid as well as Longsworth was. Workers, we found, were not prone to begrudge income disparities as such. Many of those who were openly bitter about Longsworth would point out that they didn't resent him for his income—a

---

gruntled employee had been invited to attend a Parking Committee meeting and had come away with "a better understanding of some of these issues" ("A Visitor Aide Speaks up on Employee Parking," *Colonial Williamsburg News* 43.2 [March–April 1990]: 11, 14). Once again, we see management's faith that good communications solves work-site problems.

Stories about having buildings moved are legendary at Colonial Williamsburg. Compare the story we told above, about the executive's wife and the outbuilding, with Kopper's celebratory tale of the Rockefellers as at once "old-shoe neighbors" of Williamsburg's ordinary citizenry and the town's most extraordinary residents: "Because rank hath its privileges, they were able to do certain things that might have been prohibited to others." When "Mrs. Rockefeller was awakened at night by the screams of patients in . . . Eastern State Hospital," a mental asylum, the Rockefellers negotiated with the state government and the College of William and Mary to have "the hospital moved across town"—after which "Colonial Williamsburg was able to acquire the original site" (Kopper 1986:213–14).

salary he deserved, they'd emphasize, precisely because he was so skilled at cultivating VIP donors.

An unfortunate shortcoming of our interviews with such employees was our failure to probe more deeply into what they meant by "insensitivity." We like to think that the employees we talked to were using the word *insensitivity* in much the same way as we use the word *hypocrisy*. We would like to think that, to them, the executives' expensive bicycles and cars revealed an essential dishonesty in corporate rhetoric, and that in saying "insensitivity" the workers were using that language against itself—to make it reveal its hidden contradictions—and thus displaying the capacity to think beyond the language. But it may be they had simply bought the implications of this language at a deeper level than we could measure. Were executives insensitive because they had revealed themselves to be incompetent managers of interpersonal interactions? Was the problem not that they lied or that they lied and believed their lies, but that they inadvertently told discomforting truths without knowing they had done so? Have the president and vice presidents failed, in the workers' estimation, because they have not been good public relations men?

Whether or not such critiques represented a profound exposure of the hypocrisies of corporate-speak, they revealed the universal capacity of the less enfranchised to seize the rhetoric of their "masters" and use it (to borrow from Certeau) "tactically" as a weapon to attack particular leaders.[26] At least among the workers we talked to most—those who worked in various capacities on the hybrid corporation's education side—it was resistance to persons, not resistance to premises, that was most likely to occur in the environment of Colonial Williamsburg's corporate culture. This is hardly surprising, for, as we shall see, the brunt of worker discipline on the front lines at Colonial Williamsburg revolves around the appearance of good interpersonal relationships.

7 ■ *The Front Line: Smile Free or Die*

Compliments

"About the only thing you can get fired for around here is being rude to a visitor." This was one of the first pieces of wisdom bestowed on us at the beginning of our field research. It came from an education-side vice president, and he said it with a smile, to make the point that the corporate culture of Colonial Williamsburg was benign. Several months later, while reading old issues of the *Colonial Williamsburg News,* we came across an editorial from President Longsworth touching on the same subject, but the president's tone seemed anything but benign. Reviewing the foundation's performance in 1981, Longsworth remarked that "some of the discourteous or uninterested employees are 'no longer with us' and can no longer spoil your record."[1] We read this as a veiled threat, and our reading was confirmed by at least a few of the frontline employees who were willing to express a critical attitude toward their work. "You're being paid to be hospitable," one of them told us. "You cannot be sharp or short [with visitors] because . . . it's a hospitality and courtesy violation for which you can be fired."

When the vice president mentioned rudeness as cause for dismissal, the larger point he was making is that Colonial Williamsburg is an intellectually open environment: people can say or think whatever they want about history, as long as they remain polite in their dealings with visitors. But for the frontline guide, dismissals for rudeness pointed to a different interpretation of the foundation. Like the vice president, she thought that costumed employees—interpreters, craftspeople, the workers who staff the cash registers in the Historic Area stores—can tell any historical story they want and get away with it as long as they don't offend anyone. But from that fact she concluded not that Colonial Williamsburg is a domain of intellectual freedom, but that it is a big entertainment center and not an educational institution. As she and several other interpreters told us, employees who work on Colonial Williamsburg's streets quickly learn that the place is a business that must sell itself, through them, to countless visitors. These salespeople for the foundation are known as "frontline" employees. Every working day, they meet and converse with dozens of visitors. And, as many of them told us, those who don't like that kind of work don't last long.

Although we were not able to study in sufficient detail the total social life of corporate Colonial Williamsburg, we did make a sustained attempt at understanding what it meant to manage and be managed as a "frontline" employee on the education side of the foundation. We spent a great deal of time observing (and conversing with) the education side's costumed employees as they worked with the public and as they were trained to do this work. When we heard the costumed employees at Colonial Williamsburg described as "the front line," the term seemed entirely apt, revealing of their status and the kinds of dilemmas they faced in their work. "Front line" is a term, widespread in the corporate world, for a certain kind of work that museum employees share with workers in the service and sales industries. To us, "front line" shouts a basic truth about the way employees experience their workaday lives at Colonial Williamsburg, a corporate juggernaut in the labor-intensive leisure industry. "Front line" calls up images of war. In the service and sales industries, corporations compete with one another in an endless campaign to capture market share, to win over consumers. But consumers are not merely booty, they also can, on occasion, become the enemy if they learn to dislike the product or the producers of a particular corporation. Frontline employees at Colonial Williamsburg are such not only because they must win over the visitor, but because they must defend the foundation against its potential enemies, the visitors. To us, then, frontline employees were the foot soldiers in Colonial Williamsburg's war to get and maintain market share. Moreover, as we learned more about their work, we began to suspect that frontline workers would experience typical kinds of combat fatigue: they would grow weary of putting on a good face to the mass of visitors and they would tire of the directives of superiors—and in both cases they would be forced to conceal any emerging discomfort or hostility.

But frontline employees, to our chagrin, didn't hear the martial overtones of "front line," if they heard the term at all. To most of them, it was a dead metaphor—a term in the common lexicon of corporate-speak. Working in that world, they heard it all the time—so they didn't notice it anymore. The few who did notice it, or whose attention we called to it, found the term offensive. It implied, as one put it, that they were not individuals but numbers; they were cannon fodder.

To be cannon fodder means not only that one is under someone else's command, perhaps a commander who is capricious or incompetent, but also that one is one of many, expendable. To be a number, not an individual, is a comment on the excesses of regimentation from the perspective of an individualistic ethos. As we saw in chapter 6, corporate Colonial Williamsburg is a congeries of hierarchical bureaucratic structures, yet it erects egalitarian facades to mask those structures and ultimately tries to ameliorate, at least in its rhetoric, hierarchy and anonymity in favor of equality and individuality. Colonial Williamsburg's managers and administrators worked hard to "flatten" hierarchy and to "empower" individuals. As we shall see presently, the inevitable tensions that arise in trying to reconcile the need for organization and order coupled with the anxious desire for freedom and equality are exacerbated in work routines on the front line. This is so, first, because the frontline "product," what must be managed, is personhood itself; and second, because the anxiety-provoking encounter involves not only a manager and an employee, but also an employee and visitors—all of whom hope the encounter will enhance their sense of personal worth and individuality.

The corporate answer to the anxieties provoked by frontline work routines is a preoccupation with maintaining the appearance of what counts for middle-class Americans as interpersonal authenticity—a managed egalitarian and individuating friendliness we began early in our research to call "good vibes." For the most part, good vibes works. Most frontline employees we talked with and observed did not feel they were cannon fodder for incompetent or autocratic managers. Most of them stressed the individuating potentials of their job. And most echoed what might count as the "official" version of what this work was like—the version Mildred Arthur articulated so succinctly in "The Joy of Hostessing," an article she wrote for *Colonial Williamsburg Today* (predecessor to *Colonial Williamsburg,* the glossy quarterly sent to donors). In it, she noted that because interpreters' "backgrounds are as diverse as their personalities" and the visitors one encounters "are as individual as snowflakes, . . . no two tours are exactly alike." Extolling the pleasures of being able to work in "a beautiful costume that truly sets us apart," Arthur could modestly conclude that "sometimes I feel that I am actually walking among those staunch individualists of that exciting era when the matrices for our country were being shaped." A unique individual interpreting (almost embodying) the lives of great individualists to an audience composed of appreciative individuals—this is the way Arthur sketched the epitome of the joys of hostessing.[2]

Managers, for their part, encouraged this way of thinking. The joy of the work is to be recognized as an individual. Or, as a curator put it to a group of interpreters-in-training: "What the visitors remember most often about their visit . . . is the people like you that they encounter." They would not, he said, remember "those of us that put furniture in the rooms or make decisions— which chairs are appropriate and so forth." Visitors, he said, are impressed most by "what you say, how you say it, and how you look. . . . And it's interesting to keep that in mind, because hopefully you'll get some nice compliments." He hoped that the trainees would have a chance to read the visitors' comments, which, as we knew from our work in the foundation's archives, can come in the form of letters to the president or in visitor survey materials. "Sometimes," he added, "they'll remember your whole names, sometimes not—'she was most gracious, hospitable, we enjoyed talking to her.'"

Well-managed frontline employees receive nice compliments, sometimes in person, sometimes via their managers—and it is the latter route that is more important in the corporate culture of Colonial Williamsburg. When visitors write to the foundation, the recipients of those letters—usually the president or vice presidents (or their secretaries)—pass the compliments along to the front line. This circuitous routing allows management to reiterate the idea that success at Colonial Williamsburg is an encounter that produces a compliment whose object is a memorable, even named, individual. Ironically, the fact that compliments to employees become most significant when they are delivered to, and then through, management suggests that the value of a compliment in corporate culture is not spontaneous individual recognition but its appearance and management.

Beyond compliments, employees have their individuating value routinely confirmed in corporate rhetoric. Management tells them that "hospitality and courtesy are lasting elements of the average employee's makeup."[3] Employees ostensibly need very little direction to know what they have to do to get the right responses from their audiences. But as we have already seen, the apparently natural deployment of hospitality and courtesy, of good vibes, is enforced by the ultimate sanction at management's disposal, termination of employment. This points to the contradiction at the heart of frontline work: interpersonal authenticity is thought to be spontaneous and natural, yet it must be managed, routinized, and disciplined.

In this chapter we trace the origins and development of frontline work routines at Colonial Williamsburg. We will look at insiders' accounts of the history of interpretation at the site. We will also look at the way neophyte interpreters were trained during the period of our research. But first, we turn to two influential general statements concerning museums and the interpretation of heritage and history: *Interpreting Our Heritage,* by Freeman Tilden, and *Interpretation of Historic Sites,* by William Alderson and Shirley Payne Low. Tilden's book is the virtual bible of frontline work for Colonial Williamsburg, and other sites as well. In the training sessions we observed, trainers used the adjective "Tildenesque" and urged their charges to "remember Tilden's principles." Tilden's essay on interpretation, first published in 1957, codifies a humanistic interpretive philosophy developed at museums and national parks in the thirties and forties. Alderson and Low's book, first published in 1976, builds on Tilden's but is more concerned with rationalized management techniques. Low was supervisor of hostess training at Colonial Williamsburg from 1954 to 1972, and her published work reflects the way the foundation began to rationalize Tilden's notion of interpretation. A comparison of the two works will thus suggest how increasing professionalism has influenced interpretive philosophies at Colonial Williamsburg.

The Philosophy and Management of Interpretation

Interpreting Our Heritage is the work of a cultivated scholar capable of making his own translations from the Greek classics. Freeman Tilden writes like and quotes liberally from Emerson, and his insistence that museum interpretation direct itself to the experience and sensibilities of the ordinary person is both profoundly romantic and fervently democratic. Tilden's essay is a plea for the preservation of beauty in an ugly, "mechanized and controlled" world—for the cultivation of the spirit and the whole personality in an age of increasing specialization, fragmentation, and leisure-time boredom.[4]

The alienated, distracted, inauthentic existence of the average visitor is the starting point of Tilden's interpretive philosophy. Visitors, Tilden says, come to museums "with mere idle curiosity, or to kill time, or from boredom"; they come seeking "new experience, relaxation, adventure, imitation of friends who have told [them] 'you mustn't miss it,' . . . information, affirmation, and one thousand-odd other motives." Tilden recommends six interpretive principles through which museum educators can satisfy such visitors. Educators must train their "art" on relationships rather than facts, on the meaning of the whole rather than the enumeration of parts, on the "provocation" rather than the "instruction" of "the whole man." All six principles are implied in the first, which is the most important: "Any interpretation that does not somehow relate what is being displayed or described to something within the personality or experience of the visitor will be sterile."[5]

According to Tilden, a style of interpretation that is focused on "discrete facts" and conveyed in a "stereotyped performance," a memorized "recital," will miss the whole man and fail to connect with the visitor's personality. In such a performance, "the audience and the interpreter himself become bored and listless." The antidote is to aim one's interpretation at a meaningful whole to which the visitor can feel related. Tilden is deliberately vague about the holism required, admitting that any site or exhibition can be seen in many contexts and from many perspectives. What is crucial, however, is an interpretive plot that allows visitors to imagine themselves within it. Here Tilden echoes a theme common among museum educators, particularly those working in history museums: the multisensory engagement between object and visitor that museum exhibits make possible allows a holistic learning experience because visitors can imagine themselves in the world of the exhibition. The chance to place oneself in another world, three-dimensionally exhibited, and to try out that world, as it were, is precisely what museum learning offers that school and book learning lack. This is particularly true of outdoor museums and historic sites, where such techniques as demonstrations, visitor participation, and living-history animation can bring the past into the present and "establish a vital relationship between the visitor and the memorialized people and events."[6]

We can describe this interpretive philosophy as romantic, because the meaningfulness of the museum object is thought to depend on the visitor's experience and personality; the objective world becomes meaningful only as it is re-created in the eye of the beholder.[7] Accompanying this romanticism is an abiding concern for the democratic style of social interaction that Tilden thinks ought to obtain between interpreter and visitor. As we saw, Tilden condemns interpretation based on the memorization of unconnected facts, for such information cannot restore the alienated and distracted visitor to a condition of wholeness. But there is another problem with rote presentation:

it is an obvious admission that the relationship between interpreter and audience is an insincere or impersonal one. If the visitor is to achieve an authentic existence during his museum experience, there can be no explicit sign that the museum is an impersonal institution whose aim is to package and sell such experiences to an anonymous public of consumers. Interpretation must project itself as a personal relationship, and the parties to such a relationship must be able to feel that they "like" one another.

Thus Tilden's admonition to engage the personality of the visitor refers as much to encounters between interpreters and visitors as it does to those of visitors with exhibits. The visitor, we are told, "does not so much wish to be talked *at* as to be talked *with*. He knows, and the interpreter knows, that this is not directly possible. It cannot be a round-table conversation. Hence we have to try to achieve something of this purpose in some oblique way."[8] Consider the unintended irony of this passage. Visitors desire an egalitarian and personalized social interaction; they do not wish to be lectured in authoritarian fashion, nor to be treated as faceless consumers. Since, however, visitors are but faces in a crowd, and since a personal relationship between the interpreter and each visitor is impossible, museum personnel must work to create a facade of personalized interaction. Notwithstanding the educational aims of museums, the immediate "success" or "failure" of any interpreter-visitor interaction is almost always spoken of in terms of the interpersonal rapport that has been established or botched. Thus Tilden quotes an anonymous interpreter to emphasize that a particular demonstration is effective because it has "the effect of pulling my group closer to me all the rest of the tour."[9]

The rationalized production of such apparently spontaneous rapport is a central theme in *Interpretation of Historic Sites*. Alderson and Low adopt Tilden's romantic humanism but go beyond his work to detail the administrative procedures by which museums can achieve his interpretive goals. A well-managed historic site must have "objectives," they say—a tale to tell, a message to teach—and those objectives should be fixed from above, by the directors and managers of sites. But a tale fixed in advance and bureaucratically imposed on the employees who must tell it can too easily become the sort of routinized script that Tilden and Alderson and Low shun. Thus, much of the discussion in *Interpretation of Historic Sites* focuses on how interpreters can give the appearance of individuality while hewing to the institutionally sanctioned tale. For example, at least six among a list of thirteen "Do's and Don'ts of Interpretation" concern the creation of the appearance of personal rapport between interpreters and visitors:

2. Change your interpretation a bit each time you speak to visitors. . . .

3. If you make a mistake, say so and laugh it off. Visitors identify with the human qualities of an interpreter who is not infallible. . . .

6. Keep some information for questions, rather than immediately telling all you know. Visitors like to ask questions. . . .

7. Speak in a natural, informal way, never in singsong. Try to give the impression that you just happened to think of a particular point that visitors might enjoy hearing about. . . .

10. Remember that you are the historic site, so far as visitors are concerned—the front line. You can make or break visitors' interest in the site. . . .

The stress here is on the management of appearances. Interpreters are supposed to appear natural and spontaneous. Moreover, to do so, they are required (as another of the don'ts spells it out) to leave themselves and their "personal opinions on controversial subjects" out of their interpretations.[10] As Low put it in an earlier article, "Real professionals will leave their personal problems at home and will not parade them on the job. They will keep their personal opinions on modern controversial issues out of their contacts with the public."[11] In other words, interpreters are to avoid interactions in which spontaneous, hence unpredictable and potentially unfriendly, dialogue might develop. As rule 10 tells them, they "are the historic site," but in becoming such, they must abandon personal opinions while showing themselves to possess what the authors elsewhere call "a pleasing personality."[12]

Compared with Tilden's work, the work of Alderson and Low concerns the management rather than the philosophy of museum interpretation. The administrators of a history museum must establish the story to be disseminated by their institution, and they must ensure that their employees convey that story and not some other. But employees must also be taught to manage visitors, not simply through the use of crowd control and security measures but with interpersonal skills designed to give visitors an experience they can evaluate as being not only educational but friendly. Thus, in *Interpretation of Historic Sites,* the well-managed history museum above all manufactures the illusion of personalized experience.

Like a Hostess in the Home

Insider histories of the development of interpretation at Colonial Williamsburg reveal how deep is visitors' desire to have a personalized experience, how quickly the sheer volume of visitors made such experiences hard to generate consistently, and how early the tension between desire and actuality was resolved through increasingly rationalized forms of interpersonal management. According to oral history accounts, it was Dr. Goodwin who first thought to ask local women to serve as hostesses for the visitors coming to Colonial Williamsburg. In the early 1930s, some Williamsburgers were already hiring themselves out to tourists as guides, but their amateur services were not always well received. Accordingly, Goodwin's son, Rutherfoord, in the employ of Colonial Williamsburg, started a hostess training program late in 1933, and shortly thereafter an administrative subdivision was established to take charge of public education.[13]

We are fortunate to have some rather subtle accounts of the work of interpretation at Colonial Williamsburg during the thirties and forties. There are, first, the oral histories of two of the early hostesses, Mrs. Henderson and Mrs. Sneed, recorded in 1956. There is also the *Diary of a Williamsburg Hostess,* by Helen Campbell, which describes several months of hostessing during the Second World War. This gently satirical account, published by a major national publisher, continues to provoke an ambivalent response among Colonial Williamsburg insiders, but for our purposes it provides a useful perspective complementary to that of the more straightforward and loyal accounts of Mrs. Henderson and Mrs. Sneed.

The early hostesses, whom Mrs. Campbell called "carefully selected dowagers," were asked to greet visitors and say a few things about the buildings, "just as your wife would be a hostess in your home." Mrs. Sneed, who began work in 1938, insisted in her reminiscences on the "charm and graciousness" of the early hostesses: "They just did the job of hostessing naturally." Mrs. Henderson, who supervised and trained hostesses during parts of four decades, was more careful in her explanation of the hostess-in-the-home cliché. According to her, Dr. Goodwin "wanted each of them [hostesses] to be as gracious a hostess in the exhibition buildings 'as she would be in her own home.' But I don't think Dr. Goodwin meant that literally: He meant it literally from the standpoint of graciousness, but I'm positive he meant also as competent as an interpretive hostess. . . . If Dr. Goodwin had said to my mother, 'Mrs. Lee, I will let you teach a little history along with this,' he would never have gotten my mother for a hostess."[14]

In this retrospective account of the rationale of the early hostess program, we find a tension between domestic graciousness and professional pedagogy. Mrs. Henderson, as a manager of hostesses, expected both graciousness and the skills of a professional educator, but she knew that the Williamsburg ladies whom management wanted for the work were not accustomed to think of themselves as either workers or professionals. A senior administrator reviewing the history of hostessing at the foundation told us that "it was looked upon as a way for a genteel, somewhat impoverished, southern gentlewoman to work outside the home but in a way that . . . carried no particular stigma." Indeed, the early Colonial Williamsburg hostesses were considered, and considered themselves, to be something of an aristocracy. They undertook Dr. Goodwin's work of showing the buildings out of a sense of civic and class responsibility. They were, as the man just quoted told us, "the embodiment of a kind of social presence, a kind of social grace. . . . It was remarkable to see how they could . . . take a group in hand, through a house or a building, and embody, as it were, their concept of the gracious lady of the eighteenth century."

Priding themselves on their graciousness and on the upper-class gentility of their visitors, those early hostesses considered Colonial Williamsburg to be several cuts above more commonplace tourist attractions. Recalling her admiration for the work of her fellow hostesses, Mrs. Sneed remarked, "I felt how sweet and how charming, how different from a guide." Not only were Colonial Williamsburg hostesses not guides, their visitors were not tourists, a word tabooed on the site. Both Mrs. Sneed and Mrs. Henderson thought early visitors to Williamsburg were "people who appreciated the finer things," people "far superior to the average at Coney Island."[15]

The training of hostesses during the thirties and forties seemed appropriately informal to Mrs. Henderson and Mrs. Sneed, both of whom looked with skepticism at various postwar innovations designed to professionalize Colonial Williamsburg's interpretive program. Mrs. Henderson described the training of hostesses in the early years as an "unset, informal, but directed educational program" in which the ladies studied history in order to acquire the background necessary to show the buildings. Difficult questions posed by visitors were referred to Rutherfoord Goodwin, who responded with a memo giving the answer. "The pride in doing a job well," she related, "has made real students of most of the hostesses." Mrs. Sneed described a training routine for the late thirties identical with that described by Mrs. Campbell for the war years: initiates were "given books to read" in order to answer fifty questions given them at the outset, and asked to observe experienced hostesses.[16]

These early accounts all suggest that the authoritative presentation of historical knowledge to the public created several dilemmas for the hostesses. As we saw, Dr. Goodwin stressed a domestic rather than instructional role to the first ladies he approached. Mrs. Sneed expressed a related sensibility in her assertion that Colonial Williamsburg should be a "shrine" and not an "educational institution." "The role of the hostess," she said, "is not to be an instructor to the people but to present what she can of the importance of these buildings and let them enjoy it. I don't think we would be expected to be walking encyclopedias." Indeed, some visitors were suspicious of hostesses' claims to authoritative knowledge; Mrs. Campbell presented the following overheard remarks of visitors: "We got a lady in our town . . . says she's been here many's the time, and no two of these guides ever tell the same story twice. . . . She reckons they make it up as they go along." On the other hand, some guests complained when hostesses, mindful of the limits of historical knowledge, refused to provide authoritative information. Mrs. Sneed recalled being asked, "Do you all *know* anything? Everywhere I've gone the person who has been taking me through has said, 'we think so,' 'we suppose so.' I wonder if you *know* anything."[17]

Thus hostesses had to be able to assert their scholarly authority without overwhelming visitors with it. They were expected to study standard historical sources on their own, but to turn to Colonial Williamsburg staff members when faced with questions they could not answer themselves. Each hostess was encouraged to cultivate "some particular trend which appeals to her" and to emphasize that in her talks with visitors. Similarly, a hostess was to ascertain visitors' particular interests and "adapt . . . her conversation to include that interest." Above all, hostesses were to be "natural and informal" and to avoid "sounding like a record."[18]

Even in the early days, then, when there was a relatively informal training program, we find institutional control of the stories interpreters were to tell coupled with an explicit injunction that hostesses be natural, spontaneous, and gracious in their interactions with visitors. To work within those constraints, hostesses learned to criticize or otherwise argue with their visitors, despite the taboo against such "unfriendly" interaction, by using double-voiced or ironic responses to visitors who annoyed them. Mrs. Sneed, for example, reported that hostesses who disapproved of summer visitors' skimpy attire were "not allowed to even raise our eyebrows at them." To get round that injunction, Mrs. Sneed often told the offenders that "in the eighteenth century there were definite standards of dress and conduct and that in the twentieth century we don't seem to have those any more." But, she added, "I have to be particularly careful not to say anything personal." At the same time, hostesses had to learn to smooth over situations in which visitors took personal offense at the mention of an apparently impersonal historical fact. Thus Mrs. Campbell was surprised when her praise of the durability of eighteenth-century wallpaper offended the "wife of a wallpaper manufacturer," who asserted that "modern papers are just as permanent as anything that could have been made that long ago." Summarizing her experience of such innocent blunders, Mrs. Campbell expressed her amazement "at the number of wrong things that can be said to the wrong people."[19]

Mrs. Campbell's *Diary* suggests that in addition to the disguised (ironic) criticism of visitors in their presence, among themselves hostesses formulated "unfriendly" opinions of guests laced with feelings that ran the gamut from whimsy to disgust. Indeed, Mrs. Henderson, who found nothing of good in the *Diary* (though she claimed to "like Mrs. Campbell very much"), particularly complained that "she [Campbell] held the visitor to Williamsburg in absolute ridicule" throughout the book. Mrs. Henderson also objected to Mrs. Campbell's depiction of the staff's propensity to control hostesses with an incessant stream of memos: "Her interpretation of certain inter-office memos as directives from an umpire, unanswerable, ironclad . . . was ridiculous. . . . [W]e received . . . very few orders of any kind. From the beginning we were told to use our discretion."[20]

Unfortunately, Mrs. Henderson, who described having ridden local buses to overhear visitors' reactions to the hostesses in her charge, did not comment on the *Diary*'s most spectacular example of institutional monitoring of hostesses: management's placement of hidden microphones in the exhibition buildings to record the performance of hostesses. Mrs. Campbell recounted an immediate and decisive (the microphones were quickly removed) rebellion on the part of the hostesses, who "expressed [them]selves frankly. They have, the Senior Hostesses said, large funds of information and expressions developed by themselves through long years of individual research, study and experimentation. If these are made common property by Department recordings, all individuality will be removed from their own work. . . . Senior Hostesses have gone on record against regimentation." These hostesses, then, were satisfied with the degree of individual freedom they perceived as attaching to their positions. To oppose what they saw as management's infringement on that freedom, they appealed to the very individualism that Colonial Williamsburg demanded of their presentations to visitors.[21]

All the Charm of the Thing Is Lost

Whatever the feelings of early hostesses concerning the institution they served, changing times and Colonial Williamsburg's growing popularity soon altered the conditions of their work. The three accounts we have been examining all agree that larger crowds made hostessing more arduous and less rewarding because less individualistic. Increased crowds were in part a stimulus to, and in part a result of, the postwar bureaucratic reorganization of Colonial Williamsburg and the increasing professionalization and commercialization of historical interpretation that accompanied it.

Colonial Williamsburg staff members agreed that the arrival in 1946 of Edward Alexander, who left his position as director of the State Historical Society of Wisconsin to head the foundation's interpretive program, marked a decisive step in the evolution of their institution. Even before Alexander's arrival, administrators were starting to complain that their hostesses' presentations were "object oriented, when visitors wanted to know more about the people and the social system that had existed in Williamsburg."[22] In response to that situation, Alexander developed five interpretive priorities for Colonial Williamsburg (colonial government, colonial society, furnishings, buildings, and the restoration itself), which required an increasingly rationalized employee training program to implement. He also encouraged more systematic use of audiovisual techniques, better research, a more extensive publications program, an expanded crafts program, and the creation of new special events (such as fairs, antiques forums, and the like) to attract larger and more varied audiences.

To meet the demands of these expanded programs, Alexander established what were perceived to be higher standards for the hiring of interpretive personnel, more sophisticated training programs, and more elaborate techniques for monitoring what was said during tours. A retired administrator whom we interviewed, who had been brought to Colonial Williamsburg in 1955 to take charge of interpretive training, described some of the changes taking place at that time. "If you have five priorities of interpretation," he told us, "people have got to know what to say." He discovered that the hostesses "knew a lot about what went on in Williamsburg" without knowing the wider historical context. To remedy that deficiency, he established three historical survey courses as well as a series of short courses on narrower topics. He also introduced training in pedagogy to teach the hostesses "how learning takes place." Troubled by the problem of repetition, he worked to establish "proper connections" between the stories people heard at Colonial Williamsburg's various buildings. He taught the hostesses that the "broadened background of information" they gained in the new training courses would enable them to speak to the particular interests of each group they guided. He stressed that they consciously eschew rote repetition to avoid the singsong effect typical of other guides. At the same time, he tried to break down some of the hostesses' aristocratic pretensions, a legacy of the prewar era.

How did interpretive personnel respond to the extensive changes? Mrs. Campbell's *Diary* shows that even during the war years the work of hostessing was changing as visitor demographics changed. In the early 1940s, Colonial Williamsburg hosted thousands of armed service personnel and their families, people who differed significantly in social class from the genteel antiques collectors in whom early hostesses had taken such pride. At the outset of her venture into hostessing, Mrs. Campbell had been warned that the "exertion [of the job was] entirely too great, and [the] remuneration entirely inadequate." She knew that the job opening for which she had applied had resulted from "the desertion of trained Hostesses to the higher-paid war industries." Niggling considerations of relative remuneration must have been foreign to those early "dowager" hostesses, who found newly hired hostesses "remiss and thoughtless . . . [with] a lack of regard for the responsibilities of the Ladies who show the buildings." For their part, the newcomers were amused by the aristocratic pretensions of the senior hostesses; but when visitors complained about a hostess's "lofty manner," Colonial Williamsburg managers were distressed.[23]

The high point of Mrs. Campbell's narrative describes her physical collapse brought on by the rigors of mass tourism: "Memory of the rest of the day is of leading tottering lines of touring-service families across the Court, in the Palace door, through the hall, up the stairs, down the stairs, through the Ballroom, and thrusting them out of the Supper Room door (my mouth open and going under its own power, while my drugged brain wandered far afield with no consciousness of what I said) and then dodging back again through oncoming hordes who followed the route I had just completed, to arrive at Hostess Room barely in time to start out again."[24] Mrs. Campbell's description, however humorously phrased, is borne out in the reminiscences of Mrs. Sneed and Mrs. Henderson, which cover the postwar period through the mid-1950s. Voicing her disapproval of school groups, Mrs. Sneed remarked that "the regular people are pushed around, and all the charm of the thing is lost." Mrs. Henderson described the "daily grind" in these terms: "No time for graciousness or information. Sometime ago there were two of us only at the Wythe House, and we had over a thousand visitors. . . . Well, there's nothing . . . that two people can do in taking care of a thousand people but punch their tickets. I went away that night feeling thoroughly discouraged."[25]

Moreover, both Mrs. Sneed and Mrs. Henderson were critical of some of the new interpretive techniques and training methods brought in after the war. Mrs. Sneed complained that "today [1956] they have some idea of presenting 'concepts.' (I don't like the word even.) . . . I think that before this *we* got over the importance of Williamsburg in a more subtle way." Both women were against the "scripts" that had been written for the buildings in the early 1950s. "By scripts," Mrs. Sneed explained, "I mean you had to 'people the buildings' . . . [T]hey harped on that." But according to her, such scripts destroyed spontaneity, for only a particularly talented performer could bring a script to life "without its being obvious that you are just doing something that you have been told to do." Mrs. Henderson's argument against scripts is similar: "See that their information is correct—but let it be in their own words."[26]

In the views of Mrs. Sneed and Mrs. Henderson, then, some of the new interpretive techniques introduced after Alexander's arrival worked against a hostess's ability to "get over" the buildings in an individualized manner. Perhaps a hostess's personal style and routine seemed individualistic to her but "singsong" to her supervisors. Recall that Mrs. Campbell's co-workers wanted to protect the routines they had developed ("through long years of individual research, study and experimentation") against management's attempt to institutionalize those routines by recording them. And both Mrs. Sneed and Mrs. Henderson valued their ability to perform their routines *in such a way as to convince visitors of their spontaneity.* Thus Mrs. Sneed reported that her talks at the House of Burgesses—which she described as "about the best thing I do," thereby indicating a polished performance—prompted visitors to request a copy of the talk. To such requests Mrs. Sneed described herself as replying, "Oh no, we don't have any set speech. We just talk as we please, more or less." Similarly, Mrs. Henderson thought that "the nicest thing that anybody can say to me is, 'I know you've done this many times before, but as far as we're concerned, it might be the first.'" Thus both visitors and hostesses valued the *appearance* of spontaneous personal interaction, even though both knew that such spontaneity was performed.[27]

Professionalism and Divided Consciousness

Since the time of Campbell, Henderson, and Sneed, the trend in the museum world has been to make frontline work more explicitly professional. The process of professionalization begun at Colonial Williamsburg by Edward Alexander has continued unabated. During the time of our research, and in the period immediately preceding it (to which employees frequently referred), there were constant changes in the structure and organization of frontline work. (In 1991, one frontline interpreter told us she'd "lived through" three reorganizations in seven years.) An important effort at administrative reorganization, begun in 1983, was designed to eliminate the long-standing distinction between hostesses (those charged with showing the exhibition buildings) and escorts (those charged with leading visitors over the entire site). The two groups of workers were merged and redesignated "historical interpreters" (the prevailing term at the time of our research).* The reorganizations have explicitly attempted to give professional status to interpreters, transforming hostesses into "museum educators," as one manager put it. Moreover, that attempt seems related to the changing place of women in the labor market and changing notions of job satisfaction.

As we saw, the early hostesses claimed to be motivated by a sense of civic responsibility, with little regard for their salary. Mrs. Sneed noted that hostesses' wages (from $.30 or $.40 an hour when she began in 1938 to $1.50 an hour in 1956) were insufficient for independence. Mrs. Campbell's *Diary* suggests that by the early 1940s Colonial Williamsburg was losing some of its hostesses to higher-paying jobs elsewhere. Both Mrs. Sneed and Mrs. Campbell agreed that women were attracted to hostessing as a diversion, one made to seem glamorous by the hostesses' costumes. The position was also valued for the opportunity it afforded to meet interesting people.[28]

When they recorded their reminiscences in 1956, both Mrs. Sneed and Mrs. Henderson believed that Colonial Williamsburg was finding it more difficult to attract "the type of person that they *need* to interpret the buildings," as Mrs. Sneed put it. Similarly, Mrs. Henderson thought that younger recruits, women in their twenties, were unsuitable: "They haven't the interest in the work that the older ones do, and they haven't the experience or the poise necessary to deal with the great American public."[29] It is difficult to know if such old-guard opinions were shared by management or were simply

---

*Perpetual administrative reorganizations are remarkably difficult to track. A senior administrator sketched the changing organization of the interpretive corps since his arrival at the foundation in 1962. In the mid-1950s, he told us, hostesses and escorts had been merged into one unit, but they were separated again in the early 1960s, which made four groups of interpreters: hostesses and hosts, craftworkers, escorts, and gaolers-guardsmen ("a small cadre who did the Gaol and Magazine"). In 1973 the gaoler-guardsman position was dissolved; the Gaol was incorporated into the administrative unit responsible for the exhibition buildings, and the Magazine was assigned to the Trades Department. In 1983 hostesses and escorts were merged again, but by the time of our research they were again being separated.

expressions of intergenerational rivalry. It seems clear, however, that well into the 1960s Colonial Williamsburg still depended on upper-middle-class married women to do the hostessing. Thus a Colonial Williamsburg manager who had begun work when her husband attended the College of William and Mary during the 1960s explained to us her reasons for taking the position. It was, she said, a difficult job to get, one still considered prestigious, even though the wages were only $1.86 an hour. However, hostessing had advantages, too: the work could be part time ("casual" as opposed to "regular," in Colonial Williamsburg parlance), the costume was provided, the job was intellectually stimulating, one's co-workers had similar intellectual needs and interests, and the work involved meeting interesting people among the public.

These perceived attractions of hostessing seem not far removed from those described in Mrs. Campbell's *Diary*. Yet by the late 1970s they were, apparently, insufficient to attract qualified people to work as hostesses. In part, then, the move to transform hostesses and escorts into museum educators can be seen as an attempt to enhance the professional status of museum workers so that Colonial Williamsburg could compete in the labor market. As it was explained to us, in the 1930s hostessing was a job for unskilled but cultivated women. In the 1990s, however, more women are educated and seeking professional careers. Without professional incentives the foundation cannot attract such women, but neither can it turn to less well educated people who might work in the absence of such incentives.

The 1983 structural reorganization designed to respond to this situation involved eliminating the distinction between hostesses and escorts, replacing them with historical interpreters, and subdividing that position into four levels. Historical interpreters could advance from level one to level four by mastering the new skills (pedagogical and historiographical) required at each level. The "objective" of this system, as explained in the Department of Historical Interpretation handbook, was to provide personnel with "job security and opportunities for advancement based on performance; to recognize individual contributions; and to ensure job satisfaction."[30] One manager deeply involved in this reorganization explained that the foundation's goal had been "to define a promotional ladder that our interpreters could pursue." This was necessary, she said, to entice "good people" to remain at Colonial Williamsburg by offering better pay and greater opportunity.

By the period of our research it was clear that there had been dramatic shifts in the nature of frontline work, but it was also clear that there were enduring similarities to the earlier decades. Despite the promise of "professionalization," for example, the majority of frontline employees continued to be casual workers—ten-month employees who received no benefits and were paid about six dollars an hour. Full-time employees had access to insurance benefits, lower than market-rate home equity loans, childcare, and a retirement plan, but their hourly wages were still low. It also happened that during the period of our research, Colonial Williamsburg experienced a large decline in visitation and responded by downsizing. For frontline employees, this meant that fewer temporary employees were hired in the peak season, that people who quit were not immediately replaced, that those who remained were expected to take up the slack, and that the rungs immediately above them on the career ladder had, for the most part, been eliminated.

Not surprisingly, then, almost every employee we talked to was quick to complain about job conditions generally and about the way managers were mishandling the economic crisis. Yet, most also claimed that they liked, even loved their work. And they were eager to stick to their jobs for reasons very similar to the reasons that attracted old-style hostesses to the place. As one visitor aide, who had quit a much higher paying job in the hotels to work in the Historic Area, put it: "Something attractive about this job—it's unstructured. Basically, when we're out here . . . we are just going to sit around and gossip. We are not kept to a very strict time schedule, as far as our boss breathing down our necks." By contrast, according to her, hotel employees "aren't trusted to . . . come in and out of a door properly. They're treated like children. We're respected a lot more than hotel employees are."

Like this employee, many other frontline workers we spoke to found in the work a certain prestige, along with freedom and the opportunity to enhance their personhood, their individuality. If in the 1990s there were few if any old-style hostesses with their "lofty manners," almost all of the historical interpreters or visitor aides we encountered were eager to emphasize their professional status by identifying with either the corporation itself or with its professional intelligentsia. Rather than emphasizing the distance between themselves and their employer, the corporation, many collapsed the distance. "We're about as low on the totem pole as you can go," one visitor aide told us. "But it's the most important job here, because people that come to see the town see us first. . . . We're the PR people for Colonial Williamsburg. . . . There are days here that are as rough as being a psychiatrist, when you're trying to appease everybody and feel how they feel before they get up to you in line, knowing that you're going to reflect Williamsburg to them."

In short, the frontline employees we encountered were not concerned with losing their individuality as they worked the front lines and submitted to the discipline of good vibes. What they worried about instead was losing their professional status. Yet it was precisely this status (as a teacher who does research, for example, rather than a costume, a piece of furniture meant to enliven and entertain)—it was precisely the individuating potentials of an ostensible professional status—that frontline work seemed most to wear away. This problem was especially acute among visitor aides—costumed employees who checked tickets in front of exhibition buildings, maintained "crowd control," and on busy days circulated among the lined-up visitors, answering questions ("How long until we get into the building?") and giving impromptu history lessons ("This building dates from the early 1800s"). Visitor aides were constantly complaining to us that visitors "don't take us seriously" and "think we're playacting." Almost every day, they told us, someone encountering an aide sitting on a stool at, say, the silversmith's or the Magazine would joke that it sure would be nice to have the aide's job because it "looks like loafing." Worse, there were some who, on finding out that the visitor aide was a full-time employee and not a part-time volunteer, would exclaim, "Is that all you do for a living? . . . not a very intellectual job." What visitor aides craved were encounters with "people who will sit down and ask you intelligent questions and treat you as an intelligent person."

By and large, historical interpreters were more sanguine that visitors accepted them as intellectual authorities, although many of them were also anxious, as we noted earlier, that somewhere in the anonymous crowd lurked someone far more professional than they—a real historian with a degree, or a "magpie" with more expertise than they had on a particular topic related to their tour. They recognized that the day-to-day exigencies of the work made it all but impossible to play the role of teacher-researcher. Those at busy "stations" might see a couple thousand people; and while most of this mass would silently shuffle by, gazing right through them to the artifacts that decorated the room, dozens would inevitably ask the same silly question about the same thing.

In the Palace, for example, according to a veteran interpreter, "you've got the public in front of you asking about the venetian blinds every two seconds." Many Americans think venetian blinds are a modern invention. They don't expect to find them in a colonial-era site. So, a routine question provokes a rote response, and the effort to make each response fresh causes, as the veteran put it, "tears to run down the insides of your cheeks." Having to respond to the same question again and again is "like being confined with kids in a car and every five minutes they want to know how long it's going to take to get there." The experience can make interpreters "really antagonistic" toward visitors, even though frontline workers know that it's not the visitors' fault. The experience can also make interpreters physically ill: "When you see that many people in front of your face, moving, I've gotten . . . nauseated [by] the movement."

According to this interpreter, work in what amounted to a "touring factory" hardly allowed one to act the role of teacher-professional. Worse, management, with its eye on the bottom line, wanted to increase the deindividuating flood of visitors while bending over backward to see that no visitor to the touring factory had a bad experience. "One complaint from a visitor can cause heads to roll." For management, according to our interlocutor, interpreters working at stations were as replaceable as assembly-line workers. "It's the tissue theory of management: you dispose of one and you get another, fresh one." To stay employed, a frontline worker had to keep up the facade of friendliness while tears of frustration and hostility rolled down on the inside. The veteran interpreter asserted that one way of getting around the dilemma was to answer the question about the venetian blinds before the visitor had a chance to voice it. Thus one could reveal, at least to oneself, the hypocrisies of requiring individuating spontaneity in a touring factory that precluded it.[31]

Such analytically coherent bitterness was, however, a rarity among frontline personnel. In conversations with us, most interpreters exhibited a more contradictory divided consciousness about their work. Most recognized that their profession hardly lived up to rhetorical expectations and that the corporate structure was at least in part to blame for their predicament, yet they continued to identify with the foundation as a lofty enterprise and to get considerable job satisfaction out of doing so. They were willing, as a result, to put up with or ignore or discount quite a bit of discomfort and claim that, despite everything, they loved what they were doing.

This divided consciousness is typified in a conversation we had with a middle-aged, divorced historical interpreter who had been a teacher for sixteen years but quit because of the stress. It was, she told us, unbearable to teach "students who had to be there because the law said so." She had hoped things would be different at Colonial Williamsburg but instead had found that "most people come here to be entertained, like at Busch Gardens, not to learn." Moreover, most visitors "aren't prepared. They don't know history. They don't know why they are here."

Like many of the frontline employees we interviewed, she was quick to voice her frustrations with her work so that they might be recorded (if anonymously) in our book. She told us, for example, that one of the initial enticements of the job was the promise that she'd eventually be able to move up into a supervisory position. But she felt cheated because, after years of work, the supervisor's job had yet to materialize and she now realized that it never would. What made her angriest was that "someone with my education can be paid so little. I'm a ten-month employee and don't make enough to rent my own apartment." So she, a middle-aged divorcee, had to rent a room in the house of another woman—also divorced, also of a certain age and in straitened circumstances.

To cut through the gloom, we asked her if she was ever satisfied with her job. She responded: "Yesterday, a woman was bitching at me about the ticket price. She didn't think it was fair that she had to wait in the hot sun to get in after paying all that money. So I told her that her ticket underwrites the cost of running the museum. That satisfied her. She said, 'Oh!' and that flash of insight made me feel like I'd done something worthwhile." Then, laughing, she said that she liked the job because she enjoyed "wearing a costume." The visitors who see her in the costume respect her, she explained, because of what the costume "represents." At first we thought she meant that the costume represents a certain class in a particularly admirable era (Archer's "staunch individualists"). But she corrected us—the costume is an emblem of the foundation and its reputation for excellence: "When they see me in it, they know I work for Colonial Williamsburg."

By finding job satisfaction in defending the foundation against disgruntled visitors—by acting as a successful corporate PR agent—this interpreter was perhaps able to avoid being overwhelmed by the sad paradoxes her work entailed. She had left teaching because nobody wanted to learn and had become an interpreter at Colonial Williamsburg—where people ostensibly visited because they wanted to learn but really cared nothing about history. So her professional status as a teacher was—and she sensed this—as much an illusion as was the "lofty" status of her hostess precursors. Moreover, she was deeply dissatisfied with the way the corporate ladder really worked. Her job was a dead end. She was an ill-paid employee in the tourist industry, or, as one of her colleagues put it, "a living building"—a decorative object, a walking costume. But at least the costume she wore, she hoped, was a symbol of a great corporation, Colonial Williamsburg.

Professionalization involved another paradox, about which frontline employees were less forthcoming. Many interpreters suspected that their claim to be professional teacher-researchers was a weak one. They knew they often tended to say the same routinized things to the same uncaring audience. They knew the research they did was minimal—a handful of hours in the foundation's library on a handful of days each year. Many, in short, were willing to admit that "the only thing you have to do to work here is enjoy people and be of normal intelligence." But what the vast majority were less willing to confront was the degree to which the ability to "enjoy people," or to maintain an atmosphere of interpersonal agreeability, had become the chief preoccupation of professionalization at Colonial Williamsburg. They did not like to imagine that being friendly involved considerable discipline—that it was, in their terms, artificial rather than authentic—or that this effort, if one had to make it, was prompted by external coercion, however mild. Even when we encountered them on the job exhibiting what to us was obvious, if veiled, hostility, they denied it. Consider a conversation we had with a visitor aide—a conversation that began with an altercation.

We were about to enter the silversmith's shop to observe yet another tour, but our complimentary pass—the pass management had given us so that we might freely conduct our research—had expired. A visitor aide whose job it was to check tickets noticed the date on our pass and wouldn't let us in. After pleading with her for a few minutes in the summer sun (she admitted to knowing about us, to knowing that we had virtually free access to the place, but a rule is a rule), we gave up and asked her instead how she felt management was handling the recent decline in visitation. She noted that in these "hard times," it was mainly the costumed employees who were being fired, which made "no sense because costumed employees are our product." It didn't take much prompting to get her to denigrate management, who, she said, "had no brains." She was particularly irked by her superiors' failure to see that visitors to the site were made to pay. People strolling down the restored streets were always slipping past the often less than diligent frontline employees and getting into buildings free. Worse, "they"—that is, the powers-that-be who run the foundation—"give away thirty thousand complimentary tickets a year."*

She was also annoyed that she and other visitor aides were always having

*A few months after this encounter, the *Colonial Williamsburg News* ran a column by Steve Elliott on employees' perceptions of ticket prices and value. Elliott reported that among "a large sample of front-line personnel," one quarter said they would not "recommend to a visiting close friend that he or she buy a ticket to see Colonial Williamsburg." "We also found," he continued, "that only half of the visitors not displaying tickets are asked for them when entering facilities where tickets are needed." Elliott went on to urge employees to be "informed and enthusiastic about our products and services," citing the arguments we examined in chapter 6: "Admissions revenue is vital to each employee. . . . Ticket sales fund our paychecks" (Elliott 1992:9, 11).

to deal with disgruntled visitors who swore that "last time" or "ten years ago" they had been able to go into this or that site without a ticket or with a different ticket. So she had begun her own study in the archives of the "history of ticketing" at Colonial Williamsburg. That way, she explained, she'd have the documented facts to prove that the visitors' memories were in error. Indeed, the part of her job she enjoyed most, she told us, was turning away such visitors. Perhaps so we wouldn't feel singled out, she told us that she got particular pleasure in standing up to the wife of a top foundation executive. "She had a ticket that hadn't been validated since 1987. She argued and argued, so I finally let her in, but I told her next time I'd make no exceptions."

We thought she was getting back at her ostensible superiors by playing tough with tickets. But when we ventured that she liked turning away people such as ourselves or the executive's wife because it was her way of protesting against management's arrogance or incompetence, she claimed that her enjoyment was nothing more nor less than the pleasure of a job well done: "You can get philosophical about it. But I'm just doing it because it's my job and I'm going to do my job as best I can."

Ouch!

When we added up encounters such as these, we came to some provisional and hardly remarkable conclusions about work on the front line at Colonial Williamsburg. About the only thing an employee could be fired for was being rude to a visitor. But many employees had discovered ways to be rude, as it were, without getting caught. They could, as the visitor aide had done, obey the rules to the letter, be the perfect gatekeeper. Or they could tell jokes at a visitor's expense. Or they could do things like "answer" a question about venetian blinds before the visitor had the chance to ask it, thus revealing the absurdities of individuating spontaneity in a mass environment. But in all cases the hostility had to be covert; it was never openly admitted. And worse, perhaps, any hostility toward management, or toward the work structure itself, was deflected onto the visitors. The visitor became the scapegoat in a struggle between managers and workers. Because frontline work generated a certain tension that could not be openly expressed, the empowering and individuating promises of frontline work were (we thought) illusory.

We presented this thesis to a group of senior frontline workers—interpreters and craftspeople—at a forum titled "The Visitor's Experience in

Museums." The session had been organized by the head of interpretive training as an "elective" course for the (required) continuing education of interpreters who had completed all the basic and core courses. We asked the fifteen or so persons seated around the conference table to respond to our hypothesis, which we stated in the following terms: "When so much pressure comes down to you from management to engage in a friendly way with people, you get this reservoir of hostility which comes out the back door—does that make sense?"

We suggested that the way they habitually talked about "the visitor" was evidence of this hostility. The mass of visitors were reduced to a single being—a caricature. Rarely was the anonymous visitor described in complimentary terms. In public discourse—and by this we mean in conversations both formal and informal, during orientation and training sessions, and during backstage coffee breaks—the visitor was likely to be portrayed as a rube or a boor. For example, during the new employee orientation that we described in chapter 2, the facilitator began by asking the novice employees why people came to Colonial Williamsburg, prefacing her question with a quick and cutting sketch of visitors "from the Northeast," who "wear their purses around their shoulders" because they're abnormally mistrustful. After the neophyte employees had listed the various reasons such people might come to Colonial Williamsburg (history, recreation, and so on), she concluded that visitors don't know why they're there: "The typical visitor is clueless . . . they're clueless, clueless." The novice employees learned the same thing later in the orientation when they took their first formal tour of the reconstructed town, during which they were told, among other things, that some visitors were so "clueless" that they "thought the bird sounds were electronic."

As we were outlining our findings to the forum, one of the craftspeople interjected, "We say that they come to Williamsburg and leave their brain at home." A historical interpreter agreed provisionally with the craftsperson but wanted to emphasize that such views were unproductive: "Some individuals enjoy . . . making everybody else look stupid." She went on, "You can have this one-on-one discussion where it's an exchange of information, and you both come out looking good, or you can take the attitude that 'you're stupid, I'm smart.'" She also wanted to emphasize that derogatory comments were rarely directed at visitors in public. Rather, they served as "our pressure valve," a way of "blowing off steam" when "the door's closed and the visitors are gone and we're by ourselves." She went on to revise our hypothesis: "I think angry feelings toward the visitor is the wrong way to phrase it. I think sometimes it's frustration. . . . I don't know that I've ever really felt anger at a visitor."

We agreed that "anger" was perhaps not the right term and offered a more general one: "a range of negative feelings"—at which point another interpreter interjected, "and not on a visitor, but on how things are." This prompted the craftsman to add: "What can give you an angry feeling, when we have—like in our shop, people come in, and the kids run wild doing the things nobody would ever let their kids do. And I say [to myself], why is that dumb parent letting that kid do that? Is he from New Jersey? And so, you know, you can feel anger like that, but you never express it."

That angry and conflicted encounters are inevitable in frontline work was our point in the discussion, but it was one that most experienced frontline employees would not entertain. Instead, they either did not admit to feeling angry or believed they were, in fact, never angry—frustrated, perhaps, but never angry. Whenever we brought up evidence that contradicted their stance or tried to point out how much managerial work went into making friendliness a natural outcome of working at Colonial Williamsburg, we got the same range of responses. Interpreters would claim not to be angry. They'd note, to be sure, that others—inexperienced interpreters, or "bad" (but never named) interpreters—got angry and acted inappropriately. Those were precisely the people who didn't last long at Colonial Williamsburg. But our interlocutors always emphasized that *they* would never behave that way.

As we reiterated our hypothesis, a matronly interpreter finally exclaimed, "Aren't you implying that we're nice because we're told to be nice? What if we're just nice? I like to think I'm nice because I'm nice!" Being told by us that management was telling them to be nice against their natural inclinations prompted another interpreter to add: "I don't think we need management to keep . . . wasting paper and sending memos out: 'Hospitality and courtesy burn like a flame.' You know, and all we do is cut them up and make notes out of them. And they send lots of these little drawings out about hospitality and courtesy, and I think for the most part people already do that." Shredding memos suggests a certain awareness of, and resistance to, management's attempts to control their affect—yet these senior frontline personnel were uncomfortable with our depiction of corporate discipline. Since our argument challenged their sense of themselves as naturally "nice" persons, they heard our critique of management as an attack on them, and so rejected it. In sum, the discipline of hospitality and courtesy was barely visible as a discipline, which may explain why Colonial Williamsburg is such a pleasant place to visit.*

Frontline employees, then, did not feel they needed to be managed in order to act in a naturally friendly or hospitable manner. By the same token, managers encouraged a certain kind of behavior even as they were loathe to admit they were doing so. When, for example, at another seminar, this time with trainers of interpreters, we noted how much of training involved coaching techniques for creating the appearance of friendliness, a trainer responded, "Ouch! I thought that was where you were going." It bothered her to have "the cynicism" of their work—"that we're teaching a manipulative skill"—exposed. When we asked for clarification—"Do you think you are, or not" teaching a manipulative skill?—the trainer hedged in a revealing way: "Well I don't think so. But maybe we are. And I guess we are. And the problem then becomes—is that an ultimate put-down to both the interpreter and the visitor—by training people to manipulate them?" Ideally, friendliness emerges spontaneously out of the encounter between interpreter and visitor. From her perspective as a trainer, it was also important not to leave spontaneity to chance. But she recognized that teaching techniques to make the encounter appear naturally friendly could be perceived as teaching a manipulative skill. Such are the generic paradoxes entailed in frontline work, and to those who oversee this kind of work, such a way of thinking about it produces an embarrassed "ouch."

In talking with the interpreters about expressions of hostility, we inadvertantly allowed our larger hypothesis about frontline work at Colonial Williamsburg to be reduced to a question of whether they were free to feel and to express one extreme emotion—anger. In responding to what we felt were their overly defensive denials, we lost sight of our wider hypothesis as we tried to convince our reluctanct interlocutors that they were feeling something they believed they were not feeling. In what follows, we would like to

---

*The ironies of this invisible discipline are epitomized in a 1952 editorial we found in the *Colonial Williamsburg News* ("News and Comment," 4. 11 [March 1952]: 2). It reprinted an editorial from the newsletter of a nearby military base, encouraging service personnel to "act as gentlemen" in order to avoid "a strained public opinion." Using the words of this military editorial, the *News* addressed this admonishment to Colonial Williamsburg employees: "We must constantly strive to act as normal human beings should." That employees should have to monitor themselves to be "normal" recognizes what the naturally "nice" interpreter refused to see: good vibes is a discipline. On normality as a discipline, see Erving Goffman's brilliant *Stigma* (1963).

retrieve that wider hypothesis, which we will state here bluntly: good vibes becomes a corporate goal, and employees for the most part become willing participants in achieving it. Good vibes differs from spontaneous friendliness in that it is a managed comportment. It is acting a role. Moreover, as we shall see presently, as a self-consciously managed form of comportment, it seems to its creators and users to have practical utility because they are deeply anxious that a particular relationship—that between interpreter and visitor—is potentially fraught with conflict. It is as a program for avoiding signs of interpersonal difference—inequalities, distinctions—that good vibes becomes a management preoccupation. To the degree that frontline employees learn to embody good vibes, the end result, as we shall argue, is that it becomes highly unlikely that such employees will be a good medium through which to communicate the messages of a critical history.

Training Today

That good vibes is a poor medium for communicating the new social history is perhaps most obvious when we analyze what happens when teaching "manipulative skills" goes along with training neophyte interpreters how to talk about history. The training at Colonial Williamsburg is, like the corporation itself, a kind of hybrid. It combines the pedagogical techniques of business with those of culture—the liberal arts. In the training sessions we attended, the trainers were erstwhile interpreters who had risen to become part-time managers. Their job was herculean. They had to supply a group of relatively well educated and enthusiastic amateurs with enough knowledge of the history of Williamsburg in the colonial era, the history of the reconstruction of the site, and the nuts and bolts of crowd control so that the neophytes would be able to lead tours without supervision within four weeks in three different buildings: the Wythe House, the Peyton Randolph House, and the Brush-Everard House. Treated to lectures on the decorative arts, architecture, and slave life by professional historians and curators, supplied with a thick loose-leaf binder filled with "documents" color-coded to distinguish between administrative memos (on, say, opening and closing the buildings or how to ask questions) and historiographical materials (such as facsimiles of room inventories or excerpts from biographies), the neophytes had to decide what material was important to read and memorize and what could be skimmed and ignored. They were aided in this editing by what their trainers said to them in class. The trainees learned, for the most part, not by reading but by imitating. They watched experienced interpreters lead tours; they viewed videos in which those same interpreters portrayed varieties of effective and ineffective interpretation. The upshot was that priority in training was placed on the cultivation of a certain style, a certain appearance.

As the new interpreters mastered the material for each house, they went through a process known as "clearing"; that is, they were tested, or "cleared," by giving a tour of the house to a group of visitors while being monitored by the trainers. What they were "cleared" on was outlined in a two-page document ("Standards for Clearing") included in their loose-leaf binders. "Standards for Clearing" divided an interpreter's work into six major categories ("Communication Skills," "Leadership Skills," "Interactive Skills," "Group Control," "Mechanics," and "Clothing Standards") and dozens of subcategories, each with three spaces in front which would be checked to indicate whether the trainee had performed this segment of the work "below standard," "standard," or "above standard." The document itself was a distillation (which the trainers had achieved on their own initiative) of another, longer document called "The Effective Interpreter."[32] This latter was the provisional result of an attempt by more senior managers to come up with clearly defined standards for good interpretation. Those standards were, in turn, a condensation of the philosophy of interpretation contained in Tilden's and Alderson and Low's books, refurbished to make room for the lessons of the new social history. In keeping with newly introduced corporate culture innovations, a "task force" produced the document with the help of a professionally trained facilitator. In keeping with a corporate faith that complex activities could be defined as a finite set of "techniques," which would nevertheless have to be controlled and directed, the managers who wrote the document explicitly emphasized that frontline employees were at the bottom of a chain of responsibility, with management on top. To achieve success, the team wrote, "historical interpreters need institutional backing. . . . They need dependably authoritative research, effective on-going training, and skilled supervision. . . . They need encouragement as well as rewards—a feeling that the institution respects and supports them as the front line in carrying out its mission to the public. To achieve success, historical interpreters also need specific skills, most of which can be taught or enhanced by training. Success also requires feedback, so that interpreters know when and how they have succeeded."

"The Effective Interpreter" became the lesson plan in interpreter training sessions. It and the way it was discussed offer a window through which to glimpse the quick pedagogy of the front line, for here we can see the way printed plans and agendas can become guided verbal discussion that in turn is distilled into a visual kinesthetic. By tracing the way paper plans become pedagogic acts, we can see how the training emphasized good vibes while eliding a critical social history.[33]

"The Effective Interpreter" begins by defining "successful interpretation" in terms that dovetail with the goals of the new social history: "SUCCESSFUL HISTORICAL INTERPRETATION COMPELS VISITORS TO EXAMINE THEIR IMAGES OF THE PAST AND THEIR CURRENT ATTITUDES, VALUES, AND BELIEFS." In keeping with the constructionist viewpoint embodied in the new historiography, the emphasis is on "images," "values," and reflexive examination. When we discussed this passage with trainers, they emphasized that a chief concern was to get visitors to question stereotypes about both the past and the present. "The purpose of coming here and examining the past is to cause you to examine your life today," one of the trainers told us. "In comparing it with the past, you are challenging the belief systems today." Similarly, another trainer emphasized that the goal was "to pull" visitors "into self-learning. Pull them into experiences that are going to cause them to question . . . themselves."

These comments are exactly the kinds of glosses on Colonial Williamsburg's historiographical mission that the new social historians gave us. The past is a foreign country. You visit it and you find that certain assumptions you have made about humanity and society must be revised. In describing this work of comparing the present with the past in order to develop a critical stance toward the present, the trainers kept repeating the same constellation of words. To "examine" meant to "relate" the present to the past, and to relate or examine meant that one had to "question." To question, in turn, meant that one had to experience at least a moment of discomfort—"internal conflict"—brought about by the way the site and its interpretation "challenged" preconceptions. But as we shall see, it is precisely this kind of challenge that becomes nearly impossible to enact in an environment dedicated to good vibes.

One of the axioms of good vibes is that conflict and challenge should be minimized in favor of comfort. In the documents and in training there was a tendency to emphasize making the visitor comfortable at a variety of levels, and this had unintended pedagogic consequences. The trainers believed, following Tilden's first principle, that it would be difficult to interest visitors in learning about the past if they could not in some way interact with or identify themselves in the site and concurrently in the way the site was being interpreted. This meant, as trainers kept repeating to trainees, that visitors were to be encouraged to participate on at least two levels. Trainees were told that they had to "people" the site—to name the inhabitants of the house, using names selectively to draw in visitors: "If it's a school group, you might want to talk about the teenaged daughters." Thus, participation with the persons of the past meant, first, that trainees learned to identify them as individuals who shared easily recognizable traits of personhood with visitors.

Participation entailed not only connecting visitors to the site by emphasizing similarity rather than difference, but also getting visitors to participate in the pedagogic experience itself. Tours can easily devolve into monologues, trainers emphasized, and thus "The Effective Interpreter" stresses the participatory quality of "successful interpretation." Visitors must be encouraged to ask questions, and interpreters were encouraged to tailor what they said to the needs of particular audiences. Visitors must be engaged in the site, in the history lesson, by being engaged in the interpersonal dynamics of the tour. Thus "The Effective Interpreter" is largely a guide to personal comportment. The effective interpreter, the document teaches, "exhibits good controlled movement, . . . is a good storyteller, . . . speaks with honesty and sincerity, avoiding a condescending or phony tone, . . . is personable, and approachable . . . can respond to negative visitor responses without hostility, . . . enjoys people, shows enthusiasm, . . . keeps his or her opinions and biases out of the interpretation, . . . establishes rapport and . . . creates a sense of informality, . . . makes visitors comfortable, . . . avoids artificial questioning but stimulates thought through provocative and leading questions." In sum, the document is a congeries of lists of desirable characteristics, all of which add up to the portrait painted by Tilden, Alderson and Low, Sneed, Henderson, and Campbell.

Given the manual's emphasis on maintaining the proper communicative style, it is not surprising that a similar emphasis pervaded the training sessions—especially as the trainees viewed and discussed the all-important videotapes. In introducing the tapes, the trainers tended to put equal weight on content and form, but in the subsequent discussions "style" became the chief topic. Thus trainees were enjoined to "see if the person [the videotaped interpreter] gives a planned and structured interpretation, . . . uses the environment, the surroundings, to develop the site objectives, . . . talk[s] about all the members of the site family. . . . Is she personable and approachable?" Similarly, when the trainees were treated to a videotaped performance of an ineffective interpreter, the emphasis was on style. The interpreter in the videotape waved her arms and jerked about as she delivered a disorganized monologue in which she (as the trainer quickly pointed out) inadvertently insulted the historical inhabitants of the house as well as (potentially) the visitors. In the videotaped segment, the "bad" interpreter says (at various points): "You can see that we have a piano over here that the daughters might be playing. Some people might think that's a harpsichord but it's not! . . . Mr. Brush had a lot of the latest styles—Mr. Everard, I'm sorry. It's Mr. Everard that's the one who's living here in style. He's the one that had the finances and the success to f-fi-fill [she stutters exaggeratedly] this house with some of the newest styles . . . he's got fine wallpaper and even the latest in carpeting on the floor. This is a copy of a Wilton design. . . . Personally, I think it's very ugly. What do you think? [Several trainees laugh.] Well, they enjoyed that color scheme back then. There's no accounting for taste." The trainer (who portrayed the interpreter in the video) began the discussion by noting, "I insult a visitor when I say to someone, 'You think it's going to be a harpsicord.'" She reminded the trainees not to let their personal biases infect the interpretation and that their goal is to talk about the past and make comparisons with the present in a way that "maintains the esteem of both centuries." A trainee added: "She insulted Mr. Brush too. She said he didn't have the finances to have all these nice things," which prompted another trainee to remark about the carpets. A trainer concluded that "somebody might think it's lovely. They have it at home. Or have just come in and said, 'Oh, I love this carpet.'"

Here, personal biases as well as differences between the centuries are reduced to questions of consumer taste. But more interesting, perhaps, is what is implied by the notion of "question" itself, for when the interpreter in the video remarked that she found the carpet ugly and then asked, "Don't you agree?" the trainees laughed on cue because they had learned that the sine qua non of a successful participatory tour is the effective use of questions. Trainers spent a lot of time discussing the proper deployment of questions. For them, questions were a means to relate visitors both to the site and to the interpreter. For example, "Asking Questions," a document in the trainees' binders, teaches neophytes that "some questions encourage visitors to look around and gather information from their physical environment." This is the trainers' version of a Tildenesque technique for connecting visitors to the site. Questions also were to be used to connect visitors to interpreters. According to another training document, "Check List When Asking Questions," some of the most important reasons for asking questions are "to involve visitors," "to show interest in the visitor," and "to generate excitement."[34]

There is, of course, a danger in asking questions. The wrong question can reveal huge differences or potentially unbridgeable gaps between the interlocutors. Questions, then, not only can resolve the dilemmas of egalitarian interpersonal encounters, they can create them as well. "The Effective Interpreter" promotes "provocative" questions, but trainees were also taught that nothing in an interpreter's performance should provoke personal discomfort or disagreement. Trainers tended to resolve this potential paradox by emphasizing that questions should be used primarily for stylistic effect and to encourage an all-important sense of mutual and egalitarian involvement—that is, to erase hierarchical distinctions between a knowledgeable interpreter and ignorant visitors. Thus, a training session devoted specifically to why interpreters should use questions provoked a long discussion on "involving" visitors, on "the comfort factor," and, finally, on the importance of being able to elicit "the right answer." As one trainee put it, "If they [visitors] know the answer, it makes them feel good"—a remark that led to the following discussion:

Trainer: Alright. And I want you to keep that thought in your mind. Because there's something very important that stems from that. And that's—how do they feel [this is spoken in an emphatic whisper] if they don't know the answer? There were questions that [a staff curator] asked you today, that you didn't know the answers to. And the silence! How do you feel about that, when that happens? Or, what kind of questions can you ask?

Trainee 1: Almost with a built-in answer. Obviously. What kind of tree is that pine tree?

Trainee 2: Or with no right or wrong answer, but merely how the person feels or what their experiences are.

Trainer: Alright, now you're onto something.

Trainee 3: You don't want to ask too simple a question, because you don't want to insult them, either.

Trainer: Good for you. [She passes out "Check List When Asking Questions" and then returns to the opposite problem—that the question may be too hard and therefore embarrassing.] And that's where you get to your point, Susan, that if they don't know—What year was Jamestown founded? Who can tell me?

Trainee 3: Sixteen oh-seven.

Trainer: Sixteen oh-seven. What if you had said 1608?

Trainee 3: You'd feel embarrassed.

Trainer: You'd be wrong!

Trainee 4: Couldn't you make it a little less wrong by saying, "You're not very far wrong"? [Everybody laughs.]

Trainer: Or you can ask a question that's a little more general.

The kind of pedagogic sleight of hand exemplified in this vignette taken from a session on how to use questions effectively in interpretation is unique neither to Colonial Williamsburg nor to frontline work and training. Any teacher in America will find it familiar. You use questions to draw in your students. You make them come up with the answers you want by using subtle cues. And you stop or redirect the course of the dialogue once you've gotten what you want. In a sense, this kind of pedagogic deployment of questions is parallel, as an exercise, to the way interpreter trainees were "allowed" to discover, as if on their own and through gathering and weighing evidence, what others (curators and trainers) had already predetermined they would find in a particular furnished room (see "The Salted Mine" in chapter 4,).

Likewise, in America's wider pedagogic landscape, it is thought to be more pedagogically fruitful to respond positively or with encouragement to answers students give, rather than negatively. But to point out the similarities between training at Colonial Williamsburg and generic educational practices is not to invalidate the lessons we can draw from it. In this vignette there is an almost obsessive emphasis on "comfort." This is the pedagogic version of "the customer is always right." Questions are to be deployed not primarily to convey information, nor to get people to challenge preconceptions, but to make them feel good about themselves—and more specifically, to make them feel good about participating in the experience of learning at Colonial Williamsburg. Trainees were taught to use questions to maintain an illusion of pleasant mutuality: "If they know the answer, it makes them feel good."

That this became the primary goal of asking questions is revealed in a particularly telling way in an excerpt from a training session at the Brush-Everard House. The trainers and trainees were talking about how to use questions to convey a chief theme at the house—Everard's upward mobility. The trainer asked the trainees to give examples of questions that led from museum objects to the issue of social status. She noted that interpreters could direct the visitors' attention to objects like the piano—"something that not everybody had"—and ask them if they've seen such objects in other houses in the restored town. A trainee mentioned the wall-to-wall carpeting, at which point the trainer remarked that whatever object the visitors chose would allow the interpreter to develop the theme of class mobility: "Your question's a springboard to take you in your direction." Another trainee added, "Everybody's heard stories about a poor orphan boy who became a success. Mr. Everard's a shining example of that." This prompted the trainer to exclaim, "Good for you! That's basically a statement. But it's also a question—it's also involving the visitor. The visitor is getting into what you're talking about."

Calling a statement a question suggests the absurdities that can ensue from a discourse in which everyone must always be praised for giving a "correct" response. (This exchange also suggests that training sessions not only teach about but mimic or enact the pedagogy of museum interpretation.) At this juncture, however, a potential disruption occurred. One of the trainees wanted interpreters to call into question the assumption of class mobility itself:

> *Trainee:* That's a big American myth, you know. Course, you have Andrew Carnegie and all that stuff.
>
> *Trainer:* Sure! And it's a wonderful way—people, you'll see heads nodding all over the place with that. You'll definitely have good involvement. Watch your visitor, and grin when you see a head nod, because it's fun. You really do start feeling successful. No, that's a good question. Why were you scowling about it? [laughs]. Or you can watch your visitor scowl, too, and then you think, oh-oh, what've I got to do, I've got to turn myself around somehow.

Here, in the training session itself, a potentially productive exchange—an examination of the Horatio Alger narrative that underlies the way the Brush-Everard House is decorated and interpreted—was assimilated into a lesson on the primacy of good vibes. The trainee's "scowl"—a response to the hollowness of "a big American myth" or to the trainer's unwillingness to take up a discussion of it?—was effectively redeployed in the service of learning how to turn visitor scowls into smiles.

Complaints

After we participated in interpreter training, we gave a seminar to the trainers in which we used examples such as the ones above to suggest that the kinds of questions neophytes were learning to deploy would not be likely to "compel" visitors to "examine" their preconceptions but would simply maintain a more or less superficial interpersonal comfort. We also noted a paradox in the way questions were perceived by frontline employees. On the one hand, they tried to deploy questions to "pull in" the visitor—to personalize a generic tour. On the other hand, they found it troubling, even irritating, to be pestered with what amounted to the same questions from visitors. The discussion our observations generated revealed to us how little, ultimately, managers trusted employees to treat the visitors with the attention a well-run service industry (or an educational institution) requires.

The discussion revolved around what to do when a visitor asked (for the millionth time) about the venetian blinds. We suggested that interpreters might be able to turn a mass encounter into an individuating one, which also would fulfill their pedagogic mission (to get people to examine assumptions about the past) by responding to the question with a question—"Why do you want to know?" One of the trainers countered that answering a question with a question might be construed as "confrontational," so we suggested an alternative phrasing: "That's interesting that you ask that, but why do you ask that, because a lot of people ask that, and we're curious to find out why you want to know that?" The trainers agreed that such a gambit might work, but one was still suspicious of it: "You've got several different personalities [among the interpreters], and some tend to be more abrasive than others. . . . If they did the same thing you did . . . other people would say those exact same words, and they would be offensive. And so it's a little worrisome to teach a technique that only some people [can use successfully]. . . . Other people—if you taught that as a universal technique—it would be a problem for some people." Another trainer admitted the reasonableness of her colleague's doubts but added, "We need to provide people with a variety of different techniques that they can select according to their own personality. . . . But I agree with you that some people would not be able to do it well."

Thus, the two trainers disagreed—but not by much. Both assimilated frontline work to manageable "techniques" that ideally produce an atmosphere of pleasant interpersonal authenticity. The first, however, spoke in the voice of Fordian management. It is as if, to her, the front line is a kind of factory, and the goal is to make all the employees conform to a single manageable standard. Product quality is guaranteed by anticipating somewhat exceptional but nevertheless dangerous (one bad apple ruins the bushel) imperfections in production. One abrasive interpreter, or one who is merely going through the emotional motions, will use a perfectly good technique to produce an unpleasant ("confrontational") encounter. The second trainer, by contrast, was not wedded to a Fordian paradigm for management. She accepted frontline variety, knew that there are many standards for effective interpretation, and thought that management should make available a variety of techniques from which each employee can select those suited to his or her personality. If the first trainer worried about the odd "confrontational" encounter, the second worried about the occasional interaction that will be artificial. Both trainers wanted to minimize the risk that the encounter would be unpleasant to the visitor.

From our perspective, either approach will generate a similar emphasis on "technique," on managing appearances. To us, both reduce the visitor to an easily turned-off customer. If (as we have seen) frontline employees tended to think of the multiplicity of visitors as a single person—a rube or a boor—managers reduced this mass to the visitor who writes the angry or disappointed letter. This letter of complaint is the dark complement to the publicly extolled letter of praise we mentioned at the beginning of this chapter. It is the stick instead of the carrot. Like the letter of praise, we encountered many examples of it in Colonial Williamsburg's archives. But unlike the letter of praise, the letter of complaint was not featured in the written rhetoric of management communications to employees. In such communications, the carrot tended to predominate over the stick. Yet letters of complaint came up in conversation among employees, often as the obvious reason why, as one interpreter put it, you cannot have "free inquiry." Remarking that in academia, "you can ask probing questions that will make people uncomfortable," she went on: "You do not have that sanction in a museum that is partly here to entertain people and help people feel good and be hospitable. Because the first person that you disturb—it's like, how do you provoke people without disturbing them?"

To this interpreter, people like her—"radicals," "idealists"—quickly learned to "tone down their rhetoric" if they wished to survive on Colonial Williamsburg's front line. She learned her lesson when she took a group of local African American high school students on a tour that she tried to make provocative. She enjoined the students to notice where their parents and neighbors were working—"in landscape and . . . doing custodial work"—and then pointed out that "we have so few black people in positions of power." Her lesson caused a parent to complain bitterly to her superiors. As a result, she discovered that "you can't ask the questions that are really painful. You don't have the institutional, the structural support for that." In her view, if the customer is always right, good vibes always take precedence over good pedagogy.

Is a Critical History Possible on the Front Line?

Colonial Williamsburg's managers and many of the foundation's frontline employees disagreed strongly with our argument that interpreters were trained as much in keeping up a friendly appearance as in anything else. In our view, interpreters were free "to talk as they please, more or less," only if such talk engendered a smile and a nod from the visitor. Free to be friendly, they were also free to talk about the past as they wished, but only if their conversations did not cause or reflect hostility or anger. To do otherwise would be to climb on a soapbox and risk a reprimand, or, worse to risk frowns rather than smiles from the audience. To us, this meant that a critical history—the kind the social historians claimed they were teaching on Colonial Williamsburg's congenial streets—was a virtual impossibility.

But when we presented such a view (in seminars, in conversations, in published papers), frontline employees, their managers, and the museum's professional historians were almost unanimous—in their public statements, at least—in disagreeing with us. Responding in the *Journal of American History* to an article we had published there, the senior vice president for research went so far as to say that any book we might write on the topic "will be a work of fiction where it presumes to describe the complex process of planning and delivering educational programs" at the site. According to our critic, each interpreter "is free to be as spontaneous, creative, fresh, and original as any imaginative classroom teacher who nevertheless follows a curricular plan." He argued that interpreters are like jazz musicians who improvise on basic themes: "Over the years, not a few interpreters have become their own inspired Charlie Parkers and Dizzy Gillespies."[35]

What you have read, then, in this chapter and in the chapter before it is, according to our critic, a fiction. It is a fiction, he believes, that is based on a crude agenda—left-wing carping at the corporate hierarchy. It is given a patina of verisimilitude by the voices of disgruntled or disaffected employees ready to "whisper nonsense" into a researcher's ears—"because every large nonprofit organization employs some people who disagree with its mission or are disappointed with their own piece of the pie."[36]

Needless to say, we encountered employees who were internal critics of Colonial Williamsburg and found them more than willing to complain to us—in many cases, we imagined, because they hoped we would become their mouthpiece. We have included some of their voices in our text for two reasons. First, we wanted to remind readers that Colonial Williamsburg is not a monolithic institution—its natives do not speak as a chorus, and disagreement and critique are as much a product of the place as is a particular party line. Second, we have included those voices because we often found ourselves in sympathy with them. We found some of those internal critics to be compelling in part because what they saw dovetailed with our own sense of how the place worked.

Given what internal critics told us about their work, given what we observed in training and on tours, and given what we read in the documents the foundation routinely produces, we are not convinced by management's defense of Colonial Williamsburg. Sustained passion and critical thought are discouraged, and in their place are routines meant to mimic culturally accepted models of spontaneous intellectual exchange. Interpreters spend more time learning how to "appear" creative than learning about creativity in the historiographical process. Moreover, a certain appearance also affects historiographic content. Certain stories—those, for example, that depend on a superficial identity of affect and desire between middle-class visitors and their ostensible peers in the past—are thought to play better than others. Finally, if interpreters resist this kind of straitjacketing, they do so more by lashing out at the visitor than by reflecting—allegorically, through history— on their position in the corporation and in America. There is no consciousness raising here. Interpreters attack visitors in part because of ressentiment—visitors are at once more privileged and less deserving than they are. The lashing out is covert. In the end, then, corporately managed and disciplined frontline employees are a poor conduit for complex historiographical narratives.

8 ■ *Picket Lines*

At Issue

At the end of our first year of field research, a dramatic struggle began in the work world of Colonial Williamsburg. The foundation's subsidiary, Colonial Williamsburg Hotel Properties, Inc., and the union representing the majority of its workers, Local 32 of the Food and Beverage Workers Union (AFL-CIO), reached an impasse in negotiating a new three-year contract. In mid-December, Colonial Williamsburg asked for a federal mediator while the union voted "to levy economic sanctions against Colonial Williamsburg" by urging donors and customers to withhold their support for the foundation "until a contract is approved." On 27 December, union workers rejected management's final contract offer by a vote of 294 to 15 and the union leadership began organizing "informational picket lines."[1] The union leaders decided not to strike because they feared that in the slack tourist season after Christmas, Colonial Williamsburg could survive such an event while union workers could not. Striking employees were not eligible for government unemployment compensation, whereas employees laid off due to lack of business were. Thus, informational picketing would alert the foundation's visitors to the ongoing dispute, keeping pressure on management while safeguarding workers' incomes.

The dominant issue in the dispute, as it was presented in the local press and at union rallies we attended during January, concerned guaranteed pay raises, which the union wanted instead of the combination of the pay raises and merit bonuses offered by management. The details are summarized in the following chart:[2]

Issues	Union Sought	CW Offered
Increase in hourly wages for nontipped employees	50-cent increase in each of three years	20 cents the first year, 15 cents the second and third years
Increase for tipped employees	25-cent increase in each of three years	$150 lump sum to those with 1–6 years of service, up to $250 for 16 years
Merit pay for non-tipped employees	50-cent raise guaranteed; those who don't get merit pay can appeal via a grievance procedure	10 cents per hour the first year, 25 cents the second and third years
Bonus for perfect attendance	15-cent hourly increase all three years	5 cents per hour the first year, 10 cents the second and third years
Health premium	Employees pay 25% and get optical coverage	Employees pay 33%

The question of guaranteed raises versus merit increases was crucial for both sides. Management stressed merit pay because, they claimed, it allowed them to recognize and reward excellent work on an individual basis, thereby promoting efficiency and maintaining or increasing the quality of service Colonial Williamsburg offers its visitors. In the words of one of the foundation's vice presidents, as quoted in the newspapers: "This is not rocket science stuff. . . . The bonus is based on common things to our industry like work habits, attendance, job performance and hospitality. These are the things that make the difference between us and our competition."[3] The union, by contrast, demanded guaranteed raises for all its members, not only because they defined themselves in terms of "collective" bargaining but because merit pay was uncertain and out of employees' control. Minor Christian, the president of the local, explained during a union rally we attended in January that "workers are entitled to something, and you should not be suppressed, and you should not be talking about what you will *not* receive in the form of bonuses. You need a guarantee, my friends. You cannot go to the bank with a bonus. Because that is a promissory note that you can't cash. And what you need is to be able to determine where your lives are going for not only yourselves, but for your families."

Beyond the question of control were the dollars-and-cents issues. Colonial Williamsburg claimed that given the recession, its offer was competitive and fair; as a foundation spokesman put it, "It's as good as anybody can offer in these economic times."[4] The union countered that Colonial Williamsburg was wealthy and profitable, and that it could afford a better offer to employees who were already working for "abysmal wages." The union presented statistics to show that between 1987 and 1990, when the consumer price index increased 17 percent, the "average hourly wages for non-tipped employees increased by only 11% . . . from $5.23 . . . to $5.83 an hour." Because management had decreased the number of hours that many employees worked, however, they were actually earning less than that. Indeed, the union claimed that "employees' average income is dropping further and further below the United States poverty line." In 1987, 1988, and 1989, the union said, "the average annual income for all employees covered by the Collective Bargaining Agreement" was $10,093, $9,094, and $8,957, respectively, while the poverty line for the same years rose from $11,611 to $12,675. The situation was even worse because management denied "health care and other benefits" to employees who worked fewer than a thousand hours per year. And those with family coverage had seen their contribution to health insurance rise from $75 a month in 1987 to $107 in 1989—"a whopping $1,300 for their portion of the health insurance premiums."[5]

The labor disturbances at Colonial Williamsburg during the winter of 1990–91 were neither violent nor particularly confrontational. The union picketed and wrote letters to organizations (such as the Virginia Bar Association and the Democratic Caucus of the United States House of Representatives) that were considering Colonial Williamsburg as the site for upcoming conferences. Nonunionized workers in the hotels began a petition campaign to have the union decertified, but this effort, and the union's maneuvers, ceased at the end of April when a new contract was signed. According to a foundation spokesperson, the new contract had "the same total dollars as the one offered in December," but the increases in wages came less from merit pay and more from guaranteed raises than they had in the original offer, as the following chart shows:[6]

Issues	Rejected in December	Accepted in April
Wage increase for nontipped employees	20 cents per hour the first year, 15 cents each the second and third years	25 cents per hour the first year, 17 cents the second and third years
Wage increase for tipped employees	$150 lump sum annually to those with 1–6 years of service, up to $250 for 16 years	5 cents per hour each of 3 three years
Merit pay	10 cents per hour the first year, 25 cents the second and third years	No merit pay the first year, 25 cents the second and third years
Perfect attendance	5 cents per hour the first year, 10 cents the second and third years	Same

The newspapers reported that the union conceded they had not won much in dollars-and-cents terms but claimed an important victory in matters relating to workers' rights to union representation. The new contract allowed for a grievance procedure if merit pay should be denied "for malicious or retaliatory reasons." It also allowed the union freer reign to contact workers on the job site, both for union business and "to check on issues like worker safety." According to the president of the local, the central issue of the struggle had been management's attempt to "destroy" the union, and the new contract showed that the union had been able to withstand the assault.[7]

The Rhetoric of Conflict

At the time of the contract dispute, Local 32 of the Food and Beverage Workers Union represented between 1,100 and 1,400 workers (depending on seasonal fluctuations in the workforce). Virginia is a right-to-work state, which means, roughly put, that workers in a bargaining unit represented by a union cannot be forced to join that union. When we asked the union leadership how many of the represented workers were union members, they told us 818 out of about 1,200 employees at that time of year. The bargaining unit included all the hotels and restaurants of the foundation's subsidiary, Colonial Williamsburg Hotel Properties, Inc. (CWHPI), except one motel, the Governor's Inn, and one Historic Area restaurant, Shields Tavern.*

Attempts had been made to unionize Colonial Williamsburg's hotel and restaurant workers as early as 1974, but not until 1979 was the union—Local 23 at that time—able to win an election among workers in order to qualify to represent them. Union leaders during the conflict told us that Local 23 was not an aggressive union and that it had failed to organize the workers effectively. In March 1990, Local 32 of the same union, based in Washington and Richmond, merged with Local 23, of Norfolk and Williamsburg. By recruiting more energetically, they had managed to swell the membership roll from 200 to 800. It was this revitalized and enlarged organization, Local 32, that had become locked in a struggle with management over the terms of the next three-year contract.

Some senior managers were willing to admit that the rise of the union had been due at least in part to valid grievances on the part of workers. One of the vice presidents who told us of the sloppy personnel policies of the pre-Longsworth years explained that questions of "perceived favoritism" were linked to racial tensions: "I think there was the feeling among blacks that they were still being treated like slaves. That's why we got a union. That was their big campaign. The union came in here in seventy-eight [saying] they're still treating you like slaves. And that's a very sensitive issue, obviously, to the blacks." When the interviewer asked what happened next, the vice president responded, "They voted in a union!" He went on to explain that working conditions had in many cases been "very poor." The foundation had tried to improve those conditions, he said, but it was not always possible to achieve state-of-the-art facilities in the old buildings (in particular, he mentioned repeatedly that "break rooms" were inadequate). He admitted that if Colonial Williamsburg "really wanted to make this the best place to work"—as President Longsworth's seven-year objectives announced—"we still have a long ways to go."

---

*An organizational chart made at the beginning of 1990 showed that CWHPI consisted of the following units: the Williamsburg Inn and Sports Complex (including the Golden Horseshoe Golf Course and its restaurant, the Clubhouse Grille), the Williamsburg Lodge and Conference Center, the Governor's Inn, the Motor House and Cascades complex (a motel and associated restaurants), the four colonial taverns in the Historic Area (King's Arms, Christiana Campbell's, Josiah Chowning's, and Shields), a fast-food restaurant immediately adjacent to the Historic Area (A Good Place to Eat), the café in the Wallace Gallery, and support services, including a commissary, a laundry, hotel maintenance, reservations, sales, and administration (adapted from *Colonial Williamsburg News* 43.1 [January–February 1990]: 7).

Though this vice president acknowledged the existence of poor working conditions, when he talked about African American employees' perceptions that they were treated like slaves, it was not clear to us whether he thought the assertion might be accurate or that the union was simply exploiting such sentiments to further its cause. Union leaders were much clearer about that point. According to them, Colonial Williamsburg had long been a paternalistic (if progressive) employer to a docile local black population, and the system of labor relations that had prevailed there since the beginning of the restoration was essentially a holdover of the plantation system. One union leader told us the perhaps apocryphal story that Martin Luther King had once come to Colonial Williamsburg and left, saying he couldn't do anything with such complacent people. The union official added that he himself had never seen anything like Colonial Williamsburg: "The rest of the world happened and left this place the way it was. . . . It's worse than Biloxi, Mississippi." Another union leader told us that her aunt, who had worked in Colonial Williamsburg's laundry for many years, was "scared to death" by the union organizing of the 1970s. She had told her niece, who was engaging in union activities, "You're crazy—you don't bite the hand that feeds you." From the perspective of union officials, then, their struggle was as much about teaching CWHPI employees to stand up for their rights—and teaching management to respect those employees—as it was about wages and bonuses.

Management's lack of respect for the union was evidenced, according to union leaders, in the constant harassment of union members and activities. As they told the story, the inadequate break rooms mentioned by the vice president were a function not of aging buildings but of deliberate management actions. After the union won its election in 1979, they said, management without explanation removed televisions from employee lounges and stopped giving its annual Christmas party for hotel and restaurant workers. We heard many similar anecdotes from union officials concerning retaliation against union workers and representatives. Occasionally, frontline workers told us similar stories, such as the one about "a man who got fired for talking about the union. . . . They called it gross discourtesy to a fellow employee." But the most extensive antiunion action for which management was blamed was securing two work sites (Governor's Inn and Shields Tavern) within CWHPI as nonunion. A union official told the story this way: "They established [Shields] that way [as nonunion because] . . . they were going to use Shields to demonstrate to the employees that they did not need a union. So what they have done with Shields is, give them higher benefits than they are giving to the union employees, working in the same type of tavern." He added that management justified the nonunion status of Shields by calling it "an experimental shop" in which they could "try new things." But as he saw it, this was a ruse: "Economically, what [new things] are you trying? It's money."

During the labor dispute, the union often tried to use Colonial Williamsburg's corporate rhetoric against it to expose what they saw as the foundation's hypocrisy. For example, in a brochure entitled *Living and Working in Colonial Williamsburg: The Workers' Perspective,* the union directed the following "message" to the foundation's "Patrons and Neighbors": "The management of Colonial Williamsburg claims to 'teach what freedom, liberty and justice mean, and why we must maintain them.' Unfortunately, this philosophy does not extend to Colonial Williamsburg's employment practices. . . . Like our employer, we believe that all Americans should heed the lessons of our nation's past in order to have a better life today. For us this means having a standard of living that allows us to provide for our families. . . . Colonial Williamsburg should extend its commitment to American values to their employees and neighbors. After all, freedom, liberty and justice begin at home."[8]

Borrowing another genre of corporate discourse—the language of accounting flows and budgets—union leaders also argued that because the hotel side generated all of the corporation's profits, its employees should get a greater share of the pie. The union president explained the problem during a rally: "Fifty-five percent of the revenue that is taken in through this company comes from Hotel Properties. But yet there is a different scale of pay and . . . benefits for the employees that we represent versus the other employees. . . . [For example,] there are two groups of maintenance employees, one in Hotel Properties and the other one in the foundation. The foundation people are making four and five dollars an hour more than the employees we represent. . . . Yet the Hotel Properties areas have to *train* the people in the maintenance areas." Echoing the president's analysis, other union members complained to us that workers had to train new managers, who nonetheless were brought in over the heads of long-established workers. There was a clear implication of racial inequalities in such complaints: young, often college-educated managers, white males, came in with no practical experience to manage black workers who knew the business from the bottom up.

For their part, managers who were asked to comment on the labor dispute, either by newspaper reporters or by us, responded by sticking closely to the company line. First, they denounced the union leaders as outside agitators, troublemakers who were not members of, and did not belong in, the Colonial Williamsburg family. Second, they argued repeatedly that the union's tactics—discouraging the foundation's potential visitors and customers—were acts of self-destruction. When the union dissuaded the House Democratic Caucus from holding a conference at Colonial Williamsburg, a foundation spokesman commented: "The people who are really being hurt are the union members themselves. If there is no business, there is no work."[9] It was extremely difficult, as we will discuss in the next section, to induce managers to discuss the situation in any way that did not include the ideology of organic egalitarianism that, for them, defined the social organization of Colonial Williamsburg.

Social History on the Front Line

When the labor dispute developed, our sympathies went almost unquestioningly to the union, based on what we knew of the members' working conditions and wages. In gathering information, however, we tried to hear the arguments of both sides. This proved difficult to do. Union leaders were willing to talk to us at length about their grievances, but most of their examples were anecdotal. On the other hand, the many managers we asked about the union and the dispute would not budge from the company line. Furthermore, since many of the specific arguments revolved around financial issues, it was impossible for us, lacking detailed information that management refused to divulge, to weigh the merits of the various arguments. We were left, then, with competing rhetorics based on the opposing points of view of people whose interests clashed.

But while our sympathies were clearly with the union, we found to our surprise that such was not the case for most employees on the education side of Colonial Williamsburg. Among costumed employees—interpreters and craftspeople—there was near unanimous agreement that the union was asking for too much at the wrong time and that by driving away visitors with their picket lines it was threatening everyone's job security. Such employees tended to talk of the workers in the union as a distant "they." They had, at best, a sketchy notion of the union's demands, and a remark by an African American interpreter was emblematic of their collective attitude: "They sent us a letter explaining their demands but it was so ungrammatical it was embarrassing." Despite similarities in pay scales and benefits, the costumed employees on the education side tended to see themselves as a group apart—as "professionals," not low-level workers in a service industry. Over the years there had been attempts by labor organizers to make inroads among these workers, but always without success.

While costumed employees often expressed a certain distancing superiority to workers on the hotel side of the hybrid corporation, they also sometimes expressed resentment based on their perception of relative job security in the era of downsizing. "They see the union and say, 'Well things are bad, but at least they have jobs,'" one interpreter manager told us. "Hotels and Restaurants," after all, made money while the education side spent it—as Colonial Williamsburg's employees were constantly being told—and even as visitation declined and the stock market stagnated, the hotels and restaurants continued to show a profit. Moreover, if the Historic Area (or that part of the education side directly visible to the public) could be said to make any money at all, its income was defined in terms of ticket revenues. In the view of many costumed frontline workers, the union was making a bad situation worse. "They picket, fewer visitors come," and "we" lose more jobs.

If low-level Historic Area employees were distantly derisive about what their unionized counterparts on the hotel side were up to, managers on the education side were downright angry. It seemed sadly ironic to us that people ostensibly committed to the new social history—that is, in part to teaching about class conflict in the colonial era from the perspective of the disempowered—had no sympathy for the union's cause. One of the education-side vice presidents observed that the union, "in setting the stage for a major confrontation," was "screwing their employees." He didn't understand why the union wanted to make such an issue over merit pay—an issue "that seems so odd to the rest of us because that's what we all live under." When we asked what he thought about their point that it was impossible to get a loan for a car or a house based on a bonus, he scoffed: "Gee, I've managed to get a mortgage loan."

This particular vice president earned close to (or, it was said, above) a six-figure salary and lived with his family in one of the Historic Area's largest mansions. To us, his statement that *he* could get a mortgage loan revealed how deeply wedded he was to the egalitarianism that was central to the corporate line. Moreover, after remarking that the union's fear that merit pay was "a jerk-around favoritism thing" was "just ridiculous," he added this analysis of the roots of the union-management conflict: "And it says something about their perceptions of management. But see, unions are all about making adversaries of managers and employees. That's my view. That comes with the deal. And so that's why I think you find quickly that it kind of slides over from the union mentality into 'they're trying to bust the union.'" "They think that," but "Colonial Williamsburg is not trying to bust the union." To him, this was "paranoia" generated by the "adversarial" mindset of the unions.

Admitting that managers, too, might be somewhat paranoid and adversarial in their attitudes, he noted that "there is no question that the existence of a union has . . . made us more conscious of how we deal with our employees—to the employees' advantage." He concluded that in attacking Colonial Williamsburg in the press, however, the union leader had taken the hostility too far and had revealed a dangerous "ignorance" about the way the corporation really worked: "[The union leader's] remarks that 'Colonial Williamsburg takes better care of its horses than they do of its employees—why don't they sell some of those pastures to pay us?' Or 'Colonial Williamsburg has 62 million dollars in its retirement fund. They don't need all that money. Why don't they pay us! They're screwing us!' What that tells me is that, first of all, he doesn't understand the organization—really doesn't have a clue, or maybe doesn't care to. He doesn't understand. And that ignorance, to me, is one of the reasons that the union is bad news. From what I read in the papers, they clearly think that the hotels are what Colonial Williamsburg is about. They think that's the most important part of Colonial Williamsburg. And statements about 'let's spend the retirement fund'—[with nastiness in his voice] that's *my* retirement fund, fellah! Let's spend it on wages?"

For this vice president, the union was "bad news" because it had misread so uncharitably the corporate line. For us, the bad news was that the way the vice president talked about the union revealed the corporate line's imperviousness to the messages of the new social history. In becoming managers, in learning to speak the language of management, have the new social historians lost their ability to hear the lessons their own historiography is intended to teach? The corporate line, as we have shown, stresses that the company is made up of more or less equal individuals whose differences and disagreements can be reconciled once they learn (and they will learn) to communicate. The new social history recognizes that a society is composed of groups whose interests are, often as not, opposed, and that communication might lead only to conflict over irreconcilable differences. That a social historian turned corporate executive ended up speaking the corporate line rather than reiterating the ideology of the new social history meant that he no longer thought in its terms. "I'm no ideologue," the vice president had said at one point in our interview, claiming instead that his view of things was the balanced view of the disinterested historian looking at "the history of labor-management relations" at the institution and finding such relations by and large to be good. Managers, as a rule, had looked out for employee interests. He was a manager, a man who cared deeply about ameliorating the lives of those less fortunate than himself. That is, after all, why he had gone into museums rather than becoming a corporate lawyer. He was a "suit," and he knew that he wasn't the stock villain that union people portrayed "suits" to be. So, in a sense, he projected and enlarged his view of himself to encompass the view he promulgated of the corporation as a whole. In doing this he became a perfect spokesperson for the corporate line.

As we saw in chapter 7, frontline costumed employees have also become spokespersons for the company line. Their hostility to the union during the contract negotiations was consonant with their acceptance of the philosophy of good vibes and the view of self it entails. Despite the fact that many of those frontline employees, like their counterparts in the union, barely made a living at Colonial Williamsburg, and despite the fact that they were em-ployees who every day acted as messengers for the new social history to Colonial Williamsburg's myriad visitors, they refused or were unable to see any merit in the union's position.

A leftist might ask (and keep in mind that the new social history has a distinctly leftist tone) how those people could seem so impervious to the new social history's lessons. Why had they become perfect spokespeople for a corporate line that in fundamental ways is the antithesis of the new social history? We have noted that the employees we interviewed imagined them-selves to be very different from their counterparts in the hotels. Interpreters called themselves professionals. They likened themselves to a kind of in-house faculty. They did research; they taught. While they wore uniforms (in their case, costumes) marking them as service employees, their jobs allowed them, on occasion, to don the "suits" of the managerial class. As profes-sionals, they thought of themselves as somehow superior to the workers in hotels and restaurants. But they also seemed to think that it might be in their own self-interest to distance themselves from the workers on the hotel side. In the anxiety-provoking years of downsizing, when the bottom line had become the chief corporate preoccupation, the education-side employees, who were constantly being told that they spent the money rather than made it, realized how tenuous their jobs were. They were the company's con-sumers, not its producers; they were, they felt, the most expendable workers of all.

So, low-level employees on the education side bought, and acted in accor-dance with, the corporate line that they were economically dependent (even unproductive) professionals. To preserve what they imagined were positions of tenuous privilege, they could not condone a labor disturbance, much less participate in one. Though Colonial Williamsburg officially embraced a new social history aiming, among other things, to recover the conflicts of the past, it never intended those past conflicts to seem continuous with present-day conflicts like labor disputes. To confuse the boundaries of past and present was "anachronistic," it was a sin against mimetic realism—against Colonial Williamsburg's mission to reproduce as faithfully as possible the historical era it portrayed. It was taboo.

9 ■ *The Bottom Line*

When we began our research at Colonial Williamsburg in early 1990, the new social history appeared to be triumphant. Revisionist scholars who had come to the museum as junior administrators and researchers had become vice presidents and heads of departments. The policies they had begun to promulgate in the late 1970s to revamp the Colonial Williamsburg story were in place and being implemented. Everyone—from historians, curators, and archaeologists to business administrators and marketers to frontline interpreters—affirmed the institution's commitment to the new way of telling the American story. Yet, the more closely we examined the history Colonial Williamsburg was making, the more it seemed that the messages of social history enunciated in the social historians' planning documents and programs had not been translated into the museum's daily practices. Colonial Williamsburg was perhaps a dirtier and more democratic place than it had once been. Certainly, it enjoyed calling attention to those facets of itself in ways it had never done in the past. But despite the manure that signaled dramatic "change" in comparison with the earlier clean streets, Colonial Williamsburg, it seemed to us, was still a Republican Disneyland.

The dirtier, more democratic history means that an enlarged cast of characters and a wider range of topics are now presented to the foundation's public at Colonial Williamsburg. But our ethnography shows that those changes have not blossomed into the kind of critical history the social historians once envisioned. Rather, as we see it, new characters and topics have become vehicles for an uncritical retailing of some old American myths and dreams: the Horatio Alger story, the drama of consumer desire, the wisdom of progress, the primitiveness of the past, the universality of middle-class familial emotions. The Colonial Williamsburg we discovered in the field continued to be a place that downplayed class conflict, denigrated those who complained about their lot, and celebrated upscale consumerism, linking the latter to enduring ideas of American virtue as if prosperity were a kind of grace, a sign and reward of the virtuous. Moreover, despite the constructionist teachings of the social historians, the museum's staff members still talked as though they believed that history making is a value-free endeavor, a piecemeal and disinterested collection of "just the facts."

As we see it, the new history has not thrived in this old museum, yet no simple conspiracy theory can account for this outcome. The "good guys," the "guys in white hats," the "young Turks" (phrases the revisionists sometimes used with ironic self-mockery) have not been powerless to effect the changes they advocated. And the bad guys—however we imagine them: corporate types, right-wing donors, the ruling elite—have not been unsupportive of social history. No, the workings of hegemony, the maintenance of the status quo at Colonial Williamsburg, cannot be accounted for by a static model that aligns rulers and their interests against the ruled and theirs. We think that more powerful than "interests" have been the unexamined assumptions and entrenched cultural patterns that govern history making at Colonial Williamsburg—assumptions and patterns the revisionists either overlooked or underestimated when they designed their program. We group these into three categories: those concerning objectivity, authenticity, reality, and facts; those concerning good vibes, or pleasant interpersonal encounters in a world of anonymity; and those concerning the relationship between culture and business, between an intelligentsia and management.

Colonial Williamsburg's social historians have been clear, in their published writings, at least, that they consider history making to be an interpretive or constructionist endeavor rather than an objective one. They have argued that history is more than an accumulation of facts, because facts become meaningful only in the context of larger themes and arguments. They have argued that history museums must recognize and explicitly teach—to both their internal audiences and the visiting public—that the meaning of history derives from the stories historians choose to make the facts tell; and, more important, that because the facts can be made to tell many stories, the choices museum historians and administrators make have significant political and cultural consequences.

Yet, as we have argued in this ethnography, those messages are not the ones that predominate on the streets of Colonial Williamsburg. That venerable museum remains mired in a just-the-documented-facts rhetoric that largely negates the stated intentions of its leading historians. True, interpreters in the museum-city sometimes told visitors that history changes because the interests of today's historians are different from those entertained by historians of past generations. But that message, it seems to us, was overwhelmed by the much more frequently and routinely asserted idea that Colonial Williamsburg makes its historiographical choices based on the discovery of new facts and documents—based, that is, on an objective and disinterested search for the past "as it really was."

From our perspective, this is a pernicious confusion—one, moreover, that most museums fail to transcend. Perhaps because of their location in what Tony Bennet called "the exhibitionary complex"—cultural institutions like fairs, expositions, amusement parks, and department stores, all those museumlike sites against which the museum must define itself—museums place far too much emphasis on their possession of the "really real."[1] Museums, it is assumed, amass real things, authentic objects; and their didactic, political, and moral work, as well as their cultural prestige, stem from the display of those items. Colonial Williamsburg considers itself to be superior to Disney World and Busch Gardens because, as the interpreters will tell you, those places are not real while Colonial Williamsburg is. Colonial Williamsburg is real because its core is eighty-eight eighteenth-century buildings. It is real because those buildings have been restored, brought to life, and interpreted in terms of stories that are based on documented facts. And while critics like Ada Louise Huxtable might damn Colonial Williamsburg for adulterating its core reality, for failing to preserve and present "the real thing," both the museum and its critics share a commitment to "the real" as embodied in authentic, old objects.

By contrast, we do not think it is possible to present the past as it really was. We do not think the existence of eighty-eight "original" buildings in the environs of the Duke of Gloucester Street in Williamsburg, Virginia, is a sufficient or even necessary basis for the discovery and presentation of historical reality. There is no such thing as an original building. The buildings of Colonial Williamsburg have been restored and interpreted based on what we know now; restoring and interpreting them involve choices that are ineluctably a product of the present-day concerns of the historians and administrators who manage the site and the interpreters who staff it. Every choice made in interpreting a building—to "restore it to 1770" rather than 1760 or 1780— is a function not of some absolute reality (the building, after all, was as real in 1760 or 1780 as it was in 1770) but of an ever-changing historical sensibility that is a product *of the present, not of the past.* The buildings live on in today's reality as tourists and interpreters swarm through them and tell stories about ourselves by talking about what we imagine the past to have been. Colonial Williamsburg, like every other museum and historic site, is a present-day reality. It is not, nor can it be, the past brought to life. It is not, nor can it be, "authentic." The dream of authenticity is a present-day myth. We cannot re-create, reconstruct, or recapture the past. We can only tell stories about the past in a present-day language, based on our present-day concerns and the knowledge (built, to be sure, out of documents and evidence) we construct today.

We believe, based on their writings, that Colonial Williamsburg's historians agree with the arguments we've just made. They may be less radically constructionist than we are (and, we should add, we respect the kinds of data and evidence they relentlessly amass), but by and large historians and anthropologists know that history is made in the present in reference to the past, but that it is not, and cannot be, the past.*

Given that agreement, it is inexcusable for Colonial Williamsburg and museums like it to continue to confuse the public by claiming authority based on the institutional possession of historical reality. History is not "the real thing" but an interpretation of the past as we understand it now; history is not things, and its validity is not guaranteed by the possession of things (like

---

*It is probably the case that we, as anthropologists trained in the tradition of Boasian relativism, are more radically constructionist than the social historians who work at Colonial Williamsburg. We think that this difference stems as much from disciplinary cultures as from anything: from the anthropologist's constant awareness of how much "culture" goes into the construction of every apparently objective "fact," versus the historian's practice of trying to reconstruct past cultures by building them up from their documented remains. But this difference is not crucial: while anthropologists may be more inclined to constructionism than historians, we agree with them in valuing the empirical grounding of our disciplines; that is, we, too, have a healthy respect for the kinds of data they use, for the cultural evidence bearing on other places and times that allows them and us to know something of the people who live[d] there and then. And while many historians may be more interested than anthropologists in arranging evidence and data into stories that seem to be factual, they, too, know that cultural patterns and personal passions profoundly influence those stories.

eighty-eight original buildings). You cannot point to the past; it is not embodied in objects. "The past" exists only as we narrate it today. The past is above all the stories we tell, not objects. Objects become historical, as most interpreters at Colonial Williamsburg know from their experience leading tours, when we talk about them, when we integrate them into the stories we tell about what we conceive the past to have been. History in the museum is made only when objects are contextualized, given meaning through language. It is not, then, its collection of objects and buildings that makes Colonial Williamsburg historical; it is the narratives that surround and make use of those things. The objects may well serve as a prompt to history making, but they are not the only things that can do so. That is why we said above that objects are not a sufficient or even necessary condition of history making. We can imagine creating histories without objects, but not without language.

Mimetic realism, the reigning historiographical philosophy at Colonial Williamsburg, destroys history. To teach the public that the work of Colonial Williamsburg is to reconstruct the past as it really was erases all the interpretive work that goes into the museum's story. It erases the choices the museum makes—choices to tell one story and not another, to pursue one sort of evidence and not another, to relate the Duke of Gloucester Street to one historical context and not another—and it erases the political and cultural values that, explicitly or implicitly, underpin those choices. Mimetic realism thus deadens the historical sensibility of the public. It teaches people not to question historians' stories, not to imagine other, alternative histories, but to accept an embodied tableau as the really real.

Moreover, mimetic realism destroys the utility of history as a vehicle for social criticism. If its goal is to reproduce the past as it really was—to admire the tableau for its perfection (all the details are "correct" and in place)—how can history teach people to think critically about contrasting social worlds? To give an example: at Colonial Williamsburg, reproducing the past as it really was means, as interpreters were repeatedly told, "no anachronisms" and no "personal opinions." A particularly galling anachronism, in the view of many interpreters we heard, concerned the confusion of images of slavery drawn from the nineteenth-century Deep South and read into the scene at Colonial Williamsburg. Do not imagine, interpreters would tell their audiences, that in the Williamsburg of 1770 slaves were treated as they were in Mississippi in the 1840s. Do not imagine the cotton-picking hordes, the beatings, the rapes, the mutilations, the mutinies; imagine instead the more civilized life of urban slaves whose value to their masters ensured them a decent life ("we find that your average slave is fairly expensive, and so the cruelty we hear about is really not as prevalent here in the eighteenth century").

In this instance, the "no anachronisms" rule served to draw the critical teeth of social history. The message here was that slavery in Williamsburg was not so bad, and consequently that slaveholders and we, their national descendants, need not shoulder a moral burden in reference to it.

"No anachronisms," then, destroyed the critical potential of social history by cutting off the possibility of real conversation between the visitor and Colonial Williamsburg's interpreters. Among the crowds of mostly white American visitors were many who were eager to learn about slavery because they were curious about its relationship to current racial inequities and animosities. As we discovered, many of those visitors were more than willing to recognize that slavery was horrible and that the horrors of slavery continue to echo in deleterious ways in society today. But what did they make of the kind of slavery presented at Colonial Williamsburg—a slavery in which, by and large, masters did not beat their slaves? The "no anachronisms" rule meant that such issues remained an unspoken undercurrent. The upshot was that despite its expressed interest in having a pedagogically significant impact on the way race and racial animosities are talked about today, Colonial Williamsburg generally cut off the possibility of having such an impact.*

It is, of course, the connection to racism today that is most explicitly and consistently avoided in Colonial Williamsburg's interpretive work, and mimetic realism is the perfect tool to carry out this avoidance. After all, if one's entire energy is directed to the past as it really was, the present is erased completely, as are the relationships between past and present.

Yet, those relationships were not completely outside the awareness of people at Colonial Williamsburg. When unionized hotel and restaurant workers compared the corporation to a plantation, they were recognizing, we think the connection of past slavery and present-day social hierarchies. The comparison was explicitly drawn for us only once, by an archaeologist who worked for the foundation. He said (and here we must paraphrase him because we did not record his remarks verbatim), look at eighteenth-century

---

*While we were writing this book, Charles Longsworth (no longer president but still chair of the foundation's board) published a letter in the *Washington Post* in which he argued that "the history of slavery is everyone's history, not just that of the enslaved. A sense of the significance of that history is vital to our dealing with one of the central issues of American life: racism" (Longsworth 1994). Here is another piece of evidence suggesting that Colonial Williamsburg's leadership is committed to a critical history that they have not been able consistently to deliver on the museum-city's streets.

Colonial Williamsburg, half black, half white, with the blacks in menial, subservient positions and the whites in control. It's just like Colonial Williamsburg today!

From our perspective, a statement such as that represents useful social history. The work of social history should be to connect the structural conditions (expropriated labor and social hierarchies) and cultural patterns (deep-seated racism) of the past to those of the present. But the "no anachronisms" rule and, more generally, the dream of mimetic realism make it impossible for the museum to accomplish that work. If the goal is to dwell on the past as it really was, there is little room for a critical comparative gaze that transcends the details of one moment and forces speculation on broader social concerns. Colonial Williamsburg and places like it create tableaux and then try to seduce their publics into admiring their handiwork. Here is the past the way it really was, the museum says, and you can trust our re-creation of it because we are disinterestedly devoted to documented facts. We do not stand on soapboxes and preach to you—indeed, expressing a personal opinion is a cardinal sin of interpretation. Rather, we simply present the past as it was and encourage you to make up your own mind about it.

To which we respond: that is escapism, not history.

Good vibes, too, is a form of escapism—for at least two reasons. First, it allows administrators and managers to avoid making hard pedagogical choices in favor of a consumer preference populism. Second, it explicitly limits or excludes what is most pedagogically productive in critical history— that which provokes discomfort, disquiet, and critical "questioning." Good vibes, as we saw it in practice, dovetailed with a certain kind of participatory pedagogy that became popular in museums in the 1950s and 1960s. At face value, the intention of this pedagogy was the opposite of escapism. Its goal was to reach out and involve an often reluctant or skittish audience. But the Tildenesque emphasis on attention to the visitor as a person has been taken too far, we think. Tilden wanted to make museum history relevant to museum-goers by relating it, always, "to something within the personality or experience of the visitor." This is a pedagogic technique that is not without merit, as any teacher knows. Yet it cannot become—as it has, we believe, in too many of the lessons offered the public at Colonial Williamsburg—the dominant message. When questions are designed first of all to make visitors feel good or to trick them into thinking they've made a contribution to the educational process, when stories are constructed to make visitors recognize themselves in the past or, contrarily, to laugh at the past from the presumed superiority of the present—when, in short, involving and gratifying the visitor becomes the dominating motive of history teaching, the educational payoff of such teaching is profoundly compromised. It is time, we think, for Colonial Williamsburg to rethink its reading of Tilden's interpretive method. In their attention to "the personality or experience of the visitor," Colonial Williamsburg's history teachers have lost sight of the more important object: the historical story the museum works to tell.

Participatory pedagogy at Colonial Williamsburg makes it unlikely that a critical history will be the institution's product because it boils down to catering to the most easily satisfiable desires of its visitors as if they were middle- or low-brow customers. As a general rule, employees and administrators see nothing wrong with this. For them (and for visitors as well), good vibes is often conceived as "old-fashioned" quality and service; that is, as an escape from a present in which such amenities no longer exist and as a frank throwback to a simpler, more neighborly and trusting era. But good vibes strikes us as escapist in a more profound sense because, as we see it, the premium it puts on the interpersonal pleasantness of the educational encounter at Colonial Williamsburg makes it difficult for the museum to tell critical stories.

That is an argument most of our interlocutors at Colonial Williamsburg consistently rejected. They said that attention to hospitality and courtesy did not interfere with the front line's ability to deliver good history to the public. As we saw in chapter 4, people also argued that if the "documented facts" for critical or unpleasant stories were available, frontline personnel would tell those stories—indeed, would feel obligated to tell them. We, by contrast, argue that the training routines so emphasized good vibes that the educational content of Colonial Williamsburg's frontline history was often overwhelmed or reduced to trivialities and platitudes.

Moreover, even when they agreed with us that performative form might affect pedagogic content, Colonial Williamsburg insiders saw this as a necessary concession to consumer preference. The argument here was that the museum's visitors expect to be treated in a friendly way—that hospitality and courtesy are selling points of the place—and that any deviation from the good-vibes script would run the risk of alienating consumers. Here we also disagree with our interlocutors, but we admit that the ethnographic evidence is equivocal. The scattered evidence available to us—from our sampling of visitors' reactions, from visitors' letters to Colonial Williamsburg, and from the results of the museum's own audience and marketing research—suggests that visitors are indeed concerned about hospitality and courtesy. Their letters are full of praise for gracious employees and complaints about rude ones. But whether visitors place greater emphasis on hospitality and courtesy than on history, whether some of them feel that entertainment or hospitality and courtesy get in the way of education, whether Colonial Williamsburg could still find close to a million eagerly paying visitors a year if its frontline employees were on occasion rude, cutting, condescending, and confrontational but always scrupulously committed to maintaining an educational edge— those are questions the available data cannot answer.

Nor did it seem to us that those were questions Colonial Williamsburg was interested in posing, either to itself or to its visitors. It is, after all, Colonial Williamsburg that consistently (one might even say obsessively) markets itself as a place where one will experience a uniquely gratifying hospitality and courtesy. It consistently associates history with light or pleasant thrills— with eating in a colonial atmosphere, with comedy, with the upscale life. Colonial Williamsburg thus does more than merely respond to a public; in a sense, it creates that public and defines its expectations.

This brings us, finally, to the role that critical intellectuals can play within hybrid institutions such as Colonial Williamsburg. A puzzle that has faced us throughout this study is the power (or powerlessness) of the social historians who are ostensibly in charge of history making at the museum. Why, we have asked repeatedly, has the critical agenda of those historians been blunted as their messages and arguments have passed from their programmatic writings to the public presentations on the front line?

The simplest answer to that question is that the foundation's critical historians have much less power to effect historiographical policy than they often claim to have. Market concerns did indeed dominate pedagogy in insidious if obvious ways, yet this "fact" was systematically obscured by the production of convenient propaganda. The problem with such a simple answer is that it is hard to show ethnographically. This is because the natives (especially the professional historians) were always telling us not only that they were in charge, but that they were "free" to tell any historical story they wished. They consistently emphasized that they were under no constraints (except the minor, if inevitable, constraint of a budget). As Cary Carson put it in a published response to our work: "In all my seventeen years with the foundation . . . not once have I been told to change my tune or downplay this or that kind of history because somebody upstairs thought it might displease the ticket buyers."[2]

How is one to evaluate such claims? Are they wishful thinking, a pleasant fiction? What does the anthropologist do when his or her sense of the truth diverges so dramatically from that of the natives? Our provisional solution has been to treat the historians' claims as yet more examples of the way impression management dominates public discourse at Colonial Williamsburg. And once in a while, one of these people would give us a glimpse of a kind of consciousness that contradicted or at least called into question such glossy and glib assertions of power and freedom.

Thus, early on, one of the more radical of the social historians wanted to dissuade us from portraying the place as "monolithic"—it was not, as its critics always seemed to complain, a corporate tool. And even though plenty of corporate types worked there, he had always been able, he told us, to do work of which he was proud. During his career he had helped to plan, with the encouragement of the foundation's trustees, the construction of the Anderson Forge, the Carter's Grove slave quarter, and the Public Hospital—three monuments to the new social history that are now an important and enduring part of Colonial Williamsburg's built environment. He was particularly proud of the Public Hospital—it was America's first government-funded institution dedicated to caring for the mentally ill—because it was the last great public edifice to be reconstructed at Williamsburg and because its reconstruction, during the middle of the Reagan years, could be seen as a direct refutation of the reigning ideology of that administration. In an era when governments were cutting back drastically on aid to the mentally ill, the reconstructed hospital was intended to convey to Colonial Williamsburg's visitors that American governments had always provided a safety net for such people. The Public Hospital spoke of the social responsibility the fortunate owed to the less fortunate, the very people whose lives had been shattered by the machinery of progress. To our interlocutor, the fact that Colonial Williamsburg had gone ahead with the Public Hospital during the apogee of New Right Reaganism was proof of the foundation's essential freedom.

Yet, in another conversation about the hospital, he allowed that its reconstruction had been "a sting"—a subversive con job in which a rich right-wing patron who believed that he was buying one edifice had been tricked into paying for another. Initially, the patron had agreed to finance a new visitor center designed around a large auditorium in which would be shown in perpetuity a film that had become a pre-Vietnam-era time capsule, *The Story of a Patriot*. When top management decided that such a facility was not necessary, the patron was convinced to put up funds for a decorative arts gallery to be named in his honor.[3] According to our interlocutor, he and a few other

The Public Hospital. (photo by Molly Handler)

subversives were able to appropriate a fraction of the total gift and divert it to a socially ameliorative project that flew in the face of the conservative ideology the patron normally espoused. The Public Hospital had thus been built, but only as an above-ground facade for a larger, far more expensive below-ground museum full of fancy objects which, since the coming of the new social history, had been deemed too inauthentic for display in exhibition buildings but too valuable to store or deaccession.[4]

This tale of a sting in which the Public Hospital was coupled with a fancy gallery suggests that this social historian may sometimes recognize that he is more marginal than his optimistic rhetoric admits. If the hospital serves as a venue to teach the public about some of the least fortunate members of eighteenth-century society, the gallery continues the foundation's tradition of celebrating the cultural wealth and taste of that society's elite. Social history occupies Colonial Williamsburg's reconstructed landscape only in a delicate compromise with richer, more powerful historiographical traditions.

On another occasion, this historian averred that such older traditions were perhaps overpowering, especially as they were conveyed in media outside the direct control of educators such as himself. But he prefaced his complaints about what "business" did to social history by telling us, "Don't quote me by name, but I feel like a character in a Václav Havel play." He didn't want us to quote his bitter words about Colonial Williamsburg catering to the country club set by building yet another golf course to satisfy the businessman-visitor. Nor did he want us to attribute to him the remark that he hated what had happened to *Colonial Williamsburg*—the foundation's journal—which, he felt, had become a slick vehicle for selling expensive real estate, the kind of planned, exclusivist, nostalgic communities that cater to and are built on everything the new social history is against.

Needless to say, his criticisms were hardly surprising to us. Nor did they seem particularly damning, either to him or to the foundation. So what intrigued us was the way he framed them—"Don't quote me, . . . but I feel like a character in a Václav Havel play"—as if Colonial Williamsburg, shrine to American freedom, was really a totalitarian state and he a secretly reluctant citizen of that state.

To us, his comment speaks to the kind of abdication of responsibility that is characteristic of the intelligentsia at Colonial Williamsburg and elsewhere in American society, including its universities.* Characters in Havel plays are intellectuals who are beneficiaries of a totalitarian system they spend a great deal of time apologizing for. In totalitarian regimes, intellectuals make a comfortable living and are able to enjoy considerable personal satisfaction as long as they create useful propaganda for the party. The upshot is that if you tell white lies all the time or keep your criticisms to yourself, the whole creaky machine will appear to run as if it were a smooth and efficient apparatus. In this scheme, the totalitarian system survives because the people who might be its most powerful critics lie or keep strategically silent in order to protect themselves or the system's reputation.

So, when our interlocutor wanted to criticize Colonial Williamsburg but didn't want to be quoted by name, while simultaneously explaining that he

*Having spoken in chapter 1 about "vexing assessments of relative scholarly prestige" that mark relations between the intelligentsia in museums and universities, it seems appropriate to point out that it would be easy to make the kind of criticism of university professors that we here level at scholars and administrators working in museums. University professors are "free" to promulgate in the classroom stinging critiques of class inequalities in American life even as they ignore, for example, the relationship between the institutional resources devoted to their own salaries and those devoted to the wages of the largely invisible (to them) custodial and maintenance workers who clean up after them. Or it could be argued that they are free to be critical as long as they continue to credential the sons and daughters of the middle classes, thereby fitting them for work in a corporate world where the critical lessons they may have learned in college will not be of much use to them.

felt like a character in a Havel play, he was, of course, acting the role of the co-opted intellectual. To be quoted by name is to go on the record, to create a public document for which you bear responsibility. To decline to be quoted is to abdicate responsibility.

Worse than remaining silent, however, is to talk the party line. To us, one of the unfortunate implications of the foundation's hybridity was that the social historians, as they moved up the corporate ladder, spent as much time producing what amounted to advertising copy for the institution as they did making, much less examining, historiographical policy. This meant that those historians became adept at telling their various audiences what they wanted to hear, and less concerned with intellectual consistency.

This may have meant that the constructionist and critical strains of the new social historians were nothing more than a conversational ploy, a language they had learned to speak to one audience—their academic peers—while they reserved the language of celebratory history and mimetic realism for other audiences—the donors and visitors. When frontline interpreters occasionally remarked to us that the new social history programs were "political," they did not mean that the historians who designed those programs were "political," they did not mean that the historians who designed those programs were committed to or promoting an ideological agenda. Rather, they meant that Colonial Williamsburg was catering to funding agencies. Politics, the kind of politics their superiors practiced, was just another marketing ploy.

In any case, most of the more radical discourse of the historians was not spoken directly to the front line. Our impression was that the foundation's historians had relatively little contact with its frontline messengers. This was also the impression of frontline employees, who rarely complained of intervention but often made bemused comments about the chief educators' absence.

At the hybrid corporation, chief educator-researchers are also managers and administrators, but they are reluctant, we would argue, to wrestle with the implications of this in any sustained way. Instead, they want to be authoritative without appearing authoritarian. Thus they give interpreters little direct guidance. Indeed, they seem to fear being too closely associated with the front line. Rather than spend more time teaching the front line or in conversation with them, they tend to complain about frontline employees' shortcomings from the safe distance of cultural superiority. It was our impression that the social historians pretty much took it for granted that frontline employees are not good vehicles for the new social history. They blamed this on their politics. They conjured up a plausible image of the "hostess" with "lofty" manners, or at least lofty pretensions. She is of a certain age, of a certain class (if in straitened circumstances), and she votes Republican.

But as we have seen, there is something specific to the site and the work routines associated with it that makes such lofty pretensions appealing to the front line. Reduced to mere costumes in a consumerist passion play, frontline employees tend to select costumes and personae that enhance their prestige and personal value. In a place that is a virtual showcase for fine distinctions of status, it is compelling to play up those distinctions.[5] While a select few seem to enjoy playing the more colorful riffraff out of a Hogarth print, most want to look like masters and mistresses or to meld their identities among the majority of the middling sort. In dressing up, as it were, for the job, most find it easier to talk from the perspective of masters than from that of slaves. When an interpreter talks to a visitor, it is always "we" who have our tea or sherry here in the well-appointed parlor while a distant "they" work out back. Nobody wants to play a slave.[6]

That frontline employees are free to promulgate the visions of the past they feel are most accurate and pedagogically useful, in an institution where their ostensible superiors have become otiose authorities, reflects in a negative way the "freedom" paradigm. If Colonial Williamsburg is a shrine to freedom, then the dark shadow is the shadow of a totalitarian system, albeit one that works in relatively benign ways. There are no firing squads here. No Siberias. You can get away with almost anything as long as the visitor is happy. Frontline employees are not, as a rule, good vehicles for a critical history—especially a history critical of social class and hierarchy—because their chief managers fail to come to grips with the class implications of the way they deal (or don't deal) with them as employees.

Can Colonial Williamsburg teach history rather than escapism? Yes. We offer the following suggestions as to how this might be accomplished. First, the intelligentsia at Colonial Williamsburg need to be more responsible for the museum's historiographical end-product. Currently, it is too easy for them to distance themselves from what is produced on Colonial Williamsburg's streets while at the same time they pay lip service to a commitment to a more constructionist and critical historiography. Professional historians at Colonial Williamsburg make grand policy statements about pedagogical goals but spend very little time in educational conversations with the front line. The frontline employees are left pretty much to their own devices, and the intelligentsia distance themselves from what the front line says by pointing to their lack of sophistication, or, worse, their retrograde political beliefs.

The intelligentsia can thus claim that they are giving the front line freedom to produce a kind of populist history and thereby fulfilling the promise of a truly democratic public history. But in doing this, they ignore ample evidence indicating that frontline interpreters are, by and large, not the free creative agents the rhetoric depicts.

If the social historians want to be true to their own historiography, they should bridge the distance between themselves and the front line by recognizing rather than ignoring the powerful effects of Colonial Williamsburg's corporate hierarchy. At present, hierarchy at the foundation conforms more to the model of a service industry than a university, despite the pervasive rhetoric. Frontline employees are not "teacher-researchers," as they like to claim, and as their superiors continue to let them believe. On the front line, people advance not because they do interesting research or because they teach, but because they are given the opportunity to direct their peers' interpersonal behavior. If the intelligentsia played a more direct role in frontline education, recognizing, for example, that frontline employees are as much a worthy audience as a pedagogical conduit, they might correlate advancement among frontline personnel to scholarly and pedagogical skills rather than to skills associated with managing people. In such a system there would not be the "career ladder" that now exists (which is in any case a poor substitute for decent pay and job security). Lead interpreters, trainers, and the like would be largely unnecessary; their pedagogic functions could be divided (in rotation) among the employees at each site.

Management functions on the front line would, in this new system, be minimal because Colonial Williamsburg could safely spend no time or resources managing interpersonal behavior. Trusting that any employee would know how to be civil to visitors, management would let their frontline employees manage themselves. In a serious educational institution, it should not be the frontline employees' collective responsibility to capture and hold market share. An interpreter's job should not be endangered if a disgruntled visitor has left the place never to return because the interpreter did something wrong.

Those who make policy at Colonial Williamsburg are constantly emphasizing that they do not want the place to be merely a showcase for old (if beautiful) objects. Nor do they want the place to be simply a re-creation of the past. Rather, they want Colonial Williamsburg to act as a particularly congenial site for informed reflection, argument, and discussion about what it means, today, to be an American, given our history. Colonial Williamsburg, they reiterate, should act like a "community of memory"—a phrase we borrow from sociologist Robert Bellah and his associates that succinctly summarizes a host of phrases repeated by policy makers at this particular site. For Bellah, a community of memory means that a people agree that they do, indeed, share some kind of cultural heritage, and they talk about that heritage in ways that celebrate what is good or beautiful in it but criticize what is not.[7] We argue that for Colonial Williamsburg to serve as a site for such a community of memory, it must become more open and honest with itself about its own internal conflicts and differences; it should make simultaneously a special effort to empower the least enfranchised; and its leaders should worry less about imagined threats to its institutional integrity—it must stop, in short, trying to manage perceptions of itself as it manages the past.

Notes

1 The New History in an Old Museum

1 On making the past "dirtier" at Colonial Williamsburg, see Gable and Handler 1993a; for the trend in American history museums generally, see Schlereth 1978, 1980, 1984.

2 An important programmatic statement of social historians' aims in museums is that of Cary Carson (1981), who during the period of our research was Colonial Williamsburg's vice president for research. See also Bordewich 1988; Colonial Williamsburg Foundation (CWF) 1985; and Olmert 1985 for Colonial Williamsburg; and Carson 1996; Chappell 1989; Krugler 1991; Rath et al. 1991; and Upton 1988 for the general trend.

3 For an example of the advocated shift in epistemological emphasis, see Mayo 1992; see also Krugler 1991.

4 Among the best analyses of the relationship between the interests of the founders of museums and the ideological tendencies those institutions represent are DiMaggio 1982; Harris 1990; Keuren 1984; Sherman 1989; Wallace 1986a, 1986b, 1987; and Zolberg 1981, 1984. On the question of cultural institutions and hegemony more generally, see Lears 1985; and Levine 1988.

5 On the distinction between education and entertainment, see Greenhalgh 1989; Hinsley 1991; Kelly 1994; Price and Price 1994a; and Rydell 1984; on education and entertainment at Walt Disney World, see Fjellman 1992:35–63.

6 The version of this Associated Press article that we saw was printed in the *Roanoke Times & World-News* (Severson 1994).

7 Among the works we have found most useful are Ames 1986; Bal and Bryson 1991;

Bennett 1995; Benson et al. 1986; Blatti 1987; Bourdieu and Darbel 1966; Cantwell 1993; Clifford 1988; Duncan and Wallach 1978; Fane et al. 1991; Fisher 1991; Handsman and Leone 1989; Haraway 1985; Karp et al. 1992; Karp and Lavine 1991; Leon and Rosenzweig 1989; Lumley 1988; Pearce 1990, 1994; Sherman and Rogoff 1994; Stocking 1985; and Vergo 1989.

8 Many of the essays collected in Sherman and Rogoff 1994; Karp et al. 1992; and Karp and Lavine 1991 address these questions about messages, ideologies, and interpretations; see, especially, Baxendall 1991; and Perin 1992. For related studies by anthropologists bearing on other media, see Lutz and Collins 1993; and O'Barr 1994.

9 On museum audience research, see Alexander 1979:165–72; and Munley 1986, 1987; further references may be found in Screven 1979, 1984; and Zyskowski 1983.

10 There are exceptions to this pattern, particularly in the work of scholars whose orientation is historical: Harris 1990; Sherman 1989; and Zolberg 1974. The writings of anthropologists Edward Bruner (1993, 1994), Corinne Kratz and Ivan Karp (1993), and Richard and Sally Price (1994a, 1994b) are closest to our approach in terms of their ethnographic orientation.

11 On the complexities of constructing a public, or an audience, see Bennett 1995; Brunt 1992; Duncan 1991; and Sherman and Rogoff 1994:xii–xvi; on the problem of "the public" more generally, see Robbins 1993.

12 Hudson 1987:147.

13 These figures and descriptions are taken from a press kit pamphlet entitled *Colonial Williamsburg Facts & Figures*, dated May 1989.

14 *Colonial Williamsburg Facts & Figures.*

15 CWF 1952:5.

16 "Colonial Williamsburg Now 60 Years Old: Chronology 1926–1986," *Colonial Williamsburg News* 39.11 (November 1986).

17 "Getting to Know Our Visitors," *Colonial Williamsburg News* 43.4 (August–September 1990): 6.

18 Visitor and Group Demographic Survey, 1985, and Mail-back Survey, 1990, Colonial Williamsburg Foundation Archives. These archival sources suggest that the foundation's survey data are more complicated than their public presentation indicates. In particular, the data are smoothed out in predictable ways, depending on the audience. For example, to say that most visitors travel in pairs or with children enhances the image of family visitors, but a more detailed presentation of the data, as in the 1985 survey, shows that couples with children are a distinct minority (18 percent) of the total.

19 Lawson's results are presented in her doctoral dissertation (Lawson 1995).

20 See, especially, Ettema 1987; Fjellman 1992:35–57; Greenblatt 1991:50–52; Greenhalgh 1989; Handler, forthcoming; Harris 1990; Higonnet 1994; Sherman 1989; and Wallis 1994. On the commercialization of the past more generally, see C. Campbell 1987; Lowenthal 1985; and Williams 1982.

21 Schneider 1968:112; for an insider's critique of our prejudices, see Carson 1994a.

22 Clifford 1988:32–34.

23 Gallaher 1961:260, fn. 8; see also Gallaher's introductory chapter for a discussion of the suspicions that anthropological studies in small communities can generate. Gallaher's predecessor was Carl Withers; his book was published under the pseudonym James West (West 1945).

2   Imag[in]ing Colonial Williamsburg

1   Henry 1963:21–25.

2   On the hierarchical relations between business and culture in museums, see Sherman 1989:192–238. For the larger theoretical framework, see Bourdieu 1993.

3   Kopper 1986:149; also Gonzales 1991:25–29. Upton (1988:413–14) reminds us that "nearly every historic district and museum" has its myth of "the visionary local"—"the founder who persevered against all odds." Upton notes also that "Williamsburg publicists flogged it [the Goodwin story] tirelessly."

4   Kopper 1986:148–66.

5   Hall 1992:258.

6   Kopper 1986:154–55; Hall 1992:264.

7   Harr and Johnson 1991:5–6; Hall 1992:259–64.

8   Hall 1992:263.

9   Kopper 1986:164; also Gonzales 1991:29–30. For a similar tale of stealth in the acquisition of the properties that would become Walt Disney World, see Fjellman 1992:111–22.

10 "Williamsburg Restoration," Report of the Meeting of the Advisory Committee of Architects Invited to Williamsburg to Confer upon the Various Policies Touching the Restoration, 25–26 November 1928, 7, Colonial Williamsburg Foundation Archives.

11 Kopper 1986:154–69; the quoted material is from p. 164.

12 Hall 1992:259; Kopper 1986:166.

13 Kopper 1986:169.

14 Foster 1993:179–87; compare Kopper's more benign account (1986:164).

15 Kopper 1986:181.

16 Hall 1992:270, 276.

17 "The Reminiscences of Mrs. George P. Coleman," 1956, 6–7, 62, 52, Colonial Williamsburg Foundation Archives; Rockefeller is quoted in Wallace 1986a:147; Kopper 1986:228. Charles Longsworth, president of the foundation during the period of our research, tells the story of the erroneously sited building as an example of Rockefeller's "devotion to excellence" (Longsworth 1987:3).

18 "Reminiscences of Mrs. Coleman," 46–47.

19 Minutes of the meeting held 7 September 1937, Craft Advisory Committee, Product Management Department, Colonial Williamsburg Foundation.

20 Minutes of meetings held 12 January 1938 and 10 February 1938, Craft Advisory Committee.

21 Hosmer 1981:57; also, Kopper 1986:201; and, for the marketing of colonial revival styles throughout the United States from the time of the 1876 Philadelphia Exposition to the first decades of Colonial Williamsburg, see Marling 1988.

22 Kopper 1986:204, 208.

23 Report of the meeting held 25–26 November 1928, 4, Advisory Committee of Architects. A year earlier, in a letter to Colonel Arthur Woods, who was to become the first president of the restoration, Rockefeller asserted that "the project, after it has been completed from a physical point of view, will need an endowment of a million dollars or more, in order to maintain [it]" (quoted in Gonzales 1991:29).

24 Harr and Johnson 1988:487–88.

25 Colonial Williamsburg Foundation, *1989 Annual Report,* inside front cover.

26 Colonial Williamsburg Foundation, *1989 Annual Report,* inside front cover.

27 Kopper 1986:222–23.

28 Kopper 1986:216.

29 CWF 1970:1.

30 Ford's Colony publicity packet, 1992, in the files of the authors.

31 *Colonial Williamsburg* 14.4 (Summer 1992): 3.

32 Bush 1992:83, 85.

33 Bush 1992:85; on the problem of visitors' attachment to inauthentic Christmas exhibits, see Ronsheim 1981.

34 Ford's Colony publicity packet, 1992, in the files of the authors.

35 Portions of this section appear in somewhat different form in Gable and Handler 1996.

36 Bush 1992:85.

37 Huxtable 1992:24–25; see also Huxtable 1963.

38 Wallace 1986a:148–49; see also Leone 1981; Van West and Hoffschwelle 1984; and Wells 1993.

39 For example, Wallace 1987; and Fjellman 1992.

40 Visitor letter of 2 February 1987, and reply of President Longsworth, 3 March, Colonial Williamsburg Criticisms, D–K, Colonial Williamsburg Foundation Archives.

41 "Promotion—Survey," memorandum from Thomas McCaskey to Edward P. Alexander, 17 September 1968, General Correspondence Records, Colonial Williamsburg Foundation Archives.

42 Our sense of Colonial Williamsburg's endless attempts to maintain and refurbish its image brings to mind the work of anthropologist Dan Rose on what he called the "elite discourse of the market": "The utterances that feed into the exchange possibilities of the market are a pragmatic rhetoric where statements are relentlessly made . . . of steps to go through again and again . . . that is, imaginative, practical talk about assembling some sort of mundane project no matter how minute or extensive" (Rose 1991a:111; see also Rose 1991b).

3 Why History Changes, or, Two Theories of History Making

1 Rhys Isaac's *Transformation of Virginia, 1740–1790* (1982) epitomizes social historians' concern for the analysis of social distinctions in colonial Virginia; with respect to social distinctions expressed in colonial architecture and material culture, see Carson 1978; Chappell 1981; Quimby 1978; Upton 1988:433–47; and Upton and Vlach 1986.

2 The story is told in Kopper 1986:201–3; see also Hosmer 1981:534–36.

3 Carson 1991:89, 92; Chappell 1989:248; Carson's essay was reprinted as a "book excerpt" in the glossy quarterly that Colonial Williamsburg sends its donors, *Colonial Williamsburg* 14 (Spring 1992).

4 CWF 1985:1.

5 The quotations are from the unattributed preface to *The Restoration of Colonial Williamsburg in Virginia* (*Architectural Record* 78.6 [1935]: 357).

6 Kimball 1935:359.

7 Perry 1935:363; on the conflation of history and good taste, see Kulik 1989:12–17.

8 W. D. Rockefeller 1968:51; Perry 1935:363.

9 "Colonial Williamsburg 1936–1945," *Colonial Williamsburg News* 28.9 (18 February 1976).

10   CWF 1977:iv.

11   "President's Statement Re: Public Relations Program," *Colonial Williamsburg News* 1.5 (October 1948): 2.

12   CWF 1951:10–12; see also Van West and Hoffschwelle 1984:160–69; Hosmer 1981:60–65; Wallace 1986a:151–53; Kopper 1986:187–215; and CWF 1977:1–6.

13   "Prelude Will Feature Special Exhibition in Court House of 1770," *Colonial Williamsburg News* 4.12 (April 1952):1; "Williamsburg Declaration Is Signed by Exiled Leaders," *Colonial Williamsburg News* 5.2 (June 1952): 1; "Declaration of Rights Exhibit to Be Held Over," *Colonial Williamsburg News* 5.3 (July 1952): 3; "Rights Exhibit Due to Close on Sept. 2," *Colonial Williamsburg News* 5.4 (August 1952): 1; see also Van West and Hoffschwelle 1984:167–68; and Kopper 1986:204–16.

14   "Winter Promotion Plans," *Colonial Williamsburg News* 1.7 (December 1948): 6–7; also, Hosmer 1981:65.

15   "Student Burgesses Will Meet Here Feb. 12–16," *Colonial Williamsburg News* 19.4 (2 February 1966): 1–2; "International Assembly to Bring 56 Foreign Students Together Here June 9–12," *Colonial Williamsburg News* 21.19 (29 April 1968): 1; "Buckley to Be Keynote Speaker for Assembly," *Colonial Williamsburg News* 22.17 (30 May 1969): 1.

16   "Letter from Viet Nam," *Colonial Williamsburg News* 21.8 (21 November 1967): 2; "The Present, Also, Learns from the Past," *Colonial Williamsburg News* 22.16 (30 April 1969): 1.

17   One vice president told us that Humelsine "had a nice, clever practice—what Carl would do with the annual report was commission people inside to put together a long essay of some kind." The 1958 report focused on "archaeology, furnishings and research" (11). The 1959 report was the first to have an illustrated cover; previous reports had only the corporate logo and the words "Colonial Williamsburg, Report by the President for the Year 19XX" against a dignified—blue, gray, or brown—monochromatic background. In 1959, the annual report focused on architecture; in 1960, on archaeology; in 1961, on Market Square and the Palace green; in 1962, on taverns of eighteenth-century Williamsburg; and the report for 1963 was a photographic essay entitled "Light and Shadow," presenting Williamsburg as "an aesthetic experience" (4).

18   J. D. Rockefeller 1937:401.

19   "a unique and irresistible appeal": President's Report, 1964, pp. 2–3; "Serenity and Growth," President's Report, 1966, p. 17; "NBC 'Today' Show Devotes Entire April 22nd Program to Restored City," *Colonial Williamsburg News* 19.18 (19 April 1966): 1. Predating Rockefeller's 1937 statement, the notion of Williamsburg's multiple appeals was written into the restoration's first guidebook by its author, Rutherfoord Goodwin: "In its Composition the Restoration has many Phases and Spheres which offer many Interests and Appeals" (CWF 1935:148).

20   CWF 1977:iv.

21   Carson 1981:25.

22   Bordewich 1988:31.

23   CWF 1977:6.

24   CWF 1977:9–10.

25   CWF 1977:13.

26   CWF 1977:11.

27   CWF 1977:11–12.

28   CWF 1977:12–13.

29   CWF 1977:12–13.

30   CWF 1977:13–14.

31   There is an enormous literature on objectivity in history and social science; two works that we have found particularly helpful are Novick 1987 and Megill 1994. There is also a large literature on authenticity, beginning with Walter Benjamin's "The Work of Art in the Age of Mechanical Reproduction" (1969:217–51); see also Bruner 1994; Cameron and Gatewood 1994; Gable and Handler 1996; Handler 1986; Handler and Saxton 1988; Orvell 1989; Price and Price 1995; and S. Price 1989. On simulations, see Baudrillard 1983, 1988; Eco 1986; and MacCannell 1976.

32   We heard the metaphor of filling in the gaps frequently; Hosmer (1981:51) noted its use from the first days of the restoration.

33   Perry 1935:363; on the attention to detail of the early architectural historians, see Upton 1988:416–22.

34   CWF 1952:12–13.

35   Carson 1979:2.

36   Report of the meeting of 9 April 1935, Advisory Committee of Architects, Colonial Williamsburg Foundation Archives.

37   Hosmer 1981:48; Smith 1982:9; Kopper 1986:187.

38   "Lookin' 'Round," *Colonial Williamsburg News* 19.17 (29 March 1966): 3; for additional examples, see "Magazine to Inaugurate Many Activities in June," *Colonial Williamsburg News* 15.12 (May 1962): 1; "Poll Shows 99.6% Approval of New Scenes along Duke of Gloucester," *Colonial Williamsburg News* 16.6 (17 October 1962): 3; "Oxen Reappearing on Duke of Gloucester, Haul Wood to Shops and Buildings," *Colonial Williamsburg News* 16.23 (August 1963): 1, 4; " 'Life-on-the-Scenes' Addition Keeps Crows Out—Visitors' Cameras Busy," *Colonial Williamsburg News* 17.5 (15 October 1963): 4; "Nine Sheep Graze in Historic Area as Life-on-the-Scenes Program Grows," *Colonial Williamsburg News* 20.1 (21 June 1966): 1; "More on the Scene," *Colonial Williamsburg News* 20.16 (4 April 1967): 4; "Straw Bee Hives Adding New Dimension to Life-on-the-Scenes," *Colonial Williamsburg News* 21.4 (7 September 1967): 1.

39   Letter from James Warnke, 3 September 1981, and response from Peter A. G. Brown, 11 September 1981, Letters of Commendation, Colonial Williamsburg Foundation Archives.

40   On living history, see Anderson 1984, 1985; for a critique of living history, see Handler 1987.

41   *Visitor's Companion,* 10–16 December 1990, 8.

42   Carson 1979:2.

43   "Report by the President for the Year 1954," 10.

44   Perry 1935:363; Shurtleff 1939. Upton (1988:430) noted that "recent research" has "restored some of the elaboration of the Colonial Revival view, at least for the largest houses, and recent garden historians have depicted eighteenth-century garden design in terms closer to Arthur Shurcliff's than many would have accepted a few years ago."

4   Just the Facts

1   Lawson 1995:6–15.

2   Kopper 1986:240.

3 This section appears in slightly different form in Gable and Handler 1994:128–30.
4 We are indebted to Janice Knight for this interpretation of the use of the word "interpretation" in these titles.
5 Parker Potter and Mark Leone have made a similar argument concerning the objectivism of history museums: "Outdoor history museums are filled with unverifiable assumptions, things that can never be learned from the historical record, but which must be accounted for in some way. All these 'answers' to questions never asked make places such as Williamsburg *seem* very real" (Potter and Leone 1992:478–79).
6 Brodie 1972:49–57, 97–100; 1974:92, 389–92.
7 The relationship between evidence and the presentation of African American history at the Wythe House is discussed in Gable et al. 1992:798; participants in the workshop had read our article and drew on it in the discussion described above.
8 I. Brown 1981:298; Blackburn 1975:133.
9 I. Brown 1981:304.

5 Social History on the Ground

1 *Visitor's Companion,* 10–16 December 1990, 2.
2 This point is elaborated in Gable et al. 1992.
3 CWF 1985:28.
4 CWF 1985:28.
5 CWF 1985:6.
6 CWF 1985:4.
7 CWF 1985:8–14; for a sophisticated version of the argument, see Breen 1994.
8 CWF 1985:10; in a comprehensive and brilliant essay, Cary Carson argued the importance of consumerism for identity formation in the emergent world of modernity: "In a world in motion, migrants and travelers needed a standardized system of social communications. They required a set of conventions they could carry with them that signified anywhere they went the status they enjoyed at home. . . . Standardized architectural spaces equipped with fashionable furnishings became universally recognized settings for social performances that were governed by internationally accepted rules of etiquette" (Carson 1994b:523–24).
9 CWF 1985:12–13.
10 *Visitor's Companion,* 10–16 December 1990, 1.
11 The quoted phrase was taken from President John F. Kennedy by Colonial Williamsburg president Charles Longsworth (Longsworth 1980:1).
12 Wells 1993:100.
13 Carson 1994a:149–50, quoting Gable and Handler 1993b:27–28, and 1994:131. Wells's critique of Carson and his colleagues is much like ours: "In order to prevail [over the] wealthy and conservative donors" who have so much influence at places like Colonial Williamsburg, "social historians eventually traded the radical edge of their ideas for statements that cast their goals as soothingly universal." Wells mentioned in particular Carson's "suave definition" of social history as the history of all groups in society—a definition that allows museums to present society as a "harmonious enterprise" rather than a conflictual process (Wells 1993:92).

6   The Company Line: Aspects of Corporate Culture at Colonial Williamsburg

1   C. L. Brown 1987:6.

2   Elliott 1990:11.

3   Rose 1991a:120.

4   The figures for 1934 and 1936 are from Kopper 1986:204; the other data are from the Colonial Williamsburg annual reports (1953:23; 1957:21; 1961:34; 1973:4; 1988: 23). Since the streets of Williamsburg are public property, anyone may walk there; thus there is a distinction between visitors and paying visitors, although the annual reports do not always give statistics for both categories. Colonial Williamsburg instituted a new ticketing policy in 1973 to induce more visitors to buy tickets; see the annual reports of 1971, 1972, and 1973 for a discussion of the policy and the financial problems it was meant to address. Finally, the 1990s witnessed a significant decline in paid admissions, which fell to a low of 909,000 in 1993 (*1994 Annual Report*, 20).

5   *Colonial Williamsburg News* 1.8 (January 1949): 1, and 4.7 (27 November 1951): 6; annual reports (1960:51; 1973:16). At the beginning of our research, in early 1990, people said there were four thousand employees at the foundation; by 1992, downsizing had brought the number back toward thirty-five hundred. Precise figures are hard to establish because there are so many part-time and seasonal workers.

6   All figures are from the annual reports; methods of reporting income (and expenses) in relation to organizational structure (that is, income and expenses attributed to educational activities versus those attributed to the hotels and restaurants) change over time. In general, the annual reports distinguish revenues, expenses, and income from the foundation's endowment (this last often making up the shortfall between the first and second).

7   Chorley is quoted in "Addition and Growth of Departments Has Paralleled CW Physical Restoration," *Colonial Williamsburg News* 4.7 (27 November 1951): 6.

8   "Bowl also Marks Anniversary," *Colonial Williamsburg News* 36.1 (January 1983): 1–3.

9   The term "homogeneous, empty time" is taken from B. Anderson 1991:22–36. Our favorite analysis of Western conceptions of time remains that of Whorf in "The Relation of Habitual Thought and Behavior to Language" (1939, reprinted in Whorf 1956:134–59); the quoted phrase is from p. 140. See also Thompson 1967.

10 These examples are drawn from a Special Silver Bowl Edition of the *Colonial Williamsburg News* 45.1 (Winter 1992): 2, insert.

11 Longsworth 1981:5.

12 Taken from a pamphlet dated December 1989, entitled *Colonial Williamsburg Seven-Year Objectives, 1989–1995*.

13 See, for examples, the following articles in the *Colonial Williamsburg News*: "News and Comment" (editorial), 4.11 (March 1952): 2; "News and Comment" (editorial), 12.10 (March 1959): 2; and "Salesmen Needed" (editorial), 13.2 (July 1959): 2.

14 Longsworth 1991a, 1991b.

15 Kotter 1988, 1990; Peters 1982, 1985; for "the customer is always right" at Colonial Williamsburg during the 1950s, see the references in note 13 in this chapter.

16 One of the most eloquent analyses of this tendency of Americans to blame themselves for their position in the class hierarchy is Richard Sennett and Jonathan Cobb's *Hidden Injuries of Class* (1972).

17 For a classic debate in the sociological literature on functionalist theories of stratification

and challenges to them, see Davis and Moore 1945; Tumin 1953. For another example of the uses of egalitarian ideologies in hierarchical organizations, see Newman 1980.

18 Quoted in *Report of the Colonial Williamsburg Foundation for 1978* (published as a special edition of *Colonial Williamsburg Today,* undated [1979?]), 4.

19 All quotations are from the inside front cover of the *1987 Annual Report.*

20 All quotations are from the inside front cover of the *1987 Annual Report.*

21 Longsworth 1987:2–3; the quotation about tobacco culture is from Breen 1985. The stock stories concern the restoration of the Wren Building, the discovery of the crucial visual evidence (known in foundation lore as the Bodleian Plate, after the Bodleian Library at Oxford, where it was located) used in reconstructing the Capitol and the Governor's Palace, and Rockefeller's willingness to redo restoration work in the face of new evidence; see Kopper 1986:184–87; and p. 34 in this volume.

22 Longsworth 1987:3–4.

23 Saylor 1990a:2–3.

24 It is worth noting that before the Civil Rights movement, such recreational events were segregated; see "Picnic," *Colonial Williamsburg News* 1.1 (July 1948): 1, which mentions two annual picnics, one for white employees and the other for colored employees. See also "CWers Participate in Plans for Recreation Center and Fund Drive," *Colonial Williamsburg News* 16.17 (15 April 1963): 1, 4.

25 Longsworth 1990:6.

26 Certeau 1984.

7 The Front Line: Smile Free or Die

1 Longsworth 1982:2.

2 Arthur 1982:3–5, 8.

3 *1987 Annual Report,* 10.

4 Tilden 1977:109, 99, 104.

5 Tilden 1977:91, 45, 9.

6 Tilden 1977:41, 89, 68.

7 For this definition of romanticism, see Bayley 1982.

8 Tilden 1977:12.

9 Tilden 1977:72.

10 Alderson and Low 1985:69–70.

11 Low 1965:235.

12 Alderson and Low 1985:118.

13 "The Reminiscences of Elizabeth Lee Henderson," 9–11, Oral History Collection, Colonial Williamsburg Foundation Archives; Hosmer 1981:46; Smith 1982:10.

14 H. J. Campbell 1946:23; "The Reminiscences of Mrs. Albert M. Sneed," 18, Oral History Collection, Colonial Williamsburg Foundation Archives; "Reminiscences of Elizabeth Henderson," 18–19.

15 "Reminiscences of Mrs. Sneed," 20, 26; "Reminiscences of Elizabeth Henderson," 24; H. J. Campbell 1946:3–4, 12, 25, 42.

16 "Reminiscences of Elizabeth Henderson," 17–18, 20, 24; "Reminiscences of Mrs. Sneed," 17; H. J. Campbell 1946:5; see also Smith 1982:12.

17 "Reminiscences of Mrs. Sneed," 35–36; H. J. Campbell 1946:105.

18 H. J. Campbell 1946:6; "Reminiscences of Elizabeth Henderson," 11.

19 "Reminiscences of Mrs. Sneed," 29; H. J. Campbell 1946:52.

20 "Reminiscences of Elizabeth Henderson," 62–63.

21 "Reminiscences of Elizabeth Henderson," 38; H. J. Campbell 1946:75–77.

22 Hosmer 1981:62.

23 H. J. Campbell 1946:29, 7, 23, 25, 136–37.

24 H. J. Campbell 1946:108.

25 "Reminiscences of Mrs. Sneed," 33; "Reminiscences of Elizabeth Henderson," 35.

26 "Reminiscences of Mrs. Sneed," 50–51; "Reminiscences of Elizabeth Henderson," 25–26.

27 H. J. Campbell 1946:77; "Reminiscences of Mrs. Sneed," 60; "Reminiscences of Elizabeth Henderson," 43.

28 "Reminiscences of Mrs. Sneed," 39–40; H. J. Campbell 1946:4–8.

29 "Reminiscences of Mrs. Sneed," 38–39; "Reminiscences of Elizabeth Henderson," 35–36.

30 *Policies and Procedures Handbook,* Department of Historical Interpretation, Colonial Williamsburg Foundation, July 1987, sec. I.02.

31 For discussions, based on ethnographic observations, of the problem of repetitive questions at folklore demonstrations, see Price and Price 1994a:48, 100; and Bauman et al. 1992:47.

32 "Standards for Clearing," Department of Interpretive Education, Colonial Williamsburg Foundation, June 1990; "The Effective Interpreter," Department of Interpretive Education, Colonial Williamsburg Foundation, 20 April 1990.

33 On the uses of documents in training, see Gable and Handler 1994.

34 "Asking Questions," Department of Interpretive Education, Colonial Williamsburg Foundation, March 1990; "Check List When Asking Questions," Department of Interpretive Education, Colonial Williamsburg Foundation, May 1990.

35 Carson 1994a:141, 145.

36 Carson 1994a:150.

8 Picket Lines

1 "CW Union Seeks Sanctions," *Virginia Gazette* (Williamsburg), 12 December 1990; "Union Opts to Picket CW, Not Strike—Yet," *Virginia Gazette,* 29 December 1990.

2 Adapted from "Union Has More Demands," *Virginia Gazette,* 29 December 1990.

3 "Merit Pay at Issue," *Virginia Gazette,* 12 December 1990.

4 "Unionized CW Employees Reject Offer," *Daily Press,* 28 December 1990.

5 The quotations are from *Living and Working in Colonial Williamsburg: The Workers' Perspective,* an undated pamphlet issued during the dispute by the local; the pamphlet cites Colonial Williamsburg payroll records as the source of many of the statistics in it.

6 "A New Day for CW," *Virginia Gazette,* 24 April 1991.

7 "A New Day for CW," *Virginia Gazette,* 24 April 1991.

8 See *Living and Working in Colonial Williamsburg;* the pamphlet does not list the source of the internal quotation in this passage.

9 "Democrats' Williamsburg Conference in Jeopardy," *Daily Press,* 5 January 1991.

9   The Bottom Line

1   Bennett 1995:59–88.
2   Carson 1994a:149–50.
3   This part of the story is celebrated in Kopper 1986:238–52.
4   For an excellent discussion of the political implications of the coupling of the hospital and the decorative arts gallery, see Leone 1994.
5   For a semiotic analysis of what he called the "reproduction of social distinction" at Colonial Williamsburg, see Parmentier 1994:136–42.
6   On the psychological and interpersonal ramifications of acting the role of a slave, see Lawson 1995, chap. 4.
7   Bellah et al. 1985.

Works Cited

Alderson, William T., and Shirley Payne Low. 1985. *Interpretation of Historic Sites.* Nashville: American Association for State and Local History.

Alexander, Edward P. 1979. *Museums in Motion: An Introduction to the History and Function of Museums.* Nashville: American Association for State and Local History.

Ames, Michael. 1986. *Museums, the Public and Anthropology.* Vancouver: University of British Columbia Press.

Anderson, Benedict. 1991. *Imagined Communities: Reflections on the Origin and Spread of Nationalism.* Rev. ed. London: Verso.

Anderson, Jay. 1984. *Time Machines: The World of Living History.* Nashville: American Association for State and Local History.

———. 1985. *The Living History Source Book.* Nashville: American Association for State and Local History.

Arthur, Mildred. 1982. "The Joy of Hostessing." *Colonial Williamsburg Today* 5.1: 3–8.

Bal, Mieke, and Norman Bryson. 1991. "Semiotics and Art History." *Art Bulletin* 73.2: 174–208.

Baudrillard, Jean. 1983. *Simulations.* New York: Semiotext(e).

———. 1988. *America.* London: Verso.

Bauman, Richard, Patricia Sawin, and Inta Gale Carpenter. 1992. *Reflections on the Folklife Festival: An Ethnography of Participant Experience.* Bloomington, Ind.: Special Publications of the Folklore Institute.

Baxendall, Michael. 1991. "Exhibiting Intention: Some Preconditions of the Visual Display of

Culturally Purposeful Objects." In *Exhibiting Cultures: The Poetics and Politics of Museum Displays,* ed. Ivan Karp and Steven D. Lavine, 33–41. Washington, D.C.: Smithsonian Institution Press.

Bayley, John. 1982. "Romanticism and the Status of the Object." *Studies in Romanticism* 21: 554–55.

Bellah, Robert, Richard Madsen, William M. Sullivan, Ann Swidler, and Steven M. Tipton. 1985. *Habits of the Heart: Individualism and Commitment in American Life.* Berkeley: University of California Press.

Benjamin, Walter. 1969. *Illuminations: Essays and Reflections.* Trans. Harry Zohn. New York: Schocken Books.

Bennett, Tony. 1995. *The Birth of the Museum.* New York: Routledge.

Benson, Susan Porter, Stephen Brier, and Roy Rosenzweig, eds. 1986. *Presenting the Past: Essays on History and the Public.* Philadelphia: Temple University Press.

Blackburn, Joyce. 1975. *George Wythe of Williamsburg.* New York: Harper & Row.

Blatti, Jo, ed. 1987. *Past Meets Present: Essays about Historic Interpretation and Public Audiences.* Washington, D.C.: Smithsonian Institution Press.

Bordewich, Fergus M. 1988. "Revising Colonial America." *Atlantic* (December): 26–32.

Bourdieu, Pierre. 1993. *The Field of Cultural Production.* New York: Columbia University Press.

Bourdieu, Pierre, and Alain Darbel. 1966. *L'Amour de l'art: les musees et leur public.* Paris: Editions de Minuit. English translation: *The Love of Art: European Art Museums and Their Public.* Stanford: Stanford University Press, 1990.

Breen, T. H. 1985. *Tobacco Culture: The Mentality of the Great Tidewater Planters on the Eve of Revolution.* Princeton: Princeton University Press.

——. 1994. " 'Baubles of Britain': The American and Consumer Revolutions of the Eighteenth Century." In *Of Consuming Interests: The Style of Life in the Eighteenth Century,* ed. Cary Carson, Ronald Hoffman, and Peter J. Albert, 444–82. Charlottesville: University Press of Virginia.

Brodie, Fawn. 1972. "The Great Jefferson Taboo." *American Heritage* (July): 49–57, 97–100.

——. 1974. *Thomas Jefferson, an Intimate Biography.* New York: Norton.

Brown, Charles L. 1987. "Message from the Chairman." *Colonial Williamsburg Foundation 1987 Annual Report,* 6–7. Williamsburg, Va.: Colonial Williamsburg Foundation.

Brown, Imogene. 1981. *American Aristides: A Biography of George Wythe.* Rutherford, N.J.: Fairleigh-Dickinson University Press.

Bruner, Edward M. 1993. "Lincoln's New Salem as a Contested Site." *Museum Anthropology* 17.3: 14–25.

——. 1994. "Abraham Lincoln as Authentic Reproduction: A Critique of Postmodernism." *American Anthropologist* 96.2: 397–415.

Brunt, Rosalind. 1992. "Engaging with the Popular: Audiences for Mass Culture and What to Say about Them." In *Cultural Studies,* ed. Lawrence Grossberg, Cary Nelson, and Paula Treichler, 69–76. New York: Routledge.

Bush, George. 1992. "Christmas in Williamsburg." *Better Homes and Gardens* 70.12: 82–85.

Cameron, Catherine M., and John B. Gatewood. 1994. "The Authentic Interior: Questing *Gemeinschaft* in Post-Industrial Society." *Human Organization* 53.1: 21–32.

Campbell, Colin. 1987. *The Romantic Ethic and the Spirit of Modern Consumerism.* Oxford: Oxford University Press.

Campbell, Helen J. 1946. *Diary of a Williamsburg Hostess.* New York: Putnam.

Cantwell, Robert. 1993. *Ethnomimesis: Folklife and the Representation of Culture.* Chapel Hill: University of North Carolina Press.

Carson, Cary. 1978. "Doing History with Material Culture." In *Material Culture and the Study of American Life,* ed. Ian M. G. Quimby, 41–64. New York: Norton.

———. 1979. "Zero-Base History: Accounting for a Social Interpretation at Colonial Williamsburg." *Colonial Williamsburg Today* 1.4: 2–5.

———. 1981. "Living Museums of Everyman's History." *Harvard Magazine* (July–August): 22–32.

———. 1991. "Front and Center: Local History Comes of Age." In *Local History, National Heritage: Reflections on the History of AASLH,* ed. Frederick L. Rath et al., 67–108. Nashville: American Association for State and Local History.

———. 1994a. "Lost in the Fun House: A Commentary on Anthropologists' First Contact with History Museums." *Journal of American History* 81.1: 137–50.

———. 1994b. "The Consumer Revolution in Colonial British America: Why Demand?" In *Of Consuming Interests: The Style of Life in the Eighteenth Century,* ed. Cary Carson, Ronald Hoffman, and Peter J. Albert, 483–697. Charlottesville: University Press of Virginia.

———. 1996. "The End of History—Ad Nauseam!" *Colonial Williamsburg Foundation Research Review* 6.1: 37–40.

Carson, Cary, Ronald Hoffman, and Peter J. Albert, eds. 1994. *Of Consuming Interests: The Style of Life in the Eighteenth Century.* Charlottesville: University Press of Virginia.

Certeau, Michel de. 1984. *The Practice of Everyday Life.* Trans. Steven F. Rendall. Berkeley: University of California Press.

Chappell, Edward A. 1981. "Williamsburg Architecture as Social Space." In *Fresh Advices: A Research Supplement to Colonial Williamsburg Interpreter,* no. 2 (November), i–iv.

———. 1989. "Social Responsibility and the American History Museum." *Winterthur Portfolio* 24 (Winter): 247–65.

Clifford, James. 1988. *The Predicament of Culture.* Cambridge: Harvard University Press.

Colonial Williamsburg Foundation. 1935. *A Brief and True Report for the Traveller concerning Williamsburg in Virginia.* Williamsburg, Va.: Colonial Williamsburg Foundation [CWF].

———. 1951. *The Official Guidebook of Colonial Williamsburg.* Williamsburg, Va.: CWF.

———. 1952. *Colonial Williamsburg, the First Twenty-Five Years: A Report by the President.* Williamsburg, Va.: CWF.

———. 1970. *". . . Planning for the Long Term."* Williamsburg, Va.: CWF.

———. 1977. *Teaching History at Colonial Williamsburg: A Plan of Education.* Williamsburg, Va.: CWF.

———. 1985. *Teaching History at Colonial Williamsburg.* Williamsburg, Va.: CWF.

Davis, Kingsley, and Wilbert Moore. 1945. "Some Principles of Stratification." *American Sociological Review* 10: 242–49.

DiMaggio, Paul. 1982. "Cultural Entrepreneurship in Nineteenth-Century Boston." *Media, Culture and Society* 4: 33–50, 303–22.

Duncan, Carol. 1991. "Art Museums and the Ritual of Citizenship." In *Exhibiting Cultures: The Poetics and Politics of Museum Displays,* ed. Ivan Karp and Steven D. Lavine, 88–103.

Duncan, Carol, and Alan Wallach. 1978. "The Museum of Modern Art as Late Capitalist Ritual: An Iconographic Analysis." *Marxist Perspective* 1 (Winter): 28–51.

Eco, Umberto. 1986. *Travels in Hyperreality: Essays.* San Diego: Harcourt Brace Jovanovich.

Elliott, Steve. 1990. "Passing on the Quality Spirit." *Colonial Williamsburg News* 43.5: 11.

———. 1992. "Employees Share Concern about Ticket Price, Value." *Colonial Williamsburg News* 45.1: 9, 11.

Ettema, Michael. 1987. "History Museums and the Culture of Materialism." In *Past Meets Present: Essays about Historic Interpretation and Public Audiences,* ed. Jo Blatti, 62–85. Washington, D.C.: Smithsonian Institution Press.

Fane, Diana, Ira Jacknis, and Lise M. Breen. 1991. *Objects of Myth and Memory: American Indian Art at the Brooklyn Museum.* Seattle: University of Washington Press.

Fisher, Philip. 1991. *Making and Effacing Art: Modern Art in a Culture of Museums.* New York: Oxford University Press.

Fjellman, Stephen M. 1992. *Vinyl Leaves: Walt Disney World and America.* Boulder: Westview Press.

Foster, Andrea Kim. 1993. " 'They're Turning the Town All Upside Down': The Community Identity of Williamsburg, Virginia Before and After the Reconstruction." Ph.D. diss., George Washington University.

Gable, Eric, and Richard Handler. 1993a. "Deep Dirt: Messing Up the Past at Colonial Williamsburg." *Social Analysis* 34: 3–16.

———. 1993b. "Colonialist Anthropology at Colonial Williamsburg." *Museum Anthropology* 17.3: 26–31.

———. 1994. "The Authority of Documents at Some American History Museums." *Journal of American History* 81.1: 119–36.

———. 1996. "After Authenticity at an American Heritage Site." *American Anthropologist* 98.3: 568–78.

Gable, Eric, Richard Handler, and Anna Lawson. 1992. "On the Uses of Relativism: Fact, Conjecture, and Black and White Histories at Colonial Williamsburg." *American Ethnologist* 19.4: 791–805.

Gallaher, Art Jr. 1961. *Plainville Fifteen Years Later.* New York: Columbia University Press.

Goffman, Erving. 1963. *Stigma: Notes on the Management of Spoiled Identity.* Englewood Cliffs, N.J.: Prentice-Hall.

Gonzales, Donald. 1991. *The Rockefellers at Williamsburg: Backstage with the Founders, Restorers and World-Renowned Guests.* McLean, Va.: EPM Publications.

Greenblatt, Stephen. 1991. "Resonance and Wonder." In *Exhibiting Cultures: The Poetics and Politics of Museum Displays,* ed. Ivan Karp and Steven D. Lavine, 42–56. Washington, D.C.: Smithsonian Institution Press.

Greenhalgh, Paul. 1989. "Education, Entertainment and Politics: Lessons from the Great International Exhibitions." In *The New Museology,* ed. Peter Vergo, 74–98. London: Reaktion Books.

Hall, Peter Dobkin. 1992. "The Empty Tomb: The Making of Dynastic Identity." In *Lives in Trust: The Fortunes of Dynastic Families in Late Twentieth-Century America,* by George Marcus, 255–348. Boulder: Westview Press.

Handler, Richard. 1986. "Authenticity." *Anthropology Today* 2.1: 2–4.

———. 1987. "Overpowered by Realism." Review of Anderson 1984 and 1985. *Journal of American Folklore* 100: 337–41.

———. 1997. " 'Imagine Being the Millionth Anything': Commemoration, Business and Culture at Colonial Williamsburg." In *Commemoration, Resistance and Revitalization: Reflections on the Columbian Quincentenary and Other Commemorative Events,* ed. Pauline Turner Strong. Durham, N.C.: Duke University Press, forthcoming.

Handler, Richard, and William Saxton. 1988. "Dyssimulation: Reflexivity, Narrative, and the Quest for Authenticity in 'Living History.' " *Cultural Anthropology* 3.3: 242–60.

Handsman, Russell G., and Mark P. Leone. 1989. "Living History and Critical Archaeology in the Reconstruction of the Past." In *Critical Traditions in Contemporary Archaeology: Essays in the Philosophy, History and Socio-Politics of Archaeology,* ed. V. Pinsky and A. Wylie, 117–35. New York: Cambridge University Press.

Haraway, Donna. 1985. "Teddy Bear Patriarchy: Taxidermy in the Garden of Eden, New York City, 1908–1936." *Social Text* 4.2: 20–64.

Harr, John Ensor, and Peter J. Johnson. 1988. *The Rockefeller Century.* New York: Scribner's.

——. 1991. *The Rockefeller Conscience: An American Family in Public and in Private.* New York: Scribner's.

Harris, Neil. 1990. *Cultural Excursions: Marketing Appetites and Cultural Tastes in Modern America.* Chicago: University of Chicago Press.

Henry, Jules. 1963. *Culture against Man.* New York: Random House.

Higonnet, Anne. 1994. "A New Center: The National Museum of Women in the Arts." In *Museum Culture: Histories, Discourses, Spectacles,* ed. Daniel J. Sherman and Irit Rogoff, 250–64. Minneapolis: University of Minnesota Press.

Hinsley, Curtis. 1991. "The World as Marketplace: Commodification of the Exotic at the World's Columbian Exposition, Chicago, 1893." In *Exhibiting Cultures: The Poetics and Politics of Museum Displays,* ed. Ivan Karp and Steven D. Lavine, 344–65. Washington, D.C.: Smithsonian Institution Press.

Hosmer, Charles B. Jr. 1981. *Preservation Comes of Age: From Williamsburg to the National Trust, 1926–1949.* Volume 1. Charlottesville: University Press of Virginia.

Hudson, Kenneth. 1987. *Museums of Influence.* New York: Cambridge University Press.

Huxtable, Ada Louise. 1963. "Dissent at Colonial Williamsburg." *New York Times,* 22 September.

——. 1992. "Inventing American Reality." *New York Review of Books* 39.20: 24–29.

Isaac, Rhys. 1982. *The Transformation of Virginia, 1740–1790.* Chapel Hill: University of North Carolina Press.

Karp, Ivan, Christine M. Kreamer, and Steven D. Lavine, eds. 1992. *Museums and Communities: The Politics of Public Culture.* Washington, D.C.: Smithsonian Institution Press.

Karp, Ivan, and Steven D. Lavine, eds. 1991. *Exhibiting Cultures: The Poetics and Politics of Museum Displays.* Washington , D.C.: Smithsonian Institution Press.

Kelly, Marjorie. 1994. "Scholarship versus Showmanship at Hawaii's Bishop Museum: Reflections of Cultural Hegemony." *Museum Anthropology* 18.2: 37–48.

Keuren, David van. 1984. "Museums and Ideology." *Victorian Studies* 27: 171–89.

Kimball, Fiske. 1935. "The Restoration of Colonial Williamsburg in Virginia." *Architectural Record* 78.6: 359.

Kopper, Philip. 1986. *Colonial Williamsburg.* New York: Harry N. Abrams.

Kotter, John. 1988. *The Leadership Factor.* New York: Free Press.

——. 1990. *A Force for Change: How Leadership Differs from Management.* New York: Free Press.

Kratz, Corinne A., and Ivan Karp. 1993. "Wonder and Worth: Disney Museums in World Showcase." *Museum Anthropology* 17.3: 32–42.

Krugler, John D. 1991. "Behind the Public Presentations: Research and Scholarship at Living History Museums of Early America." *William and Mary Quarterly* 48: 347–85.

Kulik, Gary. 1989. "Designing the Past: History-Museum Exhibitions from Peale to the

Present." In *History Museums in the United States: A Critical Assessment,* ed. Warren Leon and Roy Rosenzweig, 3–37. Urbana: University of Illinois Press.

Lawson, Anna. 1995. "'The Other Half': Making African-American History at Colonial Williamsburg." Ph.D. diss., University of Virginia.

Lears, T. J. Jackson. 1985. "The Concept of Cultural Hegemony: Problems and Possibilities." *American Historical Review* 90: 567–93.

Lee, Marguerite du Pont. 1966. *Virginia Ghosts.* Baltimore: Clearfield. Reprint, 1993.

Leon, Warren, and Roy Rosenzweig, eds. 1989. *History Museums in the United States: A Critical Assessment.* Urbana: University of Illinois Press.

Leone, Mark. 1981. "Archaeology's Relationship to the Present and the Past." In *Modern Material Culture,* ed. R. A. Gould and M. B. Schiffer, 5–14. New York: Academic Press.

——. 1994. "An Archaeology of the DeWitt Wallace Gallery at Colonial Williamsburg." In *Museums and the Appropriation of Culture,* ed. Susan Pearce, 198–212. London: Athlone Press.

Levine, Lawrence. 1988. *Highbrow/Lowbrow: The Emergence of Cultural Hierarchy in America.* Cambridge: Harvard University Press.

Longsworth, Charles. 1980. "A Great Procession." *Colonial Williamsburg Today* 2.4: 1.

——. 1981. "Communicating the Past to the Present." *Colonial Williamsburg Foundation 1980–81 Report,* 3–10. Williamsburg, Va.: CWF.

——. 1982. "Viewpoints from the President." *Colonial Williamsburg News* 35.2: 2.

——. 1987. "Report from the President." *Colonial Williamsburg Foundation 1987 Annual Report,* 2–5. Williamsburg, Va.: CWF.

——. 1990. "Soon, You'll Be Able to 'Speak Out!'" *Colonial Williamsburg News* 43.3: 6.

——. 1991a. "Dealing with Recession." *Colonial Williamsburg News* 44.1: 8.

——. 1991b. "Openings Part of Our Continuing Improvement." *Colonial Williamsburg News.* 44.3: 5.

——. 1994. "Educational Williamsburg." *Washington Post,* 22 October, A17.

Low, Shirley Payne. 1965. "Historic Site Interpretation: The Human Approach." *History News* 20.11: 233–44.

Lowenthal, David. 1985. *The Past Is a Foreign Country.* New York: Cambridge University Press.

Lumley, Robert, ed. 1988. *The Museum Time-Machine: Putting Cultures on Display.* London: Routledge.

Lutz, Catherine A., and Jane L. Collins. 1993. *Reading National Geographic.* Chicago: University of Chicago Press.

MacCannell, Dean. 1976. *The Tourist: A New Theory of the Leisure Class.* New York: Schocken Books.

Marling, Karal Ann. 1988. *George Washington Slept Here: Colonial Revivals and American Culture. 1876–1986.* Cambridge: Harvard University Press.

Mayo, Edith P. 1992. "Exhibiting Politics." *Museum News* 71 (September–October): 50–51.

Megill, Allan, ed. 1994. *Rethinking Objectivity.* Durham, N.C.: Duke University Press.

Munley, Mary Ellen. 1986. "Asking the Right Questions." *Museum News* 64.3: 18–23.

——. 1987. "Intentions and Accomplishments: Principles of Museum Evaluation Research." In *Past Meets Present: Essays about Historic Interpretation and Public Audiences,* ed. Jo Blatti, 116–30. Washington, D.C.: Smithsonian Institution Press.

Newman, Katherine. 1980. "Incipient Bureaucracy: The Development of Hierarchies in

Egalitarian Organizations." In *Hierarchy and Society: Anthropological Perspectives on Bureaucracy*, ed. G. M. Britan and R. Cohen, 143–63. Philadelphia: ISHI.

Novick, Peter. 1988. *That Noble Dream: The "Objectivity Question" and the American Historical Profession*. New York: Cambridge University Press.

O'Barr, William M. 1994. *Culture and the Ad: Exploring Otherness in the World of Advertising*. Boulder: Westview Press.

Olmert, Michael. 1985. "The New, No-Frills Williamsburg." *Historic Preservation* 37 (October): 27–33.

Orvell, Miles. 1989. *The Real Thing: Imitation and Authenticity in American Culture, 1880–1940*. Chapel Hill: University of North Carolina Press.

Parmentier, Richard. 1994. *Signs in Society: Studies in Semiotic Anthropology*. Bloomington: Indiana University Press.

Pearce, Susan, ed. 1990. *Objects of Knowledge*. London: Athlone Press.

——. 1994. *Museums and the Appropriation of Culture*. London: Athlone Press.

Perin, Constance. 1992. "The Communicative Circle: Museums as Communities." In *Museums and Communities: The Politics of Public Culture*, ed. Ivan Karp, Christine M. Kreamer, and Steven D. Lavine, 182–220. Washington, D.C.: Smithsonian Institution Press.

Perry, William Graves. 1935. "Note on the Architecture." *Architectural Record* 78.6: 363–77.

Peters, Thomas J. 1982. *In Search of Excellence: Lessons from America's Best-Run Companies*. New York: Harper.

——. 1985. *A Passion for Excellence: The Leadership Difference*. New York: Random House.

Potter, Parker B. Jr., and Mark Leone. 1992. "Establishing the Roots of Historical Consciousness in Modern Annapolis, Maryland." In *Museums and Communities: The Politics of Public Culture*, ed. Ivan Karp, Christine M. Kreamer, and Steven D. Lavine, 476–505. Washington, D.C.: Smithsonian Institution Press.

Price, Richard, and Sally Price. 1994a. *On the Mall: Presenting Maroon Tradition-Bearers at the 1992 Festival of American Folklife*. Bloomington, Ind.: Special Publications of the Folklore Institute.

——. 1994b. "Ethnicity in a Museum Case: France's Show-Window in the Americas." *Museum Anthropology* 18.2: 3–15.

——. 1995. *Enigma Variations*. Cambridge: Harvard University Press.

Price, Sally. 1989. *Primitive Art in Civilized Places*. Chicago: University of Chicago Press.

Quimby, Ian M. G., ed. 1978. *Material Culture and the Study of American Life*. New York: Norton.

Rath, Frederick L., Charles B. Hosmer Jr., Edward P. Alexander, Holman J. Swinney, and Cary Carson. 1991. *Local History, National Heritage: Reflections on the History of AASLH*. Nashville: American Association for State and Local History.

Robbins, Bruce, ed. 1993. *The Phantom Public Sphere*. Minneapolis: University of Minnesota Press.

Rockefeller, John D. Jr. 1937. "The Genesis of the Williamsburg Restoration." *National Geographic Magazine* 71 (April): 401.

Rockefeller, Winthrop. 1968. "Statement by the Chairman of the Boards." In *Preserving Our Handcrafts: The President's Report, 1968*, 50–51. Williamsburg: Colonial Williamsburg Foundation.

Ronsheim, Robert. 1981. "Christmas at Conner Prairie: Reinterpreting a Pioneer Holiday." *History News* 36.12: 14–17.

Rose, Dan. 1991a. "Elite Discourse of the Market and Narrative Ethnography." *Anthropological Quarterly* 64.3: 109–25.

——. 1991b. "Worldly Discourses: Reflections on Pragmatic Utterances and on the Culture of Capital." *Public Culture* 4.1: 109–27.

Rydell, Robert. 1984. *All the World's a Fair: Visions of Empire at American International Expositions, 1876–1916.* Chicago: University of Chicago Press.

Saylor, Patrick. 1990a. "Improving Quality through Employee Involvement." *Colonial Williamsburg News* 43.3: 1–3.

——. 1990b. "Compensation and Benefits: Taking a Close Look at Pay." *Colonial Williamsburg News* 43.2: 17.

Schlereth, Thomas J. 1978. "It Wasn't That Simple." *Museum News* 56.1: 36–44.

——. 1980. "The History behind, within, and outside the History Museum." *Curator* 23.4: 255–74.

——. 1984. "Causing Conflict, Doing Violence." *Museum News* 63 (October): 45–52.

Schneider, David M. 1968. *American Kinship: A Cultural Account.* Englewood Cliffs, N.J.: Prentice-Hall.

Screven, C. G. 1979. "A Bibliography of Visitor Research Education." *Museum News* 57.2: 56–59, 86, 88.

——. 1984. "Educational Evaluation and Research in Museums and Public Exhibits: A Bibliography." *Curator* 27: 147–65.

Sennett, Richard, and Jonathan Cobb. 1972. *The Hidden Injuries of Class.* New York: Knopf.

Severson, Jack. 1994. "Authenticity: Colonial Williamsburg Strives for that 18th-Century Atmosphere, Right Down to the Road Apples." *Roanoke Times & World-News,* 10 April, F1, F6.

Sherman, Daniel J. 1989. *Worthy Monuments: Art Museums and the Politics of Culture in Nineteenth-Century France.* Cambridge: Harvard University Press.

Sherman, Daniel J., and Irit Rogoff, eds. 1994. *Museum Culture: Histories, Discourses, Spectacles.* Minneapolis: University of Minnesota Press.

Shurtleff, Harold R. 1939. *The Log Cabin Myth: A Study of the Early Dwellings of the English Colonists in North America.* Cambridge: Harvard University Press.

Smith, J. Douglas. 1982. "A Solemn Obligation." *Colonial Williamsburg Today* 5.1: 9–14.

Stocking, George W., ed. 1985. *Objects and Others: Essays on Museums and Material Culture.* History of Anthropology 3. Madison: University of Wisconsin Press.

Thompson, E. P. 1967. "Time, Work-Discipline, and Industrial Capitalism." *Past and Present* 38: 56–97.

Tilden, Freeman. 1977. *Interpreting Our Heritage.* 3d ed. Chapel Hill: University of North Carolina Press.

Tumin, Melvin. 1953. "Some Principles of Stratification: A Critical Analysis." *American Sociological Review* 18: 387–93.

Upton, Dell. 1988. "New Views of the Virginia Landscape." *Virginia Magazine of History and Biography* 96.4: 403–70.

Upton, Dell, and John Michael Vlach, eds. 1986. *Common Places: Readings in American Vernacular Architecture.* Athens: University of Georgia Press.

Van West, Carroll, and Mary Hoffschwelle. 1984. "'Slumbering on Its Old Foundations': Interpretation at Colonial Williamsburg." *South Atlantic Quarterly* 83.2: 157–75.

Vergo, Peter, ed. 1989. *The New Museology.* London: Reaktion Books.

Wallace, Michael. 1986a. "Visiting the Past: History Museums in the United States." In *Presenting the Past: Essays on History and the Public,* ed. Susan P. Benson, Stephen Brier, and Roy Rosenzweig, 137–61. Philadelphia: Temple University Press.

——. 1986b. "Reflections on the History of Historic Preservation." In *Presenting the Past: Essays on History and the Public,* ed. Susan P. Benson, Stephen Brier, and Roy Rosenzweig, 165–99. Philadelphia: Temple University Press.

——. 1987. "The Politics of Public History." In *Past Meets Present: Essays about Historic Interpretation and Public Audiences,* ed. Jo Blatti, 37–53. Washington, D.C.: Smithsonian Institution Press.

Wallis, Brian. 1994. "Selling Nations: International Exhibitions and Cultural Diplomacy." In *Museum Culture: Histories, Discourses, Spectacles,* ed. Daniel J. Sherman and Irit Rogoff, 265–81. Minneapolis: University of Minnesota Press.

Wells, Camille. 1993. "Interior Designs: Room Furnishings and Historical Interpretations at Colonial Williamsburg." *Southern Quarterly* 31: 89–111.

West, James [Carl Withers]. 1945. *Plainville U.S.A.* New York: Columbia University Press.

Whorf, Benjamin Lee. 1956. *Language, Thought, and Reality: Selected Writings of Benjamin Lee Whorf.* Cambridge: MIT Press.

Williams, Rosalind. 1982. *Dream Worlds: Mass Consumption in Late Nineteenth-Century France.* Berkeley: University of California Press.

Zolberg, Vera. 1974. "The Art Institute of Chicago: The Sociology of a Cultural Organization." Ph.D. diss., University of Chicago.

——. 1981. "Conflicting Visions in American Art Museums." *Theory and Society* 10.1: 103–25.

——. 1984. "American Art Museums: Sanctuary or Free-for-All?" *Social Forces* 63.2: 377–92.

Zyskowski, Gloria. 1983. "A Review of the Literature on the Evaluation of Museum Programs." *Curator* 26: 126–27.

Index

Abbey Aldrich Rockefeller Folk Art Center, 15

African American history, 6–7, 18, 23, 68–69, 76, 78–79, 84–92, 102–15

African American Interpretation and Programs, Department of [AAIP], 18, 23, 85–89, 92

Alderson, William T., 174–77, 197, 199

Alexander, Edward, 182–84

American Girls dolls, 160

Anachronisms, 56–58, 67–68, 219, 224–25

Anderson forge, 100, 229

Anheuser-Busch Corporation, 40–43, 155

Annenberg, Leonore, 38

Annenberg, Walter, 38

Authenticity, 3, 6, 35–36, 45–49, 70, 75–76, 82–84, 94–96, 99, 146–47, 151, 161, 172–76, 223, 242 n.31; dirt as a symbol of, 3–4, 8

Bassett Hall, 15

Bellah, Robert, 235

Blackburn, Joyce, 91

Black history. *See* African American history

Broadnax, Lydia, 85–92, 97, 105–108, 111–12, 115

Brodie, Fawn, 86, 91

Brown, Imogene, 91

Brown, Michael, 85–89

Brush-Everard House, 53–54; training at, 196–203

Bruton Parish Episcopal Church, 31, 51, 52

Busch Gardens, 41–43, 155, 160, 189, 222

Campbell, Helen, 178–86, 199

Capitol, 7, 15, 51, 52, 62, 63, 245 n.21

Carson, Cary, 60–63, 66–67, 122, 228

Carter's Grove, 15, 40, 53, 76; slave quarter, 229

Chorley, Kenneth, 34, 36, 38, 40, 62n, 63–65, 71, 132, 136

Chowning's Tavern, 113

Christian, Minor, 210

Clifford, James, 26

Colonial revival, 61–63, 77, 242 n.44
Colonial Williamsburg, Incorporated, 18–19, 33
Colonial Williamsburg Hotel Properties, Incorporated, 19, 208, 211–14
Communications, corporate, 150–53, 163, 168
Constructionism, 4–5, 59–62, 77, 78–84, 220–23, 232
Consumerism, 4–5, 69–70, 117–22
Courthouse, 68
Craft House, 133
Custis, John, 87–88

DeWitt Wallace Decorative Arts Gallery, 15, 100, 118, 158, 229–30
Diary of a Williamsburg Hostess, 178
Disney World. *See* Walt Disney World

Eastern State Hospital, 166n
Egalitarianism, 137–48, 215–17
Elliott, Steve, 125–28, 137, 191n

Facts, 80–84, 221–26
Fife and Drum Corps, 7, 64, 68, 96–97
Fjellman, Stephen, 29n
Food and Beverage Workers Union, 208, 211–14
Ford, Henry, 31
Ford's Colony, 41–43, 49
Freeman, S. D., 33

Geddy, Vernon, 35
Gone with the Wind, 113
Goodwin Building, 95
Goodwin, Rev. W. A. R., 31–34, 57, 65, 69, 73, 148, 178–79
Goodwin, Rutherfoord, 73, 178–79
Governor's Inn, 212–14
Governor's Palace, 7, 15, 41, 51–52, 62, 188–89, 245 n.21

Hall, Peter Dobkin, 32–33
Havel, Václav, 231
Hemings, Sally, 85–86, 92
Henderson, Elizabeth Lee, 178–85, 199
Henry, Jules, 29
Henry, Patrick, 24, 113

Hierarchy, corporate, 137–46
Hoffschwelle, Mary, 122
Holmes, Sherlock, 71
Hudson, Kenneth, 15
Humelsine, Carlisle, 38–41, 48–49, 62n, 65–66, 132–35, 147, 241 n.17
Huxtable, Ada Louise, 44–45, 222

Jefferson, Thomas, 24, 43, 113; and Sally Hemings, 85–86, 92

Kimball, Fiske, 36
King, Martin Luther, 213
Kingsmill (residential development), 41
Kingsmill (conference center), 155
Kotter, John, 141–42, 146, 149

Lanthorn Tour, 118–20
Lawson, Anna Logan, x, 14, 23, 79
Leone, Mark, 122, 243 n.5
Living history, 18, 74–75, 131–32
Longsworth, Charles, 38–39, 46, 62n, 125, 132–35, 139–41, 146–48, 151–52, 156–57, 165–69, 212, 225n
Low, Shirley Payne, 174–77, 197, 199

Magazine, 64, 68, 76
Market Square, 51, 241 n.17
Militia, 95–97
Mimesis, 70
Mimetic realism. *See* Objectivism
Miscegenation, 84–92
Monticello, 85, 87, 92, 160
Mount Vernon, 85, 92

National Air and Space Museum, 7
National Museum of American Art, 7
Nevins, Allan, 34
New social history. *See* Social history
Nostalgia, narrative of, 99–101, 126, 129–37

Objectivism, 4–5, 59, 61, 70–71, 75–77, 83–84, 130, 219, 222, 224–26, 232, 242 n.31
Other Half tour, 85–87

Palace. *See* Governor's Palace
Patriot's Tour, 50–59, 86, 123
Perry, William Graves, 31, 62, 71

Peters, Tom, 141–42, 146, 149
Peyton Randolph House, 7
Pollack, Jackson, 71
Powder Magazine. *See* Magazine
Products Review Committee, 35–36, 157
Progress, narrative of, 99–101, 126
Public Hospital, 52, 229

Quality Teams, 148–50, 166–67

Raleigh Tavern, 7, 36, 73, 114–15
Raleigh Tavern Society, 38–39
Randolph, Peyton, 24
Realism. *See* Objectivism
Rockefeller, Abby Aldrich, 15
Rockefeller, John D., 32–34
Rockefeller, John D., Jr., 6, 15, 31–34, 36–
    39, 57, 62–65, 69, 148
Rockefeller, John, III, 63
Rockefeller, Winthrop, 63

Schneider, David Murray, 25
Segregation, racial, 73n, 245 n.24
Shields Tavern, 212–14
Sneed, Mrs. Albert M., 178–85, 199
Social history, 4, 7–8, 61, 66–70, 75–76, 93,
    115–24, 216–19; and interpretive train-
    ing, 196–98
Story of a Patriot, The (film), 64, 67, 79–80,
    229

Teaching History at Colonial Williamsburg
    (planning document), 115–18, 121, 140
Theme parks, 28–29, 41, 44

Tilden, Freeman, 174–77, 197–99, 226–27
Training, interpretive, 81–84, 112n, 192–
    205

Van West, Carroll, 122

Wallace Gallery. *See* DeWitt Wallace Decora-
    tive Arts Gallery
Wallace, Michael, 44–45, 122
Walt Disney World, 29, 160, 222
Washington, George, 24, 113
Water Country U. S. A., 43
Wells, Camille, 122, 243 n.13
Wetherburn's Tavern, 88–89, 99, 113–14
Whorf, Benjamin Lee, 138
Wig shop, 119–20
Wilburn, Robert, 62n
Williamsburg Declaration, 64
Williamsburg Holding Company, 33
Williamsburg Inn, 36, 144
Williamsburg Lodge, 36, 136
Williamsburg Pottery, 40, 43
Williamsburg Restoration, Incorporated, 19,
    33
Winthrop Rockefeller Archaeology Mu-
    seum, 15
Wolstenholme Towne, 15
Woods, Arthur, 62n
Wren Building, 52, 245 n.21
Wythe, George, 24, 43, 102–112, 118; and
    Lydia Broadnax, 85–92
Wythe House, 36, 41, 51–53, 80–81, 85–90,
    115, 158; Christmas at, 102–112, 121;
    training at, 112n